The authors of this compendium argue persuasively and passionately from Scripture that holistic kingdom mission must include reconciliation. Blending theology, practice, and case studies, their invitations to restoring broken relationships include examples from multiple continents and contexts. This volume offers a timely appeal in our divided world.

DAVID W. BENNETT, DMin, PhD
Global Associate Director and Congress Director, Seoul 2024, Lausanne Movement

God's mission of reconciling all things to himself (2 Cor 5:19) speaks to the heart of the gospel, and therefore to us as we bear this good news of reconciliation. The need for conversations on reconciliation grows in urgency as the world around us fractures. I have been deeply challenged and inspired by this landmark publication for EMS. Bringing together diverse voices contributing to the 2022 EMS conference on reconciliation and mission, it demonstrates our growth as a society and deepening commitment to *shalom* and whole-life participation in the *missio Dei*.

ROBIN HARRIS, PhD
President, Global Ethnodoxology Network
Chair, Center for Excellence in World Arts at Dallas International University
Past president, EMS (2020–2022)

How refreshing to read this collection of articles addressing the brokenness of our world with a message of hope! Seeing reconciliation as part of our shared calling motivates these writers to reflect theologically, identify practices of reconciliation, and offer case studies for consideration. People, created in God's image and likeness, and their interactions lie at the heart of these articles. Jesus calls us to be peacemakers (Matt 5:9), and Paul says the church has been given the ministry of reconciliation (2 Cor 5; Eph 2). Peacemaking and reconciliation offer an attractive paradigm for mission in the world today.

JONATHAN BORNMAN, PhD
EMM Christian-Muslim Relations Team

Ambassadors of Reconciliation is an inspired vision to reframe mission as reconciliation with God and our neighbor in all the dimensions where sin has divided and defiled us. This compendium is a comprehensive treatment of the subject—from the broadest biblical underpinnings to its practical expressions through reconciling disciples. In our war torn, justice thirsty world this volume offers a path forward. The Suffering Servant Sovereign King sends us as his incarnational ambassadors of reconciliation, with the humility and awareness that we have much work to do.

RANDY FRIESEN
VP for Leadership Development, Global Disciples

A cynical view of the world might believe that nothing is more constant than conflict, brokenness, and war. Yet the Christian hope is that God is quietly and consistently at work restoring and reconciling the world to himself through Jesus and his Spirit. I'm glad to see this timely set of theological, practical, and contextual reflections on the centrality of reconciliation and peacemaking in gospel work. My prayer is that it will serve as a catalyst to the Christian imagination of what our communities and our world might look like if only we truly believed, and lived, as if this Christian hope is true.

DAVID GURETZKI, PhD
President and Resident Theologian, The Evangelical Fellowship of Canada

A major challenge today lies in pursuing peace and reconciliation at different levels of society. The EMS 2022 compilation is a tremendous recourse with practical and pragmatic ideas on peace building. This compilation is critical for Africa, a continent which has experienced turmoil from precolonial times to date, events which have resulted in intergenerational trauma. This book is profoundly helpful, and insightful, with remarkable case studies as it helps church leaders and others build a theological framework for reconciliation.

MARTIN KAPENDA
PRN African Regional Coordinator

This magnificent collection of theology, praxis, and real examples rekindles our imagination for how good the good news really is and how great the great commission of Jesus must be. In a world fractured and fragmented by sin, the global voices of the contributors create a compelling chorus. Get this book to be challenged to embrace and pursue with deeper consideration and renewed vigor the reconciling mission of God.

WALTER KIM
President, National Association of Evangelicals

Peace and reconciliation cannot be understood without an understanding of the mission. This book is a great help in understanding the mission for peace and reconciliation that is most needed in today's world. It is important because it encompasses a theological perspective and practical practices of mission, peace, and reconciliation.

THIR KOIRALA
Asia Coordinator, Peace and Reconciliation Network

One of the most powerful dimensions of the gospel is our reconciliation with God through Christ that makes possible reconciliation with one another. This collection of essays provides both biblical foundations and practical case studies as a welcome primer on the subject. In a world of such deep divisions politically, racially, ethnically, and domestically, we urgently need the kind of insight that is found in *Ambassadors of Reconciliation*.

CRAIG OTT, PhD
Professor of Mission and Intercultural Studies, Trinity International University

Because Jesus is "our peace" who has broken down the "dividing wall of hostility" (Eph 2:14), part of the church's call to mission is to pursue reconciliation. In this timely volume, the authors explore the theological foundations of mission as reconciliation and then bring it to the street level of mission with contemporary case studies This book will be a great resource for churches striving to engage their communities with the gospel and for mission organizations and missionaries laboring to make disciples of all nations.

EDWARD L. SMITHER, PhD
Academic Dean and Professor of Intercultural Studies &
History of Global Christianity, Columbia International University

About the cover image

The Japanese art of *Kintsugi* is the restoration of broken pottery using gold as an adherant to bring the broken pieces together again to a restored, useful vessel. Every one of us has some sort of brokenness—whether it's from choices we have made or circumstances beyond our control. Sometimes we find ourselves so broken that we don't know how things could ever be restored. While things are still far from perfect until Jesus returns to reestablish his kingdom on Earth, we have a choice. We don't have to live in brokenness.

Ambassadors of Reconciliation

God's Mission through Missions for All

Geoff Hartt, Michael A. Ortiz, Manuel Böhm, Editors

Ambassadors of Reconciliation: God's Mission through Missions for All

© 2023 by Evangelical Missiological Society. All rights reserved.

No part of this book may be reproduced, stored in a retrieval system, or transmitted in any form or by any means—electronic, mechanical, photocopy, recording, or otherwise—without prior written permission from the publisher, except brief quotations used in connection with reviews in magazines or newspapers. For permission, email permissions@wclbooks.com. For corrections, email editor@wclbooks.com.

William Carey Publishing (WCP) publishes resources to shape and advance the missiological conversation in the world. We publish a broad range of thought-provoking books and do not necessarily endorse all opinions set forth here or in works referenced within this book. WCP can't verify the accuracy of website URLs beyond the date of print publication.

Scripture quotations marked ESV are taken ESV® Bible (The Holy Bible, English Standard Version®), Copyright © 2001 by Crossway, a publishing ministry of Good News Publishers. Used by permission. All rights reserved.

Scripture quotations marked NIV are taken from the Holy Bible, New International Version®, NIV®. Copyright © 1973, 1978, 1984, 2011 by Biblica, Inc.™ Used by permission of Zondervan. All rights reserved worldwide. www.zondervan.com. The "NIV" and "New International Version" are trademarks registered in the United States Patent and Trademark Office by Biblica, Inc.™

Scripture quotations marked NRSV are taken from the New Revised Standard Version Bible, copyright © 1989 National Council of the Churches of Christ in the United States of America. Used by permission. All rights reserved worldwide.

Scripture quotations marked NLT are taken from the Holy Bible, New Living Translation, copyright ©1996, 2004, 2015 by Tyndale House Foundation. Used by permission of Tyndale House Publishers, Carol Stream, Illinois 60188. All rights reserved.

Published by William Carey Publishing
10 W. Dry Creek Cir
Littleton, CO 80120 | www.missionbooks.org

William Carey Publishing is a ministry of Frontier Ventures
Pasadena, CA | www.frontierventures.org

Cover and Interior Designer: Mike Riester

ISBNs: 978-1-64508-510-2 (paperback), 978-1-64508-512-6 (epub)

Printed Worldwide   27 26 25 24 23   1 2 3 4 5   IN

Library of Congress Control Number: 2023942231

www.emsweb.org

The Evangelical Missiological Society (EMS) is a professional organization with more than four hundred members comprised of missiologists, mission administrators, reflective mission practitioners, teachers, pastors with strategic missiological interests, and students of missiology. EMS exists to advance the cause of world evangelization. We do this through study and evaluation of mission concepts and strategies from a biblical perspective with a view to commending sound mission theory and practice to churches, mission agencies, and schools of missionary training around the world. We hold an annual national conference and eight regional meetings in the United States and Canada.

Other Books in the EMS Series

No. 1 *Scripture and Strategy: The Use of the Bible in Postmodern Church and Mission* | David Hesselgrave

No. 2 *Christianity and the Religions: A Biblical Theology of World Religions* Edward Rommen and Harold Netland

No. 3 *Spiritual Power and Missions: Raising the Issues* | Edward Rommen

No. 4 *Missiology and the Social Sciences: Contributions, Cautions, and Conclusions* | Edward Rommen and Gary Corwin

No. 5 *The Holy Spirit and Mission Dynamics* | Douglas McConnell

No. 6 *Reaching the Resistant: Barriers and Bridges for Mission* Dudley Woodberry

No. 7 *Teaching Them Obedience in All Things: Equipping for the 21st Century* Edgar Elliston

No. 8 *Working Together with God to Shape the New Millennium: Opportunities and Limitations* | Kenneth Mulholland and Gary Corwin

No. 9 *Caring for the Harvest Force in the New Millennium* Tom Steffen and Douglas Pennoyer

No. 10 *Between Past and Future: Evangelical Mission Entering the Twenty-First Century* | Jonathan Bonk

No. 11 *Christian Witness in Pluralistic Contexts in the Twenty-First Century* Enoch Wan

No. 12 *The Centrality of Christ in Contemporary Missions* Mike Barnett and Michael Pocock

No. 13 *Contextualization and Syncretism: Navigating Cultural Currents*
Gailyn Van Rheenen

No. 14 *Business as Mission: From Impoverished to Empowered*
Tom Steffen and Mike Barnett

No. 15 *Missions in Contexts of Violence* | Keith Eitel

No. 16 *Effective Engagement in Short-Term Missions: Doing It Right!*
Robert J. Priest

No. 17 *Missions from the Majority World: Progress, Challenges, and Case Studies* | Enoch Wan and Michael Pocock

No. 18 *Serving Jesus with Integrity: Ethics and Accountability in Mission*
Dwight P. Baker and Douglas Hayward

No. 19 *Reflecting God's Glory Together: Diversity in Evangelical Mission*
A. Scott Moreau and Beth Snodderly

No. 20 *Reaching the City: Reflections on Urban Mission for the Twenty-First Century* | Gary Fujino, Timothy R. Sisk, and Tereso C. Casino

No. 21 *Missionary Methods: Research, Reflections, and Realities*
Craig Ott and J. D. Payne

No. 22 *The Missionary Family: Witness, Concerns, Care*
Dwight P. Baker and Robert J. Priest

No. 23 *Diaspora Missiology: Reflections on Reaching the Scattered Peoples of the World* | Michael Pocock and Enoch Wan

No. 24 *Controversies in Mission: Theology, People, and Practice of Mission in the 21st Century* | Rochelle Cathcart Scheuermann and Edward L. Smither

No. 25 *Churches on Mission: God's Grace Abounding to the Nations*
Geoffrey Hartt, Christopher R. Little, and John Wang

No. 26 *Majority World Theologies: Self-Theologizing from Africa, Asia, Latin America, and the Ends of the Earth* | Allen Yeh and Tite Tiénou

No. 27 *Against the Tide: Mission Amidst the Global Currents of Secularization*
W. Jay Moon and Craig Ott

No. 28 *Practicing Hope: Missions and Global Crises*
Jerry Ireland and Michelle Raven

No. 29 *Advancing Models of Mission: Evaluating the Past and Looking to the Future*
Kenneth Nehrbass, Aminta Arrington, and Narry Santos

No. 30 *Communication in Mission: Global Opportunities and Challenges*
Marcus Dean, Scott Moreau, Sue Russell, and Rochelle Scheuermann

Contents

Foreword *By Dr. Tony Evans* — xi

Preface: Why Reconciliation? *By Manuel Böhm* — xiii

Part 1: Reconciliation Theology

Chapter 1: Reconciling All Things: Missional Competencies in a Broken World
Al Tizon — 3

Chapter 2: Reconciliation—A Missionary Paradigm for the Twenty-First Century
Johannes Reimer — 13

Chapter 3: Reconciliation—The Neglected Outcome of Kingdom Mission
Ken Baker — 25

Chapter 4: So That the World Will Know: Reflections on an Evangelical Theology of Christian Others and the Missiological Priority of Christian Unity
Michael Hakmin Lee — 41

Chapter 5: Toward a Theological Account of Christian Forgiveness in Intergenerational Communal Contexts
Kazusa Okaya — 55

Part 2: Reconciliation Practices

Chapter 6: Reconciling Discipleship: Living as Ecclesia Wherever We Go
Manuel and Jeanette Böhm — 73

Chapter 7: Worldview Questions in Mission Training and Praxis: The Unintended Consequences of Comfortable Oppositional Thinking
Annette R. Harrison — 90

Chapter 8: Welcomed at God's Table: Moving from Abstraction to Embodied Reconciliation through Hospitality
Aubry G. Smith — 108

Chapter 9: Marked by Suffering: Discipleship, Sovereignty, and Suffering in the Gospel of Mark and in Mozambique
Alan Howell — 125

Part 3: Reconciliation Case Studies

Chapter 10: Ethnicity, Reconciliation, and the Church in Myanmar
Arend A. C. Van Dorp — 143

Chapter 11: Community-Based Reconciliation: A Case Study of the Sawi Peace Child Story
Yakubu Jakada — 159

Chapter 12: Effective Discipleship for Reconciliation:
            Case of Genocide against the Tutsi in Rwanda
            Kwizera Emmanuel   171

Chapter 13: An Invitation to the Table: Stories of Mission, Reconciliation, and Food
            Andrea Chang and Nelson Chang   185

Chapter 14: The Missional Fruit of Reconciliation: The Impact of
            Armenian and Turkish Reconciliation over the Armenian Genocide
            James Jacob Pursley   200

Appendix: Resources for Next Steps   218

About the Editors and Contributors   220

Foreword

Dr. Tony Evans

The world is connected like never before, and I don't mean just technologically, but spatially as well. Globalization has shifted the boundaries of countries and cultures. No longer do we have to travel clear across the globe to enjoy the best paella, pad Thai, or falafel. In fact, just a few miles away from my home in Dallas, I can find diaspora people from India, China, Afghanistan, Ukraine, or Latin America just to name a few of the nations represented in my community. The world is literally at my doorstep, and I know you don't have to look very far either. We no longer must travel hours away to find people who aren't like us. As believers, we are called to proclaim to our neighbors and to the nations the good news of the gospel that reconciles all people to God.

The Holy Bible has one continuous message throughout its sixty-six books: the glory of God through the advancement of his kingdom as he restores and reconciles all things to himself (2 Cor 5:19). He is the one restoring. He is the one reconciling. Yet, he has chosen to use his people as agents of reconciliation. He first used the people of Israel to proclaim his kingdom to the nations. He sent his Son, Jesus, to span the gap between himself and mankind, becoming not only the agent proclaiming reconciliation, but also the very mode of reconciliation (Col 1:20). Now, God has sent his church to be ambassadors of the good news of reconciliation to the whole world.

And God through us intends to do a new thing (Isa 43:19) that unites people across cultures, across races, across socioeconomic backgrounds, and across languages. It is not so much about conformity to each other, but rather being conformed to his image (Rom 8:29). This is reconciliation. Jesus died on the cross, rose from the grave, demolished our divisions, initiated peace, and reconciled us to God in the same body, the church (Eph 2:15–16). This is reconciliation. He sent his church on his mission to restore and reconcile all things to himself, including us now, as his ambassadors of that reconciliation. This is reconciliation alive in our present time through us. You and I are God's ambassadors (2 Cor 5:20) of reconciliation, filled with his Spirit to go to the nations, whether near or distant.

So, we ask, are we willing to be God's ambassadors of reconciliation? *Ambassadors of Reconciliation: God's Mission through Missions for All* presents essays on the theology of reconciliation, the practice of reconciliation, and case studies on reconciliation in missions. I invite you to read what has been collected in this book. As you do so, you will be led to reflect more deeply on reconciliation in missions, and you will be stimulated to act as an ambassador of reconciliation within your sphere of influences. This collection further grounds and fosters the call to every believer to step up to the line and take the shot, to be an ambassador for Christ outside of their home and church and go to the nations at their doorstep or far away to proclaim Jesus, our Reconciler. It will encourage you to be willing!

Dr. Tony Evans
Senior Pastor, Oak Cliff Bible Fellowship
President, The Urban Alternative

Preface

Manuel Böhm

Reconciliation—a heavy word to lift if one looks at today's conflict-laden societies around the world. With a glance at the Global Peace Index, one immediately recognizes that the war in Ukraine alone "led to a large rise in the number of conflict deaths, as well as sharp deteriorations in indicators [measuring peace] such as refugees and internally displaced persons (IDP), political instability and political terror" (Global Peace Index 2022, 2). People are in conflict with each other as individuals and as nations—which makes everyone suffer. Further, there are more people than ever fleeing their homes due to conflicts (89.3 million at the end of 2021). Nature is under dire circumstances as the list of natural disasters shows—which in return leads to further migration and conflicts.[1]

The concept of reconciliation has come to the forefront in recent years with even secular organizations like the UN starting to call for leaders in reconciliation.[2] Countries like South Africa or Canada have long answered this call by installing Truth and Reconciliation Commissions to address injustices of the past. While Canadians may consider reconciliation mainly in the context of First Nation's relationships, for the US it relates to racial and political unrest.[3] According to the Canadian Commission, reconciliation is about establishing and maintaining a mutually respectful relationship between Aboriginal and non-Aboriginal peoples in their country. Attaining this goal requires awareness of the past, acknowledgment of the harm that has been inflicted, atonement for the causes, and action to change behavior (Truth and Reconciliation 2015, 6).

Though this definition includes very crucial points, does it reflect an understanding of reconciliation that brings holistic transformation? Often, human efforts seek to find the right scapegoat, to ask for retribution and justice, thinking that doing so would bring peace to people and groups in tension with each other. Thus, reconciliation is described as a matter of social inequality—how meta-relationships are lived out and should be reorganized. In any case, one thing is clear: the whole world (*cosmos*) is crying out and God's children have to wonder how they can answer and how to bring change with eternal value (Rom 8:19–22).

---

1 See further details at https://www.unhcr.org/globaltrends and https://en.wikipedia.org/wiki/Category:2023_natural_disasters.

2 Read more about the UN reconciliation leader program: https://global-leader.org.

3 As a sad fact, "The United States stands out among 17 advanced economies as one of the most conflicted when it comes to questions of social unity" (Connaughton 2021). Which leads others to specifically call out "systemic racism" (HRW Report 2022; Evans 2022, 21).

Reconciliation that excludes the spiritual dimension, crucial foundation, and agent of change will never overcome the evil of the world. Scripture reminds us: "Unless the LORD builds the house, the builders labor in vain. Unless the LORD watches over the city, the guards stand watch in vain. In vain you rise early and stay up late, toiling for food to eat—for he grants sleep to those he loves" (Ps 127:1–2 NIV). One would rightly now ask if the world of conflict defines our mission. Jesus himself told his disciples, "As the Father has sent me, I am sending you" (John 20:21). Obviously, God himself is a missionary God. So why then is reconciliation the framework of the EMS 2022 Compendium?

Based on 2 Corinthians 5, it becomes evident that the people of God are called to be ambassadors of reconciliation. Those who have been reconciled to God have received a unique task: showing others that the present and future need not be defined by the past. Societies such as those described above need the people of God, his church, to provide an alternative way of reconciliation—including a more holistic way of being sent in God's mission and representing his kingdom in this world.

Various names could be mentioned here to describe the journey of missions paradigms and how evangelicals have traditionally referred to reconciliation and Pauline theology with an emphasis on "conversion as essential" (Verster 2016, 622).[4] With more influences from the global South and voices of ecumenicals calling for social transformation (Verster 2016, 622) these old boundaries have diminished. Most missiologists now agree with the approach that Desmond Tutu describes: "To love God involves loving one's neighbor. They go together or both are false. It must incarnate the love and compassion and justice and reconciliation of Christ. It (the church) must work ceaselessly for justice for only thus can it work for reconciliation" (Tutu 1983, 110).

This compendium will show how reconciliation has become a new paradigm of missions. Starting with *Part 1: Reconciliation Theology*, the foundations are defined by authors from America and other places in the world which are then represented in *Part 2: Reconciliation Practices*, to show how theory and practice go hand in hand. The compendium closes with *Part 3: Reconciliation Case Studies*, as paradigm of missions reflected through the view of classic missionary work overseas or through the context of diaspora missions to help the local church, as well as the sending and receiving agencies as they re-consider reconciliation as the guiding principle in their own contexts.

---

4 This is well done by the authors of the articles to follow and through resources cited by them.

Preface

Reconciliation Theology

Why start with theology? Because theology matters. As Kant already recognized: "Thoughts without contents are empty, intuitions without concepts are blind" (Kant 1781). When reading McNeil's pages about the degrading theology that was developed at the Stellenbosch University in South Africa in the 1930s and 40s which further led to a segregated society, her point becomes clear: "Our theology informs our anthropology, which in turn informs our sociology. That is to say, what we believe about God will tell us what we believe about people, and what we believe about people will tell us what kind of communities and societies we believe we should strive to create" (McNeil 2015, 23). Therefore, a theological framework is laid out to reflect the missional practice properly, where the reader then will see how the practices of reconciliation are referring back to the theological foundations.

A key text calling for a theology of reconciliation is 2 Corinthians 5:18–20. The word *reconciliation*, as most theologians agree, is mainly used by Paul and stems from the Greek term *katallasso*. The term comes from the context of negotiations and refers to an exchange. Paul uses this word in his letters to describe the relationship to God and the world (five times) and people to each other (once)—which already hints at the holistic theology that the reader will encounter in part one of this book. From the EMS conference 2022 one can recognize clear threads of a missiological theology of reconciliation from the references cited alone. Throughout this collection you might find similar themes and positions across the authors. Those similarities tend to strengthen the foundation of the collective voice in this book, but also pay attention to when there are divergent views. Likewise, those too broaden the content and give us further ponder.

With a wider biblical view of reconciliation and considering it as part of the mission of God, the first part of the book will not only show how reconciliation as mission is a continuation of the relationship between God as Father, Son, and Spirit to all humankind and creation, but further how it is the expression of God's love for his creation. With this framework, part one portrays the place of the church within the reconciliatory mission of God—his *ecclesia*—as a called and sent out community of ambassadors of reconciliation.

To this end, Tizon sets the scene for the conference topic when he speaks of the actuality of reconciliation as mission. He challenges us "to break out of a reductionist view of the Great Commission and to understand it as nothing less than joining God in God's mission to reconcile all things in Jesus Christ." He develops six competencies that the church needs to acquire in order to fulfill the ministry of reconciliation. Tizon concludes that "a robust understanding of reconciliation provides the best paradigm for the church's mission today" and that "reconciliation is the new 'whole' in holistic missions."

Following this broader understanding of missions, Reimer draws from Old and New Testament accounts to place the mission of the church in the *missio Dei* and reconciliation at the heart of mission of the triune God. He shows the model of the ministry of reconciliation in Jesus's incarnational mission and from there derives six concrete steps as the foundation of the peace and reconciliation ministry of the church.

Continuing with a critical view on reductionist evangelical missiology, Baker presents a biblical understanding of reconciliation through the vertical, horizontal, and transcendent components. After assessing Scripture deeply (with a focus on Pauline theology), Baker builds his argument around twenty-first century missiological approaches to promote a cruciform witness of the church that includes social implications and communal practices of reconciliation. Baker then pinpoints the role of the church in God's mission defined by *being* rather than *doing*.

Lee then takes a deeper look at the American evangelical context. He provides an honest view of American society, naming the hidden drivers of polarization and ideological segregation that are mirrored among and even driven by Christians. As a contrast, he presents 2 Corinthians 5 and the ministry of reconciliation as the call given to the church. Next, following a historical assessment of the church in the first millennium, Lee then points out how modern ecumenicalism enables a journey to a bigger view of the church beyond one's own boundaries and concludes with practical views on the mission of the church in a fractured world.

Okaya closes part one with a valuable contribution by examining classical philosophical and prominent Christian models of forgiveness. He points out how their focus on separating the offense from the agent and expiating guilt on the cross are often not applicable to communal and inter-generational settings where guilt is difficult to locate. Okaya then proposes two emendations to the traditional model of articulating Christian forgiveness: 1) focusing on union with Christ as the driving paradigm for forgiveness, and 2) considering communal shame rather than guilt as forgiveness seeks to overcome the social division in communities. He concludes that this participatory account of Christian forgiveness would be a powerful testimony to the gospel message.

Reconciliation Practices

With the theology from part one, it becomes obvious how God as a missionary God is casting a vision of all *ethne* praising together (Rev 7), is enabling enemies

Preface

to reunite (even lion and lamb), and is providing a way to overcome dichotomies (Eph 2). To accomplish his mission, he sent Jesus, the reconciler of all things. Doing *shalom* and reconciliation work according to 2 Corinthians 5 is not an add-on to missions but at the heart of God's mission and therefore needs to be integrated into the approaches of local and global missions. Being reconciled with God, means to live out the love of Christ toward God, self, and neighbor in restored relationships including stewarding creation and enabling the local church to be (once again) a light in the city. God calls his church to be reconciled with him and to understand ourselves as sent to accomplish this calling.

How can a truly gospel-centered *missio ecclesia* be reimagined and derived from the *missio Dei* (as well as from the *missio Spiritu* and *missio Christi*) calling all people back to the heart of God that is rooted in the call to be reconciled reconcilers? The local church is a collective of disciples of Jesus, the reconciler of all things. Jesus sends his disciples with the commandment, "as the Father has sent me, I am sending you" (John 20:21). Therefore, the need of reconciliation in discipleship approaches and local church ministry is obvious. Disciples of Jesus individually and collectively need to understand their own journey of reconciliation—how they accepted the offer of God to be reconciled to him in their own lives; how they were able to overcome their own wounds and eventually forgive their opponents, enemies, and perpetrators; and how they then understood themselves as sent ones (missional disciples) into the world around them. Those who take a broader approach to missions relate disciple making to the categories of love toward God, self, and others while recognizing the need for reconciliation in these areas and applying this principle to their given context as a community of believers.

David Bosch's *Transforming Mission* shaped the beginning of a new missions paradigm—a missional church that is with the people, bears the creative tension of being in the world, but not of it, perseveres in conflict without becoming people of conflict, and paves the way to be true reconciled reconcilers. But never did he mention "mission as reconciliation." His thought was a church living in "creative tension" (Bosch 1980, 222) which together with other writers has inspired the following authors to reflect how this approach is applied in various contexts.

Manuel and Jeanette Böhm provide an integrated and holistic approach called *reconciling discipleship* rooted in the *missio Dei* and the Pauline theology of 2 Corinthians 5. From their biblical analysis of discipleship and reconciliation, paired with early church understandings of following Jesus, they explore the dimensions of discipleship and reconciliation with God, self, others, and creation into various areas of hurt, healing, restoring relationships, and even the political sphere. Their concept of *reconciling disciples* is then integrated into a local approach of ecclesia, a church as reconciliation center in a specific context.

Harrison endeavors to reassess the unintended consequences of oppositional thinking in missions training and strategy when considering a Christian worldview and its prominent questions that tend to put "the other" in a lower status. She points out homophily in many approaches and introduces a framework of a pilgrimage identity rooted in Christ as the common ground between "us" and "the other." Using the biblical concept of "neighbor," a view of reconciliation is explored that overcomes a two-sided approach where only one party can be "right," in favor of a one-sided in which all are in need of reconciliation.

Smith explores the context of Belfast, Northern Ireland and uses the model of Paul Hiebert to describe the obstacles to reconciliation between Catholics and Protestants with the boundary-set approach, while showing how a centered-set approach of reconciliation could be applied through hospitality. She argues that an embodied approach to missions is shown in hospitality based on findings of a non-profit organization helping asylum seekers arriving in Northern Ireland while using Volf's theological framework to explain the application of the reciprocal movement of the trinitarian God in reconciliation practices.

Howell then uses his experience from Mozambique to explain how the Gospel of Mark applies to a contextualized discipleship approach. He considers three aspects of the Gospel of Mark that stand out (sovereignty, suffering, and discipleship) and uses them to show how in a Muslim context and inter-religious community, the concept of a suffering king (Jesus) can open up opportunities for reconciling people with God and coming to grips with their own individual and collective trauma.

Reconciliation Case Studies

How can we speak about reconciliation and think we could minister into people's lives if we do not understand the brokenness of the world and its conflicts? To have no vision and understanding of the world means to have no clear vision of missions in these contexts. Through the lenses of specific case studies, the reader will see how a deeper or new view of the sometimes foreign-appearing world is necessary in order to build a church in it. Stories of real people and their circumstances show the understanding of different powers at play in various communities and how they influence reconciliation matters.

Preface

Beyerhaus developed the model of a tripolar understanding of the world by looking at the demonic, the anthropological, and the theonomic dimensions (Beyerhaus 2001, 128–40). Contexts of reconciliation ministries are always linked to evil that seems to prevail. Understanding the world means seeing the corrupted world in which Satan is the coauthor of individual, structural, social, political, and other forms of evil. Fallen humanity's search for good, or for God, and its desire to rule and gain power, show how people's corrupted minds lead to all kinds of atrocities, hurts, and trials to escape this world of pain.

As Paul did in Athens (Acts 15), God's church is called to seek avenues to translate the gospel of reconciliation into the local context. Finding theonomic elements in people's hearts and seeing how God has been active among various people, societies, and cultures can enable processes of reconciliation with God, self, and others. The case studies provide examples of such and demonstrate how newcomers to a place seek a healed new home, and how tribal cultures from afar practice elements of reconciliation that can be utilized by the Western church for their approaches to missions.

"An Invitation to the Table" is a study based on The Peoples Church's Newcomers Network in Toronto discussing how food plays a vital role in promoting reconciliation and community building. Andrea and Nelson Chang intertwine biblical analysis with the role of food as a medium for restoration and unity with experiences of newcomers. The study showcases in four areas how eating together provides a platform to encounter people in reciprocity, how to welcome and integrate newcomers with their abilities to restore their purpose, dignity, and hope for the future, and ultimately experience *shalom* and communion with God while at the same time explaining the need for various intercultural and spiritual competencies.

Van Dorp examines the conflict in Myanmar to explain his model for reconciliation based on the biblical analysis and missiological approaches to reconciliation by Robert Schreiter and Miroslav Volf, while acknowledging the challenges for the church in Myanmar. He points out the church's potential to administer reconciliation within Myanmar and to serve as a witness to surrounding countries.

Jakada uses the case study of "The Peace Child" of the Indonesian Sawi people to describe that lasting reconciliation in a community succeeds only if it is community based and founded on a "handle" for reconciliation that is rooted within the respected cultural and religious context of the given community. Based on 2 Corinthians 5, he discusses the biblical mandate of reconciliation and refers to other cultural reconciliation handles from Rwanda and South Africa.

Switching to an African context, Kwizera first lays a foundation for the theology of reconciliation before providing historical insights to the church's development in Rwanda in the nineteenth and twentieth centuries leading up to the genocide and following reconciliation. His paper argues for an integration of reconciliation into discipleship. Of particular interest for the North American context is part three, in which he critiques racism, and part four, which lays out how the Rwandese journey of reconciliation could inspire the global church theologically, sociologically, ecclesiologically, and anthropologically.

Pursley provides a case study of reconciliation between Turks and Armenians based on the Armenian Turkish Peace Initiative (ATPI) that was formed in 2014 and convened several meetings both prior to and after *The Pasadena Declaration*. The article discusses the history of Christianity in Turkey and the impact of the genocide of Christian communities from 1915–1923 while also providing a view to fruits of reconciliation visible in the sending of missionaries and prayer movements.

What Remains?

After reflecting on the theology, the practice, and case studies of reconciliation, the reader of *Ambassadors of Reconciliation: God's Mission through Missions for All* will have gained not only deep insight into the theory, but also the practice of reconciliation. Reconciliation as part of God's mission and continuation of the trinitarian relationship to all humankind and creation is an invitation to participate in the redeeming act of restoring corrupted minds and destructive behaviors, to heal broken relationships between people and their Creator, themselves, others, and all creation.

It is now to us, God's church, to be a prayer-focused, spirit-informed, prophetic voice in our communities, showing people the God-designed way of life. With a refreshed understanding of reconciliation and a new paradigm of missions at hand we hope that this compendium will contribute to your teaching, practicing, and promoting of God's mission. May it help you undertake a critical self-analysis, to overcome outdated missiological paradigms and to embrace different, holistic approaches to spreading the gospel.

As a compendium of only one conference, the limitations are obvious. We encourage you to stay active and contribute, network for unresolved issues, and remain an ambassador for reconciliation in your areas of influence and calling. We have included an appendix of additional resources to aid this process.

Resources Cited

Beyerhaus, Peter. 2001. "Kennen die Religionen den wahren Gott? Das Christuszeugnis in der interreligiösen Begegnung." In *Theologische Beiträge* 32, (Jahrgang): 127–43.

Bosch, David. 1980. *Witness to the World: The Christian Mission in Theological Perspective*. Atlanta: John Knox.

Connaughton, Aidan. 2021. "Americans See Stronger Societal Conflicts than People in Other Advanced Economies." https://www.pewresearch.org/fact-tank/2021/10/13/americans-see-stronger-societal-conflicts-than-people-in-other-advanced-economies/.

Evans, Tony. 2022. *Kingdom Race Theology*. Chicago: Moody Publishers.

Global Peace Index. 2022. https://www.economicsandpeace.org/wp-content/uploads/2022/06/GPI-2022-web.pdf.

Kant, Immanuel. "Immanuel Kant's Critique of Pure Reason." In *Commemoration of the Centenary of its First Publication*. Translated by F. Max Mueller. 2nd Rev. Ed. New York: Macmillan, 1922. https://oll.libertyfund.org/title/ller-critique-of-pure-reason?html=true#Kant_0330_340.

McNeil, Brenda Salter. 2015. *Roadmap to Reconciliation*. Downers Grove, IL: InterVarsity Press.

Truth and Reconciliation Commission of Canada. 2015. *Honoring the Truth, Reconciling for the Future. Summary of the Final Report of the Truth and Reconciliation Commission of Canada*. https://irsi.ubc.ca/sites/default/files/inline-files/Executive_Summary_English_Web.pdf.

Tutu, D. 1983. *Hope and Suffering: Sermons and Speeches*. Johannesburg: Skotaville.

Verster, P. 2016. "Conflicting Models for Mission and Reconciliation: Future Perspectives." *Stellenbosch Theological Journal* 2, no. 2: 621–44. https://doi.org/10.17570/stj.2016.v2n2.a28.

Part 1
Reconciliation Theology

Chapter 1

Reconciling All Things

Missional Competencies in a Broken World

Al Tizon

Today's complex, globalizing world requires the church in mission to become aware of, and adept in, key arenas of twenty-first century life. The ultimate goal here is to understand what I call *competencies in reconciliation*. But before we go there, we first need to make the case for reconciliation, broadly defined, as the missiological paradigm for our times.

If I may get right to the point, *it is time to break out of a reductionist view of the Great Commission and to understand it as nothing less than joining God in God's mission to reconcile all things in Jesus Christ*. I'm not sure how this assertion hits readers initially, but I hope by the end that they will hear it as good news, even as it requires revisiting the underside of mission to appreciate it.

Reconciliation as Mission

A few years ago, I had the privilege of writing a book entitled *Whole and Reconciled: Gospel, Church, and Mission in a Fractured World* (2018).[1] In it, I propose that reconciliation is the new "whole" in holistic mission. Holistic mission, as we know, has referred to an approach to mission that attempts to put back together the ministries of evangelism and social responsibility. Of course, 20/20 hindsight tells us that these two ministries should have never been divorced in the first place. My proposal for reconciliation as mission depends on the church's ability to keep evangelism and justice married.

I stress the importance of reconciliation because in a divided world, holistic mission can no longer be just about putting word and deed back together again; it needs to be about putting the world back together again. It needs to be about participating with God in the ministry of reconciliation between God and people, between people and people, and between God, people, and creation.

---

[1] This chapter is taken from excerpts from *Whole and Reconciled* by Al Tizon, copyright © 2018. Used by permission of Baker Academic, a division of Baker Publishing Group.

Reconciliation is a rich, biblical, theological idea that is based on God's vision to make whole the world and everyone in it. Colossians 1:20 (NRSV) beautifully sums up God's agenda when Paul says, "Through [Christ], God was pleased to reconcile to [God's own self] all things, whether on earth or in heaven."

God's vision of reconciliation only makes sense in light of the biblical story of creation and fall. In the beginning God created *shalom*—a social order wherein perfect harmony existed between the Creator, humanity, and ecosystem—but that *shalom* was shattered by sin (Gen 1–3). Reconciliation is God's initiative to restore wholeness to a shattered creation. The ministry of reconciliation, therefore, to which God has called the church (2 Cor 5:18–20), refers to our participation in God's vision to reconcile all things in Christ. This is our mission. This is the Great Commission.

I will say more about the Great Commission as it relates to reconciliation. For now, allow me to say one more important thing about the nature of biblical reconciliation, namely, it is multi-dimensional. The church's message of reconciliation involves at least three dimensions: (1) the vertical (between God and people); (2) the horizontal (between people and people); and (3) the circular (between God, people, and creation). These dimensions provide the basic framework of the paradigm of "reconciliation as mission." The vertical, horizontal, and circular, or "'triple reconciliation' for individual persons, society, and creation" (Rice 2014, 58–59) point to the main arenas of God's mission and therefore the church's mission.

> The greatness of the Great Commission requires evangelism, peacemaking, and stewardship; it requires God's whole mission of reconciliation if it is going to be truly great.

Missionally speaking, these dimensions express themselves in the ministries of: (1) evangelism, which facilitates reconciliation between God and people; (2) peacemaking, which facilitates reconciliation between people and people; and (3) stewardship, which facilitates reconciliation between God, people, and creation. The church as evangelist, peacemaker, and steward is the church as reconciler in the world; it is the church being commissioned by Father, Son, and Holy Spirit to make disciples among the nations as it participates with God in the reconciliation of all things.

Our understanding of the Great Commission must be holistic in regards to reconciliation in order to call the Great Commission "great." Let me say it another way: the greatness of the Great Commission requires evangelism, peacemaking, and stewardship; it requires God's whole mission of reconciliation if it is going to be truly great.

The Great Commission is not so great when it is one-dimensional instead of three-dimensional. Here, let me humbly reprimand us as evangelicals, among whom the very term "Great Commission" caught on like wildfire in the first place. We have essentially equated the Great Commission with the ministry of evangelism, with Matthew 28 earning the distinction of the premiere evangelistic missionary text. Inspired by it, we have gone about the task of world evangelization with abandon, creating strategies based on unreached people groups and territorial windows to help us fulfill the Great Commission.

I argue that a one-dimensional, evangelism-only theology and practice of the Great Commission is incomplete at best, dangerous at worst. It has in fact contributed to crimes against humanity under colonialism, as the church's collusion with the colonial project is undeniable.

As New Testament scholar Mitzi Smith disturbingly points out in the context of colonized Africa, "Many missionaries, in collusion with European colonizers, separated the physical, unjust, inhumane treatment and oppression of Africans ... from the saving of their souls" (Smith 2014, 128-29). Referring specifically to the one-dimensional understanding of the Great Commission, she continues her strong critique, writing: "Teaching and baptizing black souls trumped the liberating of black bodies from the shackles of their white oppressors" (Smith 2014, 129).

There are literally millions of what I call "victims of the Great Commission"— people, primarily among black and brown cultures, whose dignity, lifeways, and loved ones were destroyed in the service of the one-dimensional Great Commission-inspired evangelization of the world.

Our Fractured World

This undeniable history of colonial missions screams of the necessity of rethinking the Great Commission, and I contend that we do so by defining it in terms of God's mission to reconcile *all* things—the three dimensions of reconciliation—in Jesus Christ. With this biblical warrant, plus the fact that the world seems more broken than ever, seeing the Great Commission as participating with God in the reconciliation of all things offers freshness, a ring of relevance, a compelling way of addressing the fractures that mar our world today by way of our missionary endeavors.

These global fractures are more acute than ever. Due to governmental atrocities, there are more refugees or displaced peoples than the world has ever seen. Bully dictators are emerging everywhere, from the United States to Russia to North Korea to India to Venezuela to Colombia. Personally, I believe the United States is headed for another civil war based on the old line of racism. The misunderstanding and hatred between peoples are simply out of control.

Mass shootings in this country and elsewhere are numbing. The rich get richer and the poor poorer. Sex trafficking is the most lucrative industry on the planet right now. Youth suicides are on the rise. People the world over are fast losing hope.

I admit that this is a dismal perspective on life, but can anyone deny that this is in fact the state of our world today? To be good news, to live out the Great Commission, we need to go and make disciples of all nations, inviting them to be reconciled to God through Jesus Christ and to join God in God's mission to reconcile all things.

Competencies in Reconciliation

So how do we, as missionaries, pastors, activists, and teachers practice reconciliation in the world, as we strive in the Spirit to live out the Great Commission? Part of the answer is to develop what I call *competencies in reconciliation*. More than ever, we need to become aware of, and adept in, certain competencies that address the brokenness of our world today. These competencies speak primarily to the horizontal dimension of reconciliation; they speak in part to what the church needs to be and do if we are going to be Great Commission Reconcilers in Jerusalem, Judea and Samaria, and the ends of the earth.

Theological Competency: Embracing the Kingdom Dream

Theological competency is foundational. Theology matters, and it is for everyone. Researching and *writing* theology may not be for everyone but being theologically competent enough to know the difference between what's true and untrue, authentic, and hypocritical—that is for all of us.

By "theological competency," I mean interpreting reality through the eyes of the gospel. This requires a clear grasp of the reign or kingdom of God. The kingdom of God is the socio-political expression of biblical *shalom*—a world characterized by God's best intentions for creation and everyone in it, because Jesus Christ reigns, and where God in Christ reigns, peace, justice, and reconciliation are established between God and people, between people and people, and between God, people, and creation. To the extent that God in Christ rules, righteousness, peace, mercy, justice, and love shape reality, from the domain of the human heart to the socio-political structure of nations to the order of the cosmos.

The gospel of the good news, of the *shalom* kingdom is the embodied announcement that God in Jesus Christ is restoring *shalom* upon the earth. Naturally then, this news is especially good for the poor, the oppressed, the marginalized, and the traumatized in the world.

Theological competency requires being captivated by this kingdom vision—the kingdom dream, if we wish—so much so that other dreams begin to lose their shine. The *American* dream, for example, is not big enough for children of the king. In fact, the kingdom dream not only overshadows the American dream, but it also challenges it on two fundamental fronts.

The first front is economic. The American dream is built on the pursuit of material success, and I argue that those who were raised in market-based societies default to this pursuit. We've been programmed to climb the ladder of financial and material success, and for the most part Christians have not demonstrated anything different. As Michael Budde and Robert Brimlow argue in *Christianity Incorporated*, "the church ... has become a chaplain to capitalism, a sanctifier of the vision and goals of the American dream" (Budde and Brimlow 2002, 24). As such, the church allows itself to be shaped by the wrong dream. If this is true, one word comes to mind: Repent! For as Jesus said, we "cannot serve God and mammon" (Matt 6:24). Our theological competency enables us to see the hold that pursuing wealth has had on us, to repent of it, and to begin pursuing the kingdom dream instead.

In addition to the economic front, the American dream is characterized by an inherent nationalism that the kingdom dream also challenges. Theological competency enables us to see any version of "America-first" thinking as far too small for the people of God. The kingdom dream is for Jerusalem, Judea and Samaria, and the ends of the earth. The kingdom dream refers to God's *global* agenda, and any overly patriotic, nationalistic, militant agendas run contrary to the kingdom dream.

As the church becomes more theologically competent, we turn from mammon and nation worship and begin to embrace God, God's kingdom, God's *shalom*. Doing so is crucial for the Great Commission that sends us out to reconcile all things in Christ.

Intercultural Competency: Affirming Diversity

Another area in which we need to become adept is intercultural competency. Our world today is defined by the increasingly multicultural milieu that describes our neighborhoods and communities. Missionaries have entered deeply into that milieu; so theoretically, we're more poised than most to help the church become more competent in this area, even as we ourselves continue to grow in it.

Missionaries or not, we need tools to develop this competency. For example, the Intercultural Development Inventory (IDI) is an assessment tool that precisely measures one's intercultural competence. In the Evangelical Covenant Church, the denomination to which I belong, missionaries, pastors, and denominational staff are required to take this assessment on a regular basis. Anyone who has subjected themselves to the IDI knows that it is tough on the ego! Even the most self-aware among us score lower than they anticipate. We all need to grow in our intercultural competency.

To stimulate this growth, we need to be affirming of all cultures, even as we seek the transformation of all cultures, including our own. Furthermore, in contrast to resisting cultural diversity, we need to be more affirming of the intermingling of cultures with one another. This translates into becoming more intentional about meeting the new neighbors and serving them.

For example, consider Harvest Time Christian Fellowship (HTCF) in Philadelphia. A predominantly Black congregation, HTCF intentionally moved to a predominantly Hispanic neighborhood, which is located just on the other side of a large park that separates the two communities. More than a geographical boundary, this park has symbolized the segregation between the two communities. Replanted now on "the wrong side" of the park, HTCF not only began offering ESL classes, a need their new neighbors identified, but the church also asked a number of residents of the other side of the park to teach Spanish to the church members, as part of its efforts to bridge the two communities.

The times require this kind of reconciliatory intentionality to counter the divisiveness of our world. Continuing to have mono-cultural churches, conferences, and other Christian gatherings should make less and less sense as the world becomes more and more intercultural. They should feel as awkward as attending an all-men's or all-women's church. We should develop an acute awareness that when we gather in Christ's name for whatever reason, we need to model the multicolored gospel of reconciliation.

Interreligious Competency: Dialoguing with Other Faiths

Another area of competency in which we need to become adept is interreligious competency. We need to learn to dialogue well with those of other faiths or no faith. Inevitably, as cultures come together, so do different religious belief systems, and we need to know how to dialogue with them. Learning to dialogue is different from studying up on their religious beliefs so we can convert them.

It will become extremely important in the coming days, if not already dire, for the church to learn how to dialogue with "the religious other," to know how to listen to them and learn from them, as well as to know how to proclaim Jesus in word, deed, and life in a confident, but humble way. Christian-Muslim tensions, for example, are at an all-time high. According to Bryant Myers, "Learning to love our Muslim neighbor may be the biggest and most important missiological frontier Christians face in this century" (Myers 2017, 13).

I suspect that a theology of religions—that specialized field in theology that deals with the complexities posed by a plurality of religions in the world—will gain prominence in the age of globalization, not just in the academy, but also in lay training institutes and church adult education programs. Because churches, not just the subculture of the missionary community, need to know how to understand, interact with, and work together with people of other faiths. Interfaith dialogue at the very least involves Christian hospitality, genuine listening, sharing our own religious convictions with humble confidence, and humanitarian partnership with people of other faiths (Tizon 2012, 146–47).

> Many of today's preachers assume that the behaviors that make sense to them will automatically make sense to those to whom they minister.

Intergenerational Competency: Learning Across the Ages

Another area of competency in which we need to grow is intergenerational competency. The ministry of reconciliation must address the perpetual rift between the young and the old. Our young have before them the largest smorgasbord of knowledge, beliefs, values, and lifestyles ever known to man. To the extent that it can, the church needs to know what and how they are processing the massive amount of information at their fingertips. The church needs to be in touch with their thinking about life, God, church, sexuality, relationships, violence, and death more than ever before. We must know how to share Jesus in a way that resonates with young people, lest we completely lose the next generation to the globalization vortex.

Intergenerational competency depends largely on the church overcoming its propensity toward traditionalism—not tradition, but traditionalism, which is characterized by a resistance to change. When we old people scoff at their movie and musical icons as figures of anti-faith, the youth begin to slip away. When we refuse to have open conversations regarding outlooks, values, and philosophies that differ from church convention, they begin to slip away. In order to develop intergenerational competency, the church "must change with the continually changing culture yet preserve the truth of the gospel of Jesus Christ and the historic Christian faith" (George 2003, 35).

The other side of this coin is that young people need to respect and listen to their parents and grandparents, because these elder saints have much wisdom to impart from their greater experience. Intergenerational competency has to do with both the young and the old learning from each other. We need to see intergenerational church, theology, worship, and mission, as integral to the ministry of reconciliation. Mission today needs all hands—smooth young hands and wrinkled old ones—on deck.

Internet Competency: Contextualizing to the New World

Related somewhat to the prior competency, we also need to develop internet competency. The internet is not just another means of communication, but a hyper-medium that subsumes, links, and enhances all previous media. The internet is a culture all its own. And while our children are natives to this culture, previous generations, including mine, are immigrants. We go to the young to help us navigate this new world. The question for the church is not, "How do we share the gospel through the internet," but rather, "How do we share the gospel *in* internet." The internet is as much a place as China or any geo-cultural entity. And just like we would as missionaries ask, "How do we share the gospel in China?" if we were serving in China, we need to ask, "How do we share the gospel in internet?" Understanding the internet as a culture, we need to apply the principles of missiological contextualization and thus, become competent in navigating the new culture with the gospel.

Spiritual Competency: Joining the Mustard Seed Conspiracy

Finally, we need to develop spiritual competency that will enable us to be faithful to our mission. To do so, the church must act out mustard seed faith in the world. By that, I mean the church committing to doable, local acts of peace, justice, community, discipleship, reconciliation, and evangelism, believing that in the hands of God, these small, seemingly insignificant, drop-in-the-bucket acts do their part in reflecting what is to come in Jesus Christ.

I'm forever indebted to the work of Tom Sine for giving me a lasting metaphor for mission. As a young Christian in my early 20s, I stumbled upon his book *Mustard Seed Conspiracy* (1981). In retrospect, it has probably motivated me to lead an active, missional life more than any other book. By creatively developing Jesus's parable of the mustard seed (Matt 13:31–32; Mark 4:30–32; Luke 13:18–19), Sine made "changing the world" seem doable, as he invited the ordinary and unassuming to join the subversive work of God, to join the mustard seed conspiracy.

To engage in something as large as transforming the world in Christ ironically requires a commitment to the small, the local, the less-than-glorious. As famous activist founder of the *Catholic Worker*, Dorothy Day famously quipped, "Everyone wants a revolution, but no one wants to do the dishes."[2]

---

[2] While this quote is something Dorothy Day would say, no one seems to be able to verify that she actually said it.

This saying should hang on the wall of any would-be revolutionary as a reminder of what's required of us—not the big and flashy, but the small, the unassuming, the faithful, and the personal.

And as God gathers the church's small, mustard seed acts of faith happening all over the world, we can rest in the promise that the kingdom of God in its fullness will come. The *eschaton* belongs to Christ.

Conclusion

In conclusion, the Great Commission is to participate with God in the reconciliation of all things in Jesus Christ. These six competencies in reconciliation are the areas of our mission today for our practical consideration:

1. Theological: embracing the kingdom dream
2. Intercultural: affirming cultural diversity
3. Interreligious: dialoguing with other faiths
4. Intergenerational: learning across the ages
5. Internet: contextualizing to the new world
6. Spiritual: joining the mustard seed conspiracy

Go therefore and participate with God in the reconciliation of all things, making disciples of all nations, baptizing them in the name of the Father, Son, and Holy Spirit, and teaching them to obey everything—everything!—that Jesus has shown us. Amen.

References Cited

Budde, Michael, and Robert W. Brimlow. 2002. *Christianity Incorporated*. Grand Rapids, MI: Eerdmans.

George, Sam. 2003. "Emerging Youth Cultures in the Era of Globalization: TechnoCulture and TerrorCulture" and "TerrorCulture: Worth Living for and Worth Dying For." In *One World or Many? The Impact of Globalization on Mission*. Edited by Richard Tiplady, 33–53. Pasadena, CA: William Carey Library.

Intercultural Development Inventory. 2023. *The Roadmap to Intercultural Competence Using the IDI*. Intercultural Development Inventory, LLC (idiinventory.com).

Myers, Bryant L. 2017. *Engaging Globalization: The Poor, Christian Mission, and Our Hyperconnected World*. Grand Rapids, MI: Baker Academic.

Rice, Chris. "Cape Town 2010: Reconciliation, Discipleship, Mission, and the Renewal of the Church in the 21st Century." In *Mission as Ministry of Reconciliation*. Edited by Robert Schreiter and Knud Jørgensen, 52–65. Oxford: Regnum.

Sine, Tom. 1981. *The Mustard Seed Conspiracy*. Waco, TX: Word.

Smith, Mitzi J. 2014. "'Knowing More Than Is Good for One': A Womanist Interrogation of the Matthean Great Commission." In *Teaching All Nations: Interrogating the Matthean Great Commission*. Edited by Mitzi J. Smith and Jayachitra Lalitha, 127–56. Minneapolis: Fortress.

Tizon, Al. 2012. *Missional Preaching: Engage, Embrace, Transform*. Valley Forge, PA: Judson.

Tizon, Al. 2018. *Whole and Reconciled: Gospel, Church, and Mission in a Fractured World*. Grand Rapids, MI: Baker Academic.

Chapter 2

Reconciliation—A Missionary Paradigm for the Twenty-First Century

Johannes Reimer

Understanding the Mission of God

Christian mission is all about God's mission, the *missio Dei*. He is the source, the initiator, and practitioner of mission in the world (Vicedom 2002, 32). He, the triune God, designed, rules, and sustains the world. In his mission God says consequently "Yes" to the world. He embraces responsibility for the world. In fact, as David J. Bosch says, "Christian mission gives expression to the dynamic relationship between God and the world" (Bosch 1991, 9).

What is God's mission practically speaking? And how does God do missions? To understand these questions, we have to look at the very being of God: his divine, triune nature. God is three in one: Father, Son and Holy Spirit—a perfect unity of love. The church father John Damaskin (AD 675–749) used the image of a round dance (Greek *perichoresis*) to capture this unity.[1] Miroslav Volf speaks of a *reciprocal interiority*, suggesting that whenever one person of the Trinity acts, the other two are immanently involved (Volf 1998, 209). Jesus brings out this point when he answers Philip, who desires to see God the Father: "Anyone who has seen me, has seen the Father" (John 14:9 NLT). The Son expresses the Father in perfect love and obedience as the Spirit does toward the Son (John 16:15).

God is a missionary God, and this mission is perfectly interconnected in his trinitarian nature. What the Father designs, the Son brings to hearing, and the Spirit acts to fulfill the divine vision. This builds a perfect trinitarian cycle of mission.[2]

In his mission of the Father, *missio patri*, God lays the foundation: the meaning and the aim for the world he made. God's ultimate goal is a world designed as his kingdom, which he rules over as his creation in perfect unity between creator and creation (Isa 65:17–25). Reconciliation of the world with him is at the center of this mission (2 Cor 5:18).

---
1 See my discussion on the subject in: Reimer, *Die Welt umarmen*, 153–54.
2 See the in-depth discussion in: Reimer, *Die Welt umarmen*, 160–91.

The Son, Jesus Christ, in his mission, the *missio Christi*, sets the path of action. In him God offers a standard of mission, a method to be followed. Whoever enrolls in God's mission will do so by following the Jesus model.

And finally, God acts in the world through the Holy Spirit. The mission of the Spirit, *nissio Spiritus*, is to manage God's missionary acts on earth. He is the Lord of the ministry of God's new covenant (2 Cor 3:17).

Reciprocal interiority marks God in both his being and his mission. Foundation, methodology, and praxis are absolutely interdependent. Whatever God designs remains his will. God's words will always find fulfillment (Isa 55:11; Heb 4:12).

It is impossible, therefore, to separate creation in all its godly missionary vision from salvation as an expression of love. The cultural mandate is found in Genesis 1:26–28, where God names humanity's role in his vision for the world, commissioning them to multiply, cultivate, and civilize the earth. The Great Commission, found in Matthew 28:18–20, is sending the disciples of Jesus to the nations of the world to make them disciples for his kingdom. These two mandates mark poles of the same missionary intention—to establish a world in which God rules.

Everything God does reflects his being and mission. This broad definition may understandably create irritation. If everything is mission, one might ask, what, then, is mission? The term becomes fuzzy and not indefinite. God, however, is always real, never fuzzy or debatable, so his mission cannot be less than what he is, since his being and mission are one.

The Intention of God's Mission

In mission theology, we distinguish between the dimension and intention of God's mission (Gensichen 1971, 85). While the *missio Dei* addresses many dimensions of what God does in the world, its intention is unique, and is found in the core sending of Jesus Christ. No one else and nothing else have revealed God's heart more deeply than his Son. In fact, God's mission was in total harmony with his heart. Who ever saw Jesus saw his Father, and by looking at Jesus and his mission we will be able to pinpoint God's missional heart.

So why did God send his only begotten Son? What is God's divine intention in sending Jesus? The Apostle Paul answers our question in his letter to the Colossians by writing:

> The Son is the image of the invisible God, the firstborn over all creation. For in him all things were created: things in heaven and on earth, visible and invisible, whether thrones or powers or rulers or authorities; all things have been created through him and for him. He is before all things, and in him

all things hold together. And he is the head of the body, the church; he is the beginning and the firstborn from among the dead, so that in everything he might have the supremacy. For God was pleased to have all his fullness dwell in him, and through him to reconcile to himself all things, whether things on earth or things in heaven, by making peace through his blood, shed on the cross. (Col 1:15–20 NIV)

Jesus is God's answer to a world in trouble, to the world he loves and says "yes" too. At the same time, God must reject sin, corruption, rebellion, and the self-destruction of humans in the world. God embraces the world, but he will never embrace or even tolerate the sins of the world. Sin is the root of world turmoil. Where sin takes over death will be the outcome. "For the wages of sin is death" (Rom 6:23 NIV). God does not want death. He is all about life. He is the source of all life (John 1:1). In his mission he establishes a covenant of life and peace (Mal 2:5). Because of his love to the world, God sent Jesus, the God-Son, to the world.

Jesus was sent to reconcile the world with God and bring peace to all life in all creation. God is a God of peace (Rom 15:33; 1 Cor 14:33, etc.) and he sends Jesus as his Prince of Peace (Isa 9:6) to bring peace to those who are near and far (Eph 2:17). This message is what the New Testament calls *gospel*. Reconciliation and peace are the very heart of the gospel. The gospel is a gospel of peace (Eph 6:15), introducing God's kingdom "of righteousness, peace, and joy in the Holy Spirit" (Rom 14:17 NIV). God's mission is peace-centered. Wherever God exercises his mission, his peace permeates his actions, and the aim is reconciliation.

God's Mission of Peace

God is a Lord of Peace, as Gideon names him (Judg 6:24) and his kingdom is a kingdom of peace (Rom 14:17, 18). His mission is a mission of peace (Zech 9:10) and the kingdom in which he rules will be marked by peace. The Old and New Testaments praise God for being a God of peace (e.g., Rom 15:33; 16:20; 1 Cor 14:33; 2 Cor 13:11; Phil 4:9; Heb 13:20).

The Old Testament uses the term *shalom* to describe a reconciled space. According to Walter Eisenbeis (1969, 50) the Hebrew term *shalom* stands for "a condition of Wholeness."[3] Johannes Pedersen, defines *shalom* as a state of friendship and harmony in family, kinship, and nation (Pedersen 1926, 285–311). Where there is *shalom*, justice and relationships will be restored (Harris 1980, 930–31), harmony and health in all regards will be introduced and realized (Albertz 1983, 17). *Shalom* is the originally implied vision of created life in

---

3 Eisenbeis uses the German term "Ganzheit."

harmony with its creator. As Gerhard von Rad (1935, 400–5) rightly states, *shalom* in the Old Testament requires the presence of God. Holistic reconciliation aims for *shalom*—a culture of peace on all levels of individual and social life.

The Old Testament always relates *shalom* to God (Rad 1950, 401). *Shalom* exists because God grants his people a covenant of peace (Num 25:12; Josh 9:15; Isa 54:10; Ezek 34:25; 37:26). God is the source and the gracious giver of *shalom*. The *Theological Wordbook of the OT* states: "*missio* is the result of God's activity in covenant and is the result of righteousness (Isa 32:17). In nearly two-thirds of its occurrences, *missio* describes the state of fulfillment which is the result of God's presence" (Harris 1980, 931).

The Old Testament prophets, especially Isaiah, envision a coming kingdom of *shalom*, where God rules (Isa 52:7; 54:10–15; 55:3–5; 57:19). In fact, peace to all nations is the aim of his acts in the world (Zech 9:10).

Similarly, the New Testament speaks of peace. Paul speaks about Jesus in Colossians 1:19, 20 (NIV) when he says, "For God was pleased to have all his fullness dwell in him, and through him to reconcile to himself all things, whether things on earth or things in heaven, by making peace through his blood, shed on the cross."

Jesus, is God's peace, sent by God to reconcile the world to a state of original creation (2 Cor 5:18).

Reconciliation: The Heart of God's Mission

Craig Ott, consequently defines mission as "the sending activity of God with the purpose of reconciling to himself and bringing into his kingdom fallen men and women from every people and nation to his glory" (Ott 2010, 155). Together with other authors, he bases his conviction on Pauline theology.[4] The Apostle Paul states in 2 Corinthians 5:18–21 (NIV):

> All this is from God, who reconciled us to himself through Christ and gave us the ministry of reconciliation: that God was reconciling the world to himself in Christ, not counting people's sins against them. And he has committed to us the message of reconciliation. We are therefore Christ's ambassadors, as though God were making his appeal through us. We implore you on Christ's behalf: Be reconciled to God. God made him who had no sin to be sin for us, so that in him we might become the righteousness of God.

The text underlines three basic propositions: (1) reconciliation is God's work in Christ; (2) reconciliation aims toward restoration of God's relationship with the world; and (3) reconciliation is a core ministry of the church.

---

4 See in this regard: Breitenbach, *Versöhnung*, 60.

It is the current condition of the world in relationship to God, which brings reconciliation to the table (Bieringer 1987, 295–326). The world has become godless by forsaking and forgetting what God's plan for the world originally was. Dishonoring God, humans have fallen into a self-destructive way of life. And as a result, says Paul,

> They were filled with all manner of unrighteousness, evil, covetousness, malice. They are full of envy, murder, strife, deceit, maliciousness. They are gossips, slanderers, haters of God, insolent, haughty, boastful, inventors of evil, disobedient to parents, foolish, faithless, heartless, ruthless. (Rom 1:29–31 ESV)

All these destructive attributes are produced by a corrupted mind, by the futility of godless thinking. The apostle warns the church in Ephesus:

> So, I tell you this, and insist on it in the Lord, that you must no longer live as the Gentiles do, in the futility of their thinking. They are darkened in their understanding and separated from the life of God because of the ignorance that is in them due to the hardening of their hearts. (Eph 4:17–18 NIV)

Ignorance is the problem. Humans have lost their vision. They have turned blind and walk in darkness. Their leaders are blind leading the blind (Matt 15:14), and they do what is wrong in the sight of God, following their own thoughts and desires and deserving his wrath (Eph 2:1–3).

The loving heart of God, however, seeks renewal and restoration. God does not want sinners to perish (Ezek 33:11) and therefore he sent his only begotten Son to save and reconcile the world to himself (2 Cor 5:18). To reconcile means to bring God's plan back to mind, to ignite the original vision. This is the message of God's revelation in Scripture. "From Genesis to Revelation, Scripture witnesses to God's total mission 'to reconcile to himself all things, whether things on earth or things in heaven' (Col 1:15–20). The fullness of reconciliation is friendship with God in Jesus Christ" (Rice 2005, 11).

The reconciled are new in Christ (2 Cor 5:17) and follow Christ's mind (Phil 2:5). Reconciliation is the restoration of memory, the renewal of the mind, and the ability to understand what the will of God for life is (Rom 12:1–3). Leaving our godless past behind and striving toward a future designed by God for those who accept Christ as their Lord and Savior—this is what reconciliation does. God desires peace with his creation and, therefore peace is at the heart of his mission (Reimer 2017, 69). Pope Benedict XVI writes: "Reconciliation then, is not limited to God's plan to draw estranged and sinful humanity to himself in Christ through the forgiveness of sins and out of love. It is also the restoration of relationships between people through the settlement of differences and the removal of obstacles to their relationships in their experience of God's love" (Pope Benedict 2010, 8). Robert Schreiter summarizes properly:

What we see in these Pauline passages is how reconciliation is a central way of explaining God's work in the world. Through the Son and the Spirit, God is making peace—between God and the world, and thus also within all of creation itself. When this insight is brought together with the concept of the *missio Dei* developed a few decades earlier in missiology, we see the biblical foundations for reconciliation as a paradigm of mission, a paradigm that began taking on a particular poignancy and urgency in the last decade of the twentieth century. (Schreiter 2013, 14)

God's Mission and the Mission of God's People

God's people are invited and sent to participate in his mission. The church is "a people in God's reign," according to the German theologian Leonard Goppelt (Goppelt 1978, 254). Does this mean that all missionary activity of God's people must intentionally follow a spirit of peace and reconciliation? Yes, says the Apostle Paul to the Christians in Corinth. In 2 Corinthians 5:18–19 (NIV) we read:

> All this is from God, who reconciled us to himself through Christ and gave us the ministry of reconciliation: that God was reconciling the world to himself in Christ, not counting people's sins against them. He has committed to us the message of reconciliation.

God's people have been given a mission of reconciliation and peace. We are sent as our Lord was sent, with the same intention. The church is called to a mission of reconciliation to introduce peace to all the tribes of the world. And we are commissioned to do so in the way of Jesus.

How then did Jesus bring peace to those near and those far (Eph 2:17)? He is "God's best missionary" (Escobar 2006, 97), the message and the mission model. In Jesus the church finds what Samuel Escobar calls the "Christological pattern" of mission (Escobar 2006, 106). God's method of doing missions is expressed in his sending.[5] What is peace-building Jesus's way?

How Did Jesus Build Peace?

The New Testament tells us the story of Jesus, his life, and his works, in the Gospels. This story may be recaptured in six basic steps.

First, the mission of Jesus started with his coming into the world. John states in John 1:1–5, 14 (NIV):

> In the beginning was the Word, and the Word was with God, and the Word was God. He was with God in the beginning. Through him all things were made; without him nothing was made that has

---
5 See an in-depth discussion in: Reimer, *Die Welt umarmen*, 172–81.

been made. In him was life, and that life was the light of all mankind. The light shines in the darkness, and the darkness has not overcome it. ... The Word became flesh and made his dwelling among us. We have seen his glory, the glory of the one and only Son, who came from the Father, full of grace and truth.

Jesus enters the world as a human being in order to reveal God to humans. The evangelist Luke notes in Luke 1:76–79 (NIV) the prophecy of Zechariah about his son, John the Baptist and the coming Messiah:

And you, my child, will be called the prophet of the Most High; for you will go before the Lord to prepare the way for him, to give his people the knowledge of salvation through the forgiveness of their sins, because of the tender mercy of our God, by which the rising sun shall come to us from heaven to shine on those living in darkness and in the shadow of death, to guide our feet into the path of peace.

The Messiah comes to bring peace. At the day of his birth the angels praise him for bringing peace to the earth (Luke 2:14). Jesus, the Son of God, comes as one of us, found in everything as a man, but without sin (Heb 4:15). He understands what we go through. Incarnation, being made in flesh, marks the entry point of a ministry of reconciliation. Jesus sets out to reconcile men with God as a human being. The gospel is a human story in every regard.

Second, the initial public actions of Jesus among people around him were fascinating. Jesus started his public ministry by serving people. Sick, wounded, hungry, tax collectors rejected by the community, and desperate managers of a wedding facing the fact that they had run out of wine. All of them were served by Jesus. He turned water to wine, laid his hands on the sick and healed them, and multiplied bread and fish to feed the hungry. He cared for widows and outcasts such as the tax collectors, lepers, and demoniacs. By serving people, Jesus built his reputation. Masses were following him, entrusting him to help them and change their lives. Trust defined the point of entry of Christ's ministry, and it was built by service. The ministry of reconciliation presupposes service. The reconciler cares for the needy. In fact, his own self-understanding is pictured in Luke 4:18–19 (NIV). Jesus says: "The Spirit of the Lord is on me, because he has anointed me to proclaim good news to the poor. He has sent me to proclaim freedom for the prisoners and recovery of sight for the blind, to set the oppressed free, to proclaim the year of the Lord's favor." He comes as a servant to become the reconciler!

Third, by serving people Jesus got invited into their homes. He ate and drank with them. Many of them were neglected and even cast out by the religious elite. The scribes and Pharisees were criticizing Jesus by mocking him for eating with the sinners (Matt 9:11; Mark 2:16 NIV). Tax collectors, prostitutes, and others were among them. Serving them opened opportunities for conversation and fellowship. Table fellowship was the sign of a trusting relationship in the Jewish culture of the day. Here was the place where people shared their needs and experiences and built friendships. The reconciliation that Jesus was practicing presupposed such conversations, and established a creative, life-promoting dialogue.

Fourth, Jesus did not only serve and converse with people. The way he lived and served was provocative. The religious elite especially felt endangered by what he did. The masses following him indicated a movement which seemed to have the potential to challenge their authority and position of power. Soon they engaged Jesus in all kinds of discussions, questioning his authority. Jesus did not flee such debates. In contrast, he used them time after time to reveal hypocrisy, wrong teachings, heresy, and the wrong doings of his opponents, as in the case of the woman caught in adultery (John 8:1–11). The Pharisees use her to challenge Jesus's theology, ready to kill the woman for what she did. Jesus responds by revealing their own sinful condition by saying: "Let any one of you who is without sin be the first to throw a stone at her" (v. 7). None of them did. Ashamed, they all left and Jesus, having saved the woman from stoning, encouraged her to go and sin no more. Jesus lived a life in truth, revealing the true condition in which his fellow Jews were living. Reconciliation as done by Jesus never covered up sin, but rather revealed it. Truth precedes freedom and peace.

Fifth, Jesus forgave sin, freed people from bondage, and gave them peace. Some of them could not even move—they were brought to Jesus to experience freedom. Think of a woman like Mary Magdalene, the known sinner, who washed the feet of Jesus with her tears and anointed him with perfume (Luke 7:36–50). Jesus forgave her sins and send her home in peace.

And finally, Jesus reconciles people with a purpose. The Apostle Paul reflects on his reconciling act and says in Ephesians 2:4–10 (NIV):

> But because of his great love for us, God, who is rich in mercy, made us alive with Christ even when we were dead in transgressions—it is by grace you have been saved. And God raised us up with Christ and seated us with him in the heavenly realms in Christ Jesus, in order that in the coming ages he might show the incomparable riches of his grace, expressed in his kindness to us in Christ Jesus. For it is by grace you have been saved, through faith—and this is not from yourselves, it is the gift of God—not by works, so that no one can boast. For we are God's handiwork, created in Christ Jesus to do good works, which God prepared in advance for us to do.

Reconciliation through Jesus leads to mission, "to do good works, which God prepared in advance for us to do" (v. 10).

In summary: Jesus applied six basic steps to reconciling humans with themselves, God and one another. In simple words Jesus:

1. Joined the people
2. Served them, winning their trust
3. Talked to them about their lives
4. Confronted them with their sinful lives
5. Healed them
6. Called them to follow him in his mission

The Church: Agent of Reconciliation and Peace

Messengers of Reconciliation

The church is called to step into the mission of Christ. It has no other call, no other vision, no other methodology. The church is invited to join the people, incarnate into a given culture, serve and converse with the people, confront them with their sin, lead them to divine healing and reconciliation, and invite them to join God's mission in the world. Mission is first and foremost God's mission, *missio Dei* (Vicedom 2002, 32). Whatever we might think and say about the mission of the church, it must be rooted in God's mission, "the heart of all mission" (Brunner 1951, 17). The church exists for God's mission, it is, as Emil Brunner puts it "a proclaiming existence" (Brunner 1951, 17). And it proclaims God's redemptive heart and act. Craig Ott consequently defines mission as "the sending activity of God with the purpose of reconciling to himself and bringing into his kingdom fallen men and women from every people and nation to his glory (Ott 2010, 155). The mission of the church must therefore be defined by reconciliation.

> The church is called to step into the mission of Christ. It has no other call, no other vision, no other methodology.

1. Living a reconciled life
2. Serving troubled people
3. Dialoguing for peace
4. Naming the hard issues
5. Healing the wounded
6. Engaging in God's mission

Reconciliation as Paradigm of Mission

It is fascinating to see that the issue of reconciliation has become one of the central themes in mission circles since the early 1990s (Schreiter 2013, 13). It has developed rapidly to a vividly discussed model of mission.[6] Some authors even postulate that solving the disturbing factors and eliminating sources of societal conflict in society and aiming for a meaningful convivence (Sundermeier 1986, 86–90) will determine the future of Christian mission (Reimer 2011, 19–35). Robert Schreiter speaks of reconciliation as paradigm of mission (Schreiter 2005, 74–83). The Lausanne Movement (LOP 51) and the mainline denominations (Rice 2005, 18–19), the Ecumenical Movement (WCC 2005), and the Roman Catholic Church (Pope Benedict: *Africae Munus*) all reclaim mission as reconciliation for their future operations.

The changes occurring after the millennium in regard to reconciliation as mission are best depicted by looking at the fundamental difference in how the Lausanne Movement regards reconciliation. In 1974 Lausanne emphasized that "reconciliation with God is not reconciliation with other people." Here reconciliation was viewed as a fruit of evangelism. The 2010 statement takes a different view: "Reconciliation to God is inseparable from reconciliation to one another" and it is a model of mission (Rice 2013, 53). The mission of the church is, in the perspective of all major Christian traditions, a mission of reconciliation.

Mission as Reconciliation does not, however, replace all other ministries of the mission of the Church. Robert Schreiter states it well:

> Reconciliation as a paradigm of mission does not replace the other paradigms but can bring them into closer connection with one another within the larger frame of God's intentions for the world. So this two-fold contribution—to the larger questions of reconciliation in the world today and to the dialogue between paradigms of mission within the churches—assures a continuing role for this paradigm of reconciliation on missionary thinking for the coming decades. (Schreiter 2013, 29)

---

6 See for instance an overview of the debate in Matthey, "Versöhnung im ökumenischen missionstheologischen Dialog," 174–91.

References Cited

Albertz, Rainer. 1983. "Shalom und Versöhnung. Alttestamentliche Kriegs- und Friedenstraditionen." In *Theologia Practica* 18 (1/2): 16–29.

Bieringer, R. 1987. "2Kor 5,19a und die Versöhnung der Welt." In *EthL* 63 (1987): 295–326.

Bosch, David J. 1991. *Transforming Mission. Paradigm Shifts in Theology of Mission*. Maryknoll, NY: Orbis.

Breitenbach, Cilliers. 1989. *Versöhnung. Eine Studie zur paulinischen Soteriologie*. Wissenschaftliche Monographien zm Alten und Neuen Testament, 60. Neukirchen-Vluyn: Neukirchener Verlag.

Brunner, Emil. 1951. *Vom Missverständnis der Kirche*. Stuttgart: Evangelisches Verlagshaus.

Eisenbeis, Walter. 1969. *Die Wurzel שלם im Alten Testament*. Berlin: de Gruyter.

Escobar, Samuel. 2006. "Evangelical Missiology. Peering into the future at the turn of the century." In *Global Missiology for the 21st Century. The Iquacu Dialogue*, edited by William D. Taylor. Grand Rapids, MI: Baker: 101–22.

Escobar, Samuel. 2006. *La Palabra—Vida de la Iglesia*. Atlanta: Editorial Mundo Hispano.

Faith and Order Paper No 201. 2005. "Participating in God's Mission of Reconciliation—A Resource for Churches in Situations of Conflict." World Council of Churches, December 31, 2005. https://www.oikoumene.org/en/resources/documents/commissions/faith-and-order/vi-church-and-world/Faith-and-Order-201?set_language=en.

Gensichen, Hans-Werner. 1971. *Glaube für die Welt. Theologische Aspekte der Mission*. Gütersloh: Gütersloher Verlag.

Goppelt, Leonard. 1978. *Theologie des Neuen Testaments*. Göttingen: Vandehoeck and Ruprecht.

Harris, Laird R., Gleason L. Archer, and Bruce K. Waltke, eds. 1980. *Theological Wordbook of the Old Testament*. 2 volumes. Chicago: Moody Press.

Lausanne Occasional Paper No. 51 (October 2004) "A New Vision, a New Heart, a Renewed Call." Paper presented at the Lausanne Committee for World Evangelism in Pattaya, Thailand. https://lausanne.org/content/lop/lop-51-reconciliation-as-the-mission-of-god.

Matthey, Jacques. 2005. "Versöhnung im ökumenischen missionstheologischen Dialog." In *ZfM* 3 (2005): 174–91.

Ott, Craig. 2010. *Encountering Theology of Mission. Biblical Foundations, Historical Developments, and Contemporary Issues*. Grand Rapids, MI: Baker.

Pedersen, Johannes. *Israel. Its Life and Culture*. Reprint of the first edition from 1926. London: Geoffrey Cumberlege (I–II).

Reimer, Johannes. 2011. "Der Dienst der Versöhnung—bei der Kernkompetenz ansetzen. Zur Korrelation von Gemeinwesenmediation und multikulturellem Gemeindebau." In *Theologisches Gespräch*. Heft 1/2011: 19–35.

Reimer, Johannes. 2013. *Die Welt umarmen. Theologie des gesellschaftsrelevanten Gemeindebaus*. Transformationsstudien Bd. 1. 2 edition. Marburg: Francke Verlag.

Reimer, Johannes. 2017. *Missio Politica. The Mission of the Church and Politics*. Carlisle, UK: Langham.

Rice, Chris. 2005. *Reconciliation as the Mission of God. Christian Witness in the World of Destructive Conflicts*. Durham, NC: Duke Divinity School.

Rice, Chris. 2013. "Cape Town 2010: Reconciliation, Discipleship, Mission, and the Renewal of the Church in 21st Century." In *Mission as Ministry of Reconciliation*. Edited by Robert Schreiter and Knud Jørgensen, 52–65. Oxford: Regnum Books.

Schreiter, Robert. 2005. "Reconciliation and Healing as a Paradigm for Mission." In *International Review of Mission* 94, no. 372 (January): 74–83.

Schreiter, Robert, and Knud Jørgensen, eds. 2013. *Mission as Ministry of Reconciliation*. Regnum Edinburgh Centenary Series. Vol. 16. Oxford: Regnum Books International.

Sundermeier, Theo. 1986. "Konvivenz als Grundstruktur ökumenischer Existenz heute." In *Ökumenische Existenz Heute* 1 (1986): 86–90.

Vicedom, Georg. 2002. *Missio Dei—Actio Dei*. Edition afem—mission classics 4. Nürnberg: VTR.

Volf, Miroslav. 1998. *After Our Likeness. The Church as the Image of the Trinity*. Grand Rapids, MI: Eerdmans.

Von Rad, Gerhard, 1935. "שָׁלוֹם im AT." In Kittel, Gerhard (Ed). 1935. *Theologisches Wörterbuch zum Neuen Testament*. Zweiter Band: Δ–H, vol 2. Reprint of the first edition from 1935. Göttingen: Vandehoeck and Ruprecht, 1950, 400–405.

Von Rad, Gerhard. 1950. "שָׁלוֹם im AT." In Kittel, Gerhard, Hg. *Theologisches Wörterbuch zum Neuen Testament*. Bd. 2. Stuttgart: Kohlhammer, 401.

Chapter 3

Reconciliation—The Neglected Outcome of Kingdom Mission

Ken Baker

"Can a gospel that reconciles people to God and not people to people be the true gospel of Jesus Christ?" (Perkins 2008). We instinctively respond with a fervent "of course not!" But, does the testimony of our mission efforts reflect this belief? Do our global mission structures, strategies and methodologies tell a different story? In other words, does our orthopraxy match our orthodoxy? For the most part, I believe the answer is "no." Over several decades a focus on Unreached People Groups (UPG) has dominated global mission (at least within North American circles) and has resulted in a widely held conclusion that the outcome of global mission is church planting movements (CPMs) where the "rapid multiplication" of indigenous, reproducing churches "*sweeps through a people group*" (Garrison 2004, loc 245; italics in original). Subsequently, this focus on CPMs has spawned various, but similar, methodologies (e.g., DMM, T4T, Any3) which seek to catalyze movements to Jesus even, in some contexts, without a missionary's permanent residence among the target people (Rhodes 2022, 195).

It is my conviction that CPMs, and the missions industry promoting them, represent an incomplete description of God's kingdom purposes in the world. God intends much more for his church than catalyzing church growth movements. I have written elsewhere that popular CPM-style methods have come to reflect the *who*, *what*, and *how* of global missions engagement in recent decades, but that the critical aspect of *why* has been incompletely addressed (Baker 2021, 82).

In my prior work, I have insisted that the *why* of kingdom mission is not merely that "there would be Jesus movements within every people, but the flourishing of the reign of God through the redeeming and reconciling work of the cross, reclaiming and transforming humanity for shared intimacy and presence with God and his people" (Baker 2021, 93). As a companion to that argument, this chapter will assert that the biblical imperative of reconciling people(s) to people(s) is a neglected outcome of kingdom mission. But first, we will examine why this vision of reconciliation is a neglected outcome.

Expansion vs. Community

The UPG narrative and the push for CPMs is about the *expansion* of indigenous, reproducing churches among UPGs everywhere. This is the contemporary envisioned outcome for the blessing of the nations in God's kingdom, and the presumed, practical application of the Great Commission. However, what if this assumed outcome is incomplete? If the envisioned outcome (CPMs) does not reflect the whole of God's kingdom purposes, then, by default, the process employed (strategies and activities) of God's people is also incomplete.

I submit that kingdom mission is not only about *expansion* but also *community*, the connective bonding and cruciform life of those who are reconciled together in Christ. This perspective of *mission-as-community* focuses on how the spirit of God gathers and shapes a community of those reconciled in Christ rather than merely multiplying CPMs. Mission-as-community allows the gospel its complete intent, to reconcile and restore relational community between people and peoples in Christ.

The linchpin of our bonding and life together is reconciliation and reunion bought with the blood of Christ on the cross. Christ died so that we would be one, reunited as his community. Therefore, if we do not comprehend and embrace the reality and implications of reconciled community in Christ, our approach to global kingdom mission remains incomplete. Furthermore, this community dimension of kingdom mission provides the soil in which, and from which, the expansion activity of mission unfolds. "Jesus sends a *community* on a mission to the nations. The whole of Jesus's ministry has been to gather and form a people who will embody God's purposes for the sake of the world" (Goheen 2011, 115; italics in original).

> Mission-as-community allows the gospel its complete intent, to reconcile and restore relational community between people and peoples in Christ.

CPMs, though, are the water in which much Great Commission ministry swims—a representation of the dominant mission-as-expansion dimension of global mission. As long as this expansion outcome is perceived to be the complete picture of kingdom mission, mission-as-community will languish in neglect. We will now examine why reconciliation of people(s) to people(s), the heart of mission-as-community, must be embraced, lived, and taught as a companion outcome to mission-as-expansion.

The Nature and Fruit of Reconciliation

Holistic reconciliation recognizes that the gospel has individual, corporate, and cosmic dimensions (Gombis 2006, 5). These dimensions can be described as *vertical* (humans reconciled to God), *horizontal* (humans reconciled with each other), and *transcendent* (reconciliation of all creation). Altogether it is God's ultimate purpose "through him [Christ] to reconcile to himself all things, whether on earth or in heaven, making peace by the blood of his cross" (Col 1:20 ESV). This passage (vv. 15–23) repeatedly (seven times) emphasizes God's comprehensive intention to reconcile "all things." The blood of Jesus Christ covers all creation, not just individual sin, for it is "the guarantee of a healed creation to come" (C. Wright 2006, loc 4247).

Likewise, the reconciliation of all things in Christ gives the character, behavior, and witness of his church its orientation and meaning. However, this comprehensive vision of the reconciliation of people(s) to people(s) through the cross, *and its implications*, is essentially overlooked, for "much evangelical missiology has traditionally laid emphasis on the vertical aspect of reconciliation—the personal restoration of the human-divine relationship" (Rowan 2012, 37; see also Volf 1998, 5). Likewise, the natural consequence of an emphasis upon individual salvation, when applied to a people group, can lead to viewing the subsequent church as a collection of saved individuals without reference to corporate and transcendent understandings of reconciliation.

Indonesian theologian, Paulus Widjaja, affirms this broad fixation on individual reconciliation which neglects concern for "the embrace of others, especially the different others" (Rowan 2012, 37). Furthermore, contemporary justice narratives may discourage the pursuit of holistic reconciliation in mission due to a fear of setting aside the gospel. However, the biblical testimony of reconciliation is at the heart of the gospel (Gombis 2006, 1). The true intent of the cross, is that humans would once again be reunited with God and each other because "the mission of God in our fallen, broken world is reconciliation" (Lausanne 2004, 9). We will now look at why reconciliation is a manifestation of the kingdom of God.

The popular understanding of "reconciliation" involves the restoration of friendship or relationship, as well as settling or resolving conflict. To restore relationship invokes prior alienation and even enmity, recognizing that "enmity toward God is enmity toward human beings, and the enmity toward human beings is enmity toward God" (Volf 1998, 7). Thus, a more complete definition of reconciliation could be stated as, *overcoming alienation and enmity to restore relationship and live in peace.*

The two primary Greek words in the Greek New Testament, *katallage* (reconciliation) and *(apo)katallasso* (to reconcile), derive from "a Greek word group used in Hellenistic diplomacy ... for peace treaties [referring] to the restoration of various group and interpersonal relationships after a period of enmity" (Constantineanu 2010, 88). Biblically, though, "reconciliation" has sharper contours of meaning. Paul employs this diplomatic terminology in a unique manner by having the injured party, God himself, initiate reconciliation. In other words, "God intervenes prior to and apart from human repentance [which is] clearly expressed by Paul in Romans 5:8, 10 where Paul states that God has taken the initiative and reconciled human beings while they were still sinners and hostile to God" (Constantineanu 2010, 91; see also Rowan 2012, 27).

When we consider Romans 5:1–11 coupled with 2 Corinthians 5:11–21, as well as other passages where Paul specifically references his conversion experience on the Damascus road (Acts 9; 1 Cor 9:1; 15:8–10; Gal 1:15–16; Phil 3:4–11) we can easily see the lifelong impact of this transformative event on his ministry (2 Cor 4:4–6; Eph 2:3–11; Col 1:23, 25). Saul, on the way to Damascus, thought he was God's agent as a committed persecutor of Jesus-followers when he was suddenly confronted by Jesus himself. Jesus was alive and exactly who he claimed to be, King and Lord of all! Immediately, Saul understood that he had been in direct opposition to the Lord God, and he instantly changed sides, from one who was hostile to God to God's servant. Since "in Christ God was reconciling the world to himself, not counting their trespasses against them" (2 Cor 5:19), Saul too was reconciled to God, "the old [had] passed away ... the new has come" (2 Cor 5:17), and he was given the ministry of reconciliation. However, to be entrusted with the "message of reconciliation" (2 Cor 5:19) implies *all dimensions* of reconciliation, and Saul would embark on that same trajectory of apostolic ministry. Not only was his personal relationship with Jesus Christ transformed (vertical reconciliation), but his newfound relationships with Jesus-followers were transformed (horizontal reconciliation), as well as his understanding of new creation (transcendent reconciliation).

Remember that in the passage referenced above, Paul is writing to the Corinthian church, which was mired in conflict both with him and among themselves. They needed to understand the full implications of God's reconciliation of all things. So, Paul reminds them that the fundamental reconciliation of people with God, the resulting transformation of relationships and the experience of peace between people, requires a response to the appeal to "be reconciled to God" (2 Cor 5:20), "They were already Christians, but they had to recognize that true reconciliation with God will bring authentic reconciliation with one another" (Rowan 2012, 32).

Furthermore, Paul exhorts the believers at Corinth that "the church exists as a community of reconciliation, pointing back to the unique reconciling work of God in Christ on the cross, and pointing forward, by its work and witness, to the ultimate reconciliation of 'all things'" (Rowan 2012, 33). "Everything depends, however, on how we understand the final reconciliation and its implication for life in a world of enmity" (Volf 2019, 109). Lesslie Newbigin succinctly explains these implications for the mission of the church:

> The redemption which God has wrought in Christ is for the world. Its purpose is a new humanity, mankind made one in Christ, converted from that egocentricity which cuts man off from God and his neighbor, restored to that life of communion for which mankind was created. The firstfruits and instrument of that purpose is the church ... There is no reconciliation to God apart from reconciliation with the fellowship of his reconciled people. (Quoted in Leithart 2016, loc 3367)

The church is God's instrument in the ministry of reconciliation, which envisions far more than the task of making disciples of all nations. "God's heart for the nations is that they would be reconciled to him *and to each other* to the praise of his glory (cf. Ps 87)" (Baker 2021, 90; italics in original). The mindset which promotes mission as a task flows from the paradigm that God has a mission for his church, which overlooks the reality that God has a community of his people for his mission. The church, the body of Christ, is a manifestation of his kingdom, and we have been given the role of displaying the reign of God and the life of our King in the world. Thus, who we are, and how we live, is just as much an outcome of kingdom mission as what we do. This is the testimony of the early church. "They realized, as they worshiped the God they saw in Jesus and celebrated his good news, that a new way of being human had been launched. They looked at impossibilities and prayed their way through them. They were mocked and vilified, attacked, and driven out of communities. But the work went on. New things happened. People saw the difference. The resurrection of Jesus launched a new, and newly integrated, way of life" (N. T. Wright 2015, 116).

The early church lived the testimony of a "*contrast* community" (Goheen 2011, 194; italics mine) within their context, demonstrating before all society the oneness they had found in Christ. Though "humanity was created as one but was divided by sin" (Leithart 2016, loc 206), in Christ humanity is reunited as one, fulling the vision of our Lord when he prayed in Gethsemane for those who would believe in him "that they may all be one, just as you, Father, are in me, and I in you, that they also may be in us, so that the world may believe that you have sent me" (John 17:21).

Oneness, with and for humanity, has been God's intent since calling Abram and his descendants to be a blessing to the nations as "an answer to the sin and the scattering of Genesis 3–11" (Hays 2003, 61). "The separation of Abraham and Israel was always overshadowed by the promise that the one God would one day bless humanity as *one* humanity" (Leithart 2016, loc 230; italics in original). This is the abiding promise of the gospel of the kingdom which "announces the fulfillment of God's one plan for the one human race: the plan to unify all tribes, tongues, nations, and peoples in Christ … the reunion of humanity in Christ *is* the gospel" (Leithart 2016, loc 252, 266; italics in original).

Nowhere was the way of Christ more resolutely displayed than through the reconciled relationship between Jews and Gentiles in Christ. This was a particularly dominant gospel paradigm in the life and theology of the Apostle Paul. He lived and preached it from his ministry with Barnabas in Antioch, to his advocacy at the Jerusalem Council, to his house-church planting, to his exhortation among the early churches. The goal was peace. Peace and community oneness are the fruit of reconciliation in Christ.

Often peace and reconciliation are intertwined in the same passage (e.g., Rom 5:1–11; Eph 2:14–18; Col 1:15–22). And there is no passage which is more explicit about the result of reconciliation in Christ between Jew and Gentile than Ephesians 2:11–22. Once "separated from Christ" and "alienated" (v. 12), but now "brought near" (v. 13) and "made … one," with the "dividing wall of hostility" destroyed (v. 14), creating "one new man" and "making peace" (v. 15), reconciling both in "one body" and "killing the hostility" (v. 16), bringing "peace to those who were near" (v. 17) (see Isa 57:19), and giving "access in one Spirit to the Father" (v. 18), meaning they were "no longer strangers and aliens," but "fellow citizens" and "members of the household of God" (v. 19), which "being joined together, grows into a holy temple in the Lord" (v. 21), such that they "are being built together into a dwelling place for God by the Spirit" (v. 22). What a powerful witness of the cruciform nature of reconciled life in Christ, for "as the church takes the form of Christ … God's purposes for the world take shape" (Rowan 2012, 50). The "nearness" effectuated by the blood of Christ (v. 13) not only reconciles alienation and brings peace between humans and God (the Genesis 3 separation), but also reconciles alienation and brings peace among peoples (the Genesis 11 separation).

Reconciliation to God is inseparable from reconciliation to one another. Christ, who is our peace, made peace through the cross, and preached peace to the divided world of Jew and Gentile. The unity of the people of God is both a fact ("he made the two one") and a mandate ("make every effort to preserve the unity of the Spirit in the bond of peace"). God's plan for the integration of the whole creation in Christ is modeled in the ethnic reconciliation of God's new humanity (Cape Town Commitment 2011, 33–34).

The references to "peace" and "dwelling" remind us of the continual refrain and longing of God throughout Scripture to be reconciled with his people and dwell with them. Beginning in Exodus 6:7, God promises "I will take you to be my people, and I will be your God." He confirms this promise in Exodus 29:45, then declares in Leviticus 26:12 "I will walk among you and will be your God, and you shall be my people." He repeats the promise with the declaration of a new covenant in Jeremiah 31:33 and 32:38, and in Ezekiel 11:20, 36:28, and especially 37:27 which states, "My dwelling place shall be with them, and I will be their God, and they shall be my people." Paul quotes this passage in 2 Corinthians 6:16: "I will make my dwelling among them and walk among them, and I will be their God, and they shall be my people" (see also Heb 8:10). This constant longing for God to be with this people culminates in the glorious panorama in Revelation 21 of the new heaven and new earth, "And I heard a loud voice from the throne saying, 'Behold, the dwelling place of God is with man. He will dwell with them, and they will be his people, and God himself will be with them as their God'" (Rev 21:3).

The ongoing manifestation of this reconciliation is the one community of Christ, his body, the church of Jesus Christ, the people of God. This community is a reprise of God's original intent for eternal communion with humanity, in full continuity with the vision for Israel as an eschatological community (Goheen 2011, 124). This kingdom community, a people of peoples, is the full expression of the gospel's intent to reconcile people to God and to each other.

Redemption and reconciliation are not just for individual benefit, for "as individuals, we have been saved for life-giving relationships within kingdom of God communities, not merely for privatized walks with Jesus. We become our true selves only in community, exercising our gifts and learning to receive the gifts of others" (Gombis 2011, 46–49). Therefore, in kingdom mission, God's people, the church, the body of Christ, this people of peoples, are called (commissioned) to continue *in continuity* with Jesus's incarnational ministry, the sustained multiplication of Christ's character and presence in the world.

We are witnesses of the incarnate Son of God, which is first, an identity given to a community, and second an activity (word and deed). The incarnation event invokes the cross, which is directly relational and communal, the center of reconciliation and restoration of broken communion with God and others. Restored from the tragedy of broken relationship with God and with the rest of humanity, the "community of witnesses" is the link between the cross and the world. The church is both the embodiment of Christ's gospel and its vehicle.

Yet, this beautiful picture of blessed community as one reconciled people together is a neglected outcome of kingdom mission.

This vision of peace and community oneness among the people of God is mostly suspended as only a future hope. Within too much of the global Christian world there is a pervasive, tolerant acceptance of division and separation without the slightest sense that something is amiss. Such independence is assumed and considered normal. Attention toward oneness in the body of Christ, achieved through the blood of our Lord, and manifested in peace as a testimony before the watching world is stunningly overlooked, neglected, and functionally denied.

We learned this attitude, posture, and behavior from our Protestant forbearers who institutionalized division and separation. We have received uncritically, and passed on, this posture of independence and expediency because it allows us to do our own thing without compromise and cooperation. Even though we read in Scripture about forgiveness, love for one another (neighbors and enemies), peace, unity, and the destruction of hostility, such teaching does not seem to penetrate and convict. Instead, we appear to accommodate the accuser of the brethren. Is not our enemy wholly opposed to reconciliation and peace in any form? Satan stands against anything which brings God glory, and the divine love that leads to reconciliation, peace, love, and unity brings God great glory by pointing to Jesus as the sent one of God (see John 13 and 17). Yet, many scoff at such concerns as naïve, idealistic, and tilting at windmills—among them, David Garrison who emphasizes that a fixation with Christian unity is virtuous, but time consuming, and includes it in list of distractions called "the devil's candy" (Garrison 2004, loc 4009-68).

Jesus says, "Blessed are the peacemakers" (Matt 5:9), but we seem to have no interest in this kingdom outcome. How ironic that, as the recipients of peace with God, we have no interest in living and extending this blessing to our brothers and sisters in Christ, let alone our neighbors. It is a repeat of the Israelite syndrome whereby the nation of Israel accepted the blessings of God without the accompanying obligations. What, though, do peace and community oneness have to do with kingdom mission? They testify of the power of reconciliation which is at the heart of the gospel story. Before the reconciliation of the cross, there was no peace—only hostility. After the reconciliation purchased through the blood of Christ, there is peace. God has always pursued restored relationship with his humanity, which he made possible through the incarnation, death, and resurrection of his Son. In Christ all humanity has renewed access to God (Eph 2:18) and all people(s) have reunion with each other in new humanity, the "dwelling place for God" (Eph 2:22).

Peace with God and each other in Christ is the outcome of kingdom mission as we anticipate the complete flourishing of Christ's kingdom before the throne of God (Rev 21–22). In other words, when advocating for reconciliation as an outcome of missions I am referring not only to reunion with God and transcendent oneness, but to the *actual social appropriation* of God's reconciling work through Christ in the life of believing communities. In 2 Corinthians 6:1–10, Paul's intent "is to illustrate that the gospel message, to be the gospel message, *must be embodied*, not just spoken. There is thus an intrinsic relationship between the message of reconciliation and the messenger's own reconciliation and life" (Constantineanu 2010, 72; italics mine). "For the church to make peace, she herself must embody God's peace as a living sign of God's reconciled community" (Lausanne 2004, 19).

The Social Implications of Reconciliation

Reconciliation with God is the "foundation of all Christian discourse on reconciliation: what God has done for humanity through Jesus Christ. What is new is the deeper exploration of the 'horizontal' dimension of reconciliation; that is, reconciliation between humans, as individuals and as groups" (Schreiter and Jørgensen 2013, 13). Returning to the point of the opening question, "since reconciliation is concurrently vertical and horizontal, how can anyone be reconciled to Jesus and not to his *whole* church?" (Baker 2021, 89; italics in original). *If we belong to Jesus, then we belong to those who belong to Jesus.* This affirmation is no less true today than it was in the early church, but the sense of belonging through reconciliation is widely neglected, even forgotten. In Ephesians 1:9, 10 we read that God intends through "making known to us the mystery of his will, according to his purpose, which he set forth in Christ as a plan for the fullness of time, to unite all things in him, things in heaven and things on earth" that the church, the body of Christ, unified in one spirit, be the vanguard of God's will to unify all things. Thus:

> If the church is to be a preview of where God is taking history, it will exhibit that kind of reconciliation and unity. This stress on unity is in harmony with Jesus's prayer that his followers might be one "so that the world may believe that you have sent me" (John 17:21). Thus, disunity is a scandal not because it is unfortunate but because it contradicts the very gospel we proclaim. A missional church cannot help but be concerned with an expression of the unity of the church. But where does one begin at this point in history with close to thirty thousand denominations? (Goheen 2011, 224)

Sadly, as Goheen alludes, the history of division, separation, and denominationalism in Protestant history is a clear indication of the disinterest in Christian reconciliation as a biblical and missional imperative. Likewise, "theologians and missiologists have not tended to explore the social implications of the doctrine of reconciliation particularly for the church in its mission to the wider world" (Rowan 2012, 15). "We face not so much *mistaken explications* of the social meaning of reconciliation as a deeply disturbing *absence* of sustained attempts to relate the core theological beliefs about reconciliation to the shape of the church's social responsibility" (Volf 1998, 4; italics in original). Some may recoil at the phrase "social responsibility," transposing it into "social gospel" and assuming it is a departure from gospel ministry. However, this is not what I mean by holistic reconciliation or the social responsibility of reconciliation. Rather, the gospel is "the announcement that God has come in Jesus to begin his work of reclaiming and redeeming the world, which begins with a redeemed people—a holy people who will manifest *in their social practices* the very life of God on earth" (Gombis 2006, 1; italics in original).

Reconciliation of people(s) to people(s) is an imperative of God's gospel, the natural outflow of reconciliation with God. "The necessary relational outworking of the doctrine of reconciliation presupposes communities of local Christians who together live as peacemakers in their local context" (Rowan 2012, 44). Perhaps if we think "peacemaking" when we hear the word "reconciliation" we will be more inclined to embrace its call.

"Part of the uniqueness of the Christian gospel of reconciliation is that it unites people of all cultures, ethnic groups and languages, while at the same time allowing people to maintain the distinctiveness of their own culture" (Rowan 2012, 45). To be in Christ is a reordering of identity that does not erase differentiation, but which highlights the power of love and reconciliation between natural opponents or enemies. "Because the church is global, it should be uniquely equipped to demonstrate ethnic harmony within its ranks … the whole Christian community needs to take far more seriously the fundamental nature of the church as a reconciled, multi-ethnic family" (Dowsett 2013, 109).

Far too often in our mission strategies and approaches we do not consider the social dimension of "all things made new" through the power of the cross and the resurrection. When mission methods are highly individualistic, generically applied, or variously limited in scope, the impact of the gospel on social relations, particularly racial, ethnic, and class relations, is easily overlooked, and even denied. Without a deep understanding of contextual and cultural realities our disciple-making methods can miss social complexities which limit the comprehensive impact of the gospel of Christ. "What if a people are very ethnocentric or nationalistic but do not realize it? Not only might they assume that the gospel is foreign propaganda; they may also be full of hate toward certain other nations or tribes (e.g., China vs. Japan). Nothing in the plan of salvation suggests to people that they should examine and repent of their sense of cultural superiority. Sin typically manifests itself in countless social ways; its roots penetrate deep into a person's sense of identity" (Vaughn 2016, 5). Therefore, our disciple making from day one, should embrace, model, and teach the reconciliation of people(s) to people(s) as a gospel outcome of kingdom mission.

Addressing the social dimension of reconciliation in Christ matters. In all cultures and contexts we see that:

> Unjust balances of societal power are also a consequence of the unresolved past and present. … Against these forces of the past and present, alienated groups cannot even imagine a future of friendship, solidarity or common life. … [Therefore] When Christians are passive bystanders and refuse to become constructive agents of reconciliation amid such divisions and destructive conflicts, we are guilty of withholding love to a neighbor, the love of God is not manifested in our lives, and we give life to a defective gospel. (Lausanne 2004, 12)

If in our haste to multiply disciples we ignore, discredit, or underestimate the role of reconciliation and peacemaking then we ill-prepare emerging church communities to apply their new faith adequately and faithfully to their own social situation, not to mention other societies or cultures around them.

The Communal Practice of Reconciliation

"Peace I leave with you, my peace I give to you. Not as the world gives do I give to you" (John 14:27). "*Shalom* as God's peace envisions the wholeness, well-being and flourishing of all people and the rest of creation both individually and corporately in their interrelatedness with God and with each other. *Shalom* as God's peace encompasses all dimensions of human life, including the spiritual, physical, cognitive, emotional, social, societal, and economic" (Lausanne 2004, 15; italics in original). Our pursuit and application of reconciliation in our human context is all inclusive because it is God's transcendent intention to reconcile all things. But we must also acknowledge that this picture of reconciled, transformed life through the power of the cross is "subversive because it is counter-cultural" (Dowsett 2013, 106). Reconciliation and peace run cross-current to the human predicament, and they bring a myriad of challenges. "Reconciliation between divided peoples requires a risky, mutual journey of intentional relationship-building in which all groups are transformed and called to costly sacrifices" (Lausanne 2004, 21). Anticipating this challenge,

Paul gave explicit instructions for how God's people are to live in community as lovers, reconcilers, and peacemakers.

Romans 12:1–15:7 demonstrates the length and depth of reconciliation and peace expected *within* and *beyond* the body of Christ. It is Paul's description of what life in Christ looks like in our social world. It is the answer to the query, "in light of Christ's reconciling work on the cross, how then should we live?" Since we have been reconciled and are at peace with God, and since we are one body in Christ, and members one of another, we are to "present [our] bodies as a living sacrifice" by not being "conformed to this world," but "transformed," discerning "what is the will of God" (12:1–2). After an exhortation to "think with sober judgment" (12:3), next is the foundation from which transformed, Spirit-generated behavior is learned and tested, the body of Christ (12:4–8). Then, for the next fifty-seven verses, Paul goes into great practical detail about what reconciled and peaceful living looks like. Here is just a sampling: "love one another with brotherly affection" (12:10); "seek to show hospitality" (12:13); "live in harmony with one another" (12:16); "live peaceably with all" (12:18); "be subject to governing authorities" (13:1); "owe no one anything" (13:8); "let us not pass judgment on one another any longer" (14:13); culminating in this holistic reminder, "welcome one another as Christ has welcomed you" (15:7).

Along the way Paul gives explanatory remarks about why this posture of reconciliation and peace matters, "Love does no wrong to a neighbor; therefore love is the fulfilling of the law" (13:10); "whether we live or whether we die, we are the Lord's" (14:8); "each of us will give an account of himself to God" (14:12); "so then let us pursue what makes for peace and for mutual upbuilding" (14:19); "that together you may with one voice glorify the God and Father of our Lord Jesus Christ" (15:6).

This passage graphically demonstrates what it means for kingdom people and communities to live out the ministry of reconciliation as a testimony of Christ in the world. For the "church is God's world-changing social experiment of bringing unlikes and differents to the table to share life with one another as a new kind of family. When this happens, we show the world what love, justice, peace, reconciliation, and life together are designed by God to be. The church is God's show-and-tell for the world to see how God wants us to live as a family" (McKnight 2014, 16).

Why do we not recognize that love, peace, and community are a direct outcome of kingdom mission? Jesus gave us a mission strategy which we consistently overlook, "A new commandment I give to you, that you love one another: just as I have loved you, you also are to love one another. By this all people will know that you are my disciples, if you have love for one another" (John 13:34–35). Our love for one another is an attractive light in the darkness of the world and its alienation from God and each other. Yet, it seems that our conception and practice of global mission reflects more task-oriented mobilization and activity than love-oriented character and community.

Much has been written about Christ's call to mission as our "missionary task" (Goheen 2014, 155), a conception of mission that is received and passed along without pause and reflection. Yet, in order to accept reconciliation and community as a natural outcome of kingdom mission it is necessary to reconceive our understanding of the nature of the church in relation to its mission in the world. "[It] is not so much the case that God has a mission for his church in the world, but that God has a church for his mission in the world. Mission was not made for the church; the church was made for mission—God's mission" (C. Wright 2006, loc 697).

In other words, mission is not so much a task which God has given the church to do, as much as God has a role for his church to live (Baker 2021, 89). Unfortunately, far too much attention has been given to the missionary task to the detriment and neglect of our role as the people of God in the world. This is not merely semantics, there is a fundamental difference. Too often, following Western tendency, people and ministry are defined by what we do and not by who we are. Yes, we are witnesses of and for Christ, but we are first "in Christ" as lovers (of God, one another, neighbors, enemies), reconcilers, and peacemakers.

> It is necessary to reconceive our understanding of the nature of the church in relation to its mission in the world.

Too often it seems, we are so consumed with addressing the lostness of the world that we fail to cultivate the fruit (love, reconciliation, and peace) of our "foundness" and reunion in Christ. How we are sent into the world matters. We do not go in the world as task-bearers, but as image-bearers. It's about who we are and also how we are, not just what we are doing. We bear the image of the cruciform life of Christ, whose love for humanity compelled him to the cross, and whose blood covered our sin, so that we could be reunited with him, and each other, forever.

The soil of kingdom mission is the cruciform life of Christ. "We always carry around in our body the death of Jesus, so that the life of Jesus may also be revealed in our body" (2 Cor 4:10 NIV). "Not only is a cruciform ministry the *only way* to produce the fruit of faith in a crucified Christ, but ministry in the shape of the cross is the *only way* to unleash the power of the resurrection life of Jesus" (Gombis 2022; italics mine).

The sacrificial love of the cross reveals God's embrace of the world in all its sin, rebellion, and alienation. It invokes the image of God, arms outstretched, waiting for humanity to yield and come. "The arms of the crucified [one] are open—a sign of a space in God's self and an invitation for the 'enemy' to come in" (Volf 2019, 127). This too is our posture as the people of God, the body of Christ. This is where kingdom mission in the world begins: sacrificial love seeking reconciliation and peace. Without this foundation disciple making among the nations does not testify to the reign of God over all dimensions of life and relationships.

Approaching kingdom mission with an incomplete paradigm (e.g., CPM-style disciple making) diminishes the full purposes of God in the world, devalues the vision of societal engagement in the name of Christ, and overlooks how we are designed to live as the body of Christ in loving interdependence. Conversely, the cruciform, communal character of the reconciled church will thoroughly reshape our approach, not only to disciple making, but to the whole spectrum of kingdom mission in this broken world.

Conclusion: A (Lonely) Plea

My intent here is to paint a picture of a neglected narrative of kingdom mission. The reconciliation of people(s) to people(s), and its fruit of peace and community, does not have the flair of rapid multiplication or compounding movements. It boasts only of crucified lives seeking to breach chasms of hostility and embrace the alienated world so that the gospel story of Christ will be seen and heard. This is the soil of cruciform witness which gives the testimony of Christ's gospel, borne by his people, the power to cut through darkness, alienation, and enmity. Nevertheless, it is not hard to be pessimistic about the future of holistic reconciliation as an embraced outcome of kingdom mission (Nehrbass 2021, 298). Warning about its neglect feels like shouting in the wind in the face of the juggernaut of the CPM paradigm.

In a missions climate where the urgency of reaching the lost and rapid multiplication portends to fuel movements, anything that would seem to slow the process, like holistic reconciliation, is devalued. Such relational entanglements are viewed as unproductive because they threaten to undercut the desired outcome—a rapidly multiplying movement. Yet, God has a church for his kingdom mission, and it is not all about movements among the unreached. From Scripture we have seen God's heart for a gathered community characterized by reconciliation in love and peace—the soil out of which witness grows in word and deed. Thus, I appeal to you to join this lonely plea for a renewed embrace of reconciliation as an integral outcome of kingdom mission.

Mission endeavors that neglect to include human reconciliation, reunion, and peace in Christ do not represent the whole gospel, or the supremacy of Christ over all things.

References Cited

Baker, Ken. 2021. "Five Decades, Four Questions, and One Which Remains: Queries Concerning the Unreached People Group Movement." In *Advancing Models of Mission: Evaluating the Past and Looking to the Future* edited by Kenneth Nehrbass, Aminta Arrington, and Narry Santos, 81–96. Littleton, CO: William Carey Publishing.

Cape Town Commitment. 2010. "A Confession of Faith and a Call to Action." *Third Lausanne Congress.* https://lausanne.org/wp-content/uploads/2021/10/The-Cape-Town-Commitment.

Constantineanu, Corneliu. 2010. *The Social Significance of Reconciliation in Paul's Theology: Narrative Readings in Romans.* London: T&T Clark. E-book. https://bit.ly/3ix0QCY.

Dowsett, Rose. 2013. "Reconciliation as Reconstruction of a Wounded and Unjust Society." In *Mission as Ministry of Reconciliation*, edited by Robert Schreiter and Knud Jørgensen, 101–11. Oxford, UK: Regnum. Kindle Edition.

Garrison, David. 2004. *Church Planting Movement: How God Is Redeeming a Lost World.* Monument, CO: WIGTake Resources. Kindle Edition.

Goheen, Michael W. 2011. *A Light to the Nations: The Missional Church and the Biblical Story.* Grand Rapids, MI: Baker. Kindle Edition.

Goheen, Michael W. 2014. *Introducing Christian Mission Today: Scripture, History and Issues.* Downers Grove, IL: InterVarsity Press. Kindle Edition.

Gombis, Timothy G. 2006. "Racial Reconciliation and the Christian Gospel." *Act 3 Review* 15, no. 3 (2006): 117–128. https://timgombis.files.wordpress.com/2011/06/racial-reconciliation-and-the-christian-gospel-gombis.pdf.

Gombis, Timothy. 2011. "The Paul We Think We Know." *Christianity Today* 55, no. 7 (July): https://www.christianitytoday.com/ct/2011/july/paulwethink.html.

Gombis, Timothy. 2022. "The Apostle Paul and Measuring Up in Ministry." *Faith Improvised* (blog.) March 17, 2021. https://bit.ly/3D1hYdD.

Hays, J. Daniel. 2003. *From Every People and Nation: A Biblical Theology of Race*, edited by D. A. Carson. NSBT 14. Downers Grove, IL: InterVarsity Press.

Lausanne Occasional Paper No. 51 (October 2004) "A New Vision, a New Heart, a Renewed Call." Paper presented at the Lausanne Committee for World Evangelism in Pattaya, Thailand. https://lausanne.org/content/lop/lop-51-reconciliation-as-the-mission-of-god.

Leithart, Peter J. 2016. *The End of Protestantism: Pursuing Unity in a Fragmented Church.* Grand Rapids, MI: Brazos Press. Kindle Edition.

McKnight, Scot. 2014. *A Fellowship of Differents*. Grand Rapids, MI: Zondervan. Kindle Edition.

Nehrbass, Kenneth. 2021. *Advanced Missiology: How to Study Missions in Credible and Useful Ways*. Eugene, OR: Cascade Books. Kindle Edition.

Perkins, John. 2008. Spoken comment from keynote address at the Ethnic America Summit in St. Louis, MO.

Rhodes, Matt. 2022. *No Shortcut to Success: A Manifesto for Modern Missions*. Wheaton, IL: Crossway. Kindle Edition.

Rowan, Peter. 2012. "The Theology of Reconciliation and Its Importance in the Theology of Mission." PhD diss. Oxford: Regnum Books. https://www.academia.edu/36284735/The_Theology_of_Reconciliation_and_its_Importance_in_the_Theology_of_Mission.

Schreiter, Robert, and Knud Jørgensen, eds. 2013. *Mission as Ministry of Reconciliation*. Oxford: Regnum. Kindle Edition.

Vaughn, Brad. 2016. "Does the 'Plan of Salvation' Make Disciples?" In *Asian Missions Advance* (January): 11–17. https://bit.ly/3L6JoBM.

Volf, Miroslav. 1998. "The Social Meaning of Reconciliation." *Occasional Papers on Religion in Eastern Europe* 18.3, Article 3. https://digitalcommons.georgefox.edu/ree/vol18/iss3/3.

Volf, Miroslav. 2019. *Exclusion and Embrace, Revised and Updated: A Theological Exploration of Identity, Otherness and Reconciliation*. Nashville: Abingdon Press. Kindle Edition.

Wright, Christopher J. H. 2006. *The Mission of God: Unlocking the Bible's Grand Narrative*. Downers Grove, IL: IVP Academic. Kindle Edition.

Wright, N. T. 2015. *Simply Good News: Why the Gospel Is News and What Makes It Good*. Harper Collins. Kindle Edition.

Chapter 4

So That the World Will Know

Reflections on an Evangelical Theology of Christian Others and the Missiological Priority of Christian Unity

Michael Hakmin Lee

A Divided Nation:
Factors Driving Socio-Religious Polarization

In *American Politics: The Promise of Disharmony*, the prescient political scientist Samuel P. Huntington observed that throughout American history, there has been a cyclical pattern of mass social upheaval and unrest brought on by a moral convulsion that seems to occur every sixty years or so. Such moments of "creedal passion" are characterized by disgust with the present state of our society, an intense erosion of social trust in our public institutions, and a desire for reforms to recover lost ideals. When these convulsions recede, for better or worse, the national consciousness is transformed as societal beliefs, norms, and values are reconfigured, and power is redistributed, giving way to new structures and organizations (Huntington 1983, 91).

Building off Huntington's theory, David Brooks posited that since the mid-2010s we have been in the midst of another moral convulsion. Brooks argues that in contrast to the Boomers, who were shaped by the last moral convulsion during the 1960s, millennials and Gen Z, who have grown up in an "age of disappointment" seek "not liberation, but security; not freedom, but equality; not individualism, but the safety of the collective; not sink-or-swim meritocracy, but promotion on the basis of social justice" (Brooks 2020).

However, the experience of deep disappointment and mistrust does not just follow generational cohorts; it is a pervasive societal issue that has given rise to various competing groups who feel disillusioned and embattled and have rallied around figureheads like Donald Trump and movements like Black Lives Matter. Hardships, like the COVID-19 pandemic, have a way of exposing and presenting the opportunity to express the latent values and characteristics of individuals and societies. Stressors loosen inhibitions causing us to lower our masks, resulting in backstage behaviors playing out on the frontstage. The stark contrast in the following example is telling: 72 percent of Danes, a nation which currently enjoys relatively high social trust, reported feeling more united because of the global pandemic, compared to only 18 percent of Americans who reported the same (Devlin and Connaughton 2020).

Another parallel driver of societal polarization seems to be that Americans, who enjoy relative freedom of movement and opportunity in choosing where they live and where to worship compared to the vast majority of the world, commonly opt into homogeneity.[1] In his influential book *The Big Sort: Why the Clustering of Like-Minded America Is Tearing Us Apart*, Bill Bishop coined the phrase "the big sort" to describe the sociological phenomenon whereby for decades, Americans have been sorting themselves into homogeneous communities of people who live, think, and vote similarly. In a recent NPR interview Bishop remarked how this trend toward polarization and ideological segregation has only intensified since he wrote the book over a decade ago (Burnett 2022). Commenting on the substantial increase in super landslide counties (i.e., where a presidential candidate won at least 80 percent of the vote) from 6 percent in 2004 to 22 percent in 2020, political scientist Larry Sabato put it this way: "Biden won 85 percent of counties with a Whole Foods and only 32 percent of counties with a Cracker Barrel" (Burnett 2022).

The global COVID-19 pandemic exposed and intensified the fractures that already exist in our society, and has accelerated the migration of people, like socially conservative Californians moving to Texas, who are tired of the social and ideological friction they feel with their local government and neighbors. Just as political ideology informs where people choose to live, it also strongly informs where people want to worship. In a recent Lifeway survey, the majority of respondents, 47 percent, indicated that they prefer to attend a church where "people share my political views," while 42 percent disagreed, and 12 percent were unsure (Lifeway Research 2018).

Also, people are not only being sorted physically but virtually as well. Tristan Harris, a former tech insider who now heads up the Center for Human Technology, testified before a 2019 US Senate Commerce subcommittee hearing regarding the increasing asymmetry of power between tech companies and users. He noted that companies like Facebook and Google are becoming increasingly aggressive in their race to garner our attention and that their products are

---

[1] It is also true that social minorities do not have the same social power and opportunity to choose where they live, and so they often end up in places with other social minorities because of exclusion and denial of opportunity (e.g., housing and job discrimination). Nonetheless, this also leads to homogeneity.

socially engineered to be as addictive as possible. Harris and others have argued persuasively that the powerful, predictive algorithms that tech companies use to keep us engaged are dangerously leading us to a more polarized society.

We live in an age of outrage (Stetzer 2018) and disappointment driven in part by a toxic synergy that exists between a mass of consumers who are increasingly addicted to their cell phones and social media, and tech companies (and cable news companies) who are incentivized to make their products as addictive as possible, in part by feeding consumer-curated, bias-affirming content that keeps people in ideological echo chambers and accelerates polarization. There is also the reality of hostile actors, foreign and domestic, who are leveraging the power of social media to engage in information warfare to mislead and foment societal discord.

But what does our deep societal dysfunction have to do with what is going on in the American church? In our short history as a nation state, the American church and denominations have split over and become segregated by doctrinal distinctives, ecclesial structures and practices, racial and ethnic identity, gender roles, views of human sexuality, musical preferences, and more. There is a growing and troubling convergence of Christian identity and socio-political identity, giving rise to coalescing groups of so-called "red state Christians" and "blue state Christians" (Denker 2019).

The divisions within the Christian fellowship that have formed along ideological and political lines are of course far from being just an internal issue. To our shame, rather than being a counter cultural community of the Spirit that embodies the values of God's kingdom and our King, we mirror the same fissures that have been forming and widening in our society for decades (Dalrymple 2021). The fact is, many within the American evangelical church are not just passively complicit or negligent in allowing societal incivility and divisiveness to infect their churches; worse, they are actively engaged in perpetuating discord within the Christian fellowship and in the broader society (Gorski and Perry 2022; Jones 2020; Posner 2020). Our nation is deeply divided, and lamentably the American church is deeply divided.

Followers of Jesus have been called to a ministry of reconciliation (2 Cor 5:18). The full arc of the biblical story points to reconciliation encompassing healing and restoration of broken relationships that extends both vertically with God and horizontally within humanity. Full obedience to our call in our divided world requires that we become much more attentive to pursuing intra-Christian reconciliation alongside our proper evangelical zeal for seeing those outside the church be reconciled to God, for according to Jesus in his final recorded prayer, these works of reconciliation are inseparably linked.

Jesus's Prayer for Unity

On the night he was betrayed, Jesus prayed:

> My prayer is not for them alone. I pray also for those who will believe in me through their message, that all of them may be one, Father, just as you are in me and I am in you. May they also be in us so that the world may believe that you have sent me. I have given them the glory that you gave me, that they may be one as we are one—I in them and you in me—so that they may be brought to complete unity. Then the world will know that you sent me and have loved them even as you have loved me. (John 17:20-23 NIV)

Jesus prayed that his followers would experience the same relational unity that he enjoyed with the Father. As Millard Erickson asserts, "Unity between Father and Son is a relational reality and is the model for our unity" (Erickson 1998, 1137). And just as love characterizes the oneness relationship between the Father and Son, Jesus instructed his disciples that their love for one another would be the ultimate distinguishing mark of their common identity as his followers: "By this everyone will know that you are my disciples, if you love one another" (John 13:35 NIV).

We need not conclude that the unity that Jesus prayed for refers to a single ecclesiastical organization or to put it plainly, that somehow every local church and every Christian would fall under the authority of a single ecclesial tradition like the Roman Catholic Church. And yet it does not forbid such a scenario, for the plain logic of this prayer requires that our unity must be visible and recognizable, not just invisible or theoretical, for it to bear witness to the world. Reflecting on the meaning of Jesus's prayer for unity, Lesslie Newbigin observed:

> In our fractured world, only a united church can credibly testify to the reconciling power of the gospel.

> Our Lord says that He has given this glory to those who believe in Him 'that they may be one even as we are one.' Being children of God must mean being—in some recognizable sense—members of one family. All our rationalizations of schism and all our evasions of the plain meaning of scripture will not enable us to side-step the logic of that argument. In some sense those who are children of one Father must be recognizable as members of one family. (Newbigin 1961, 20)

In our fractured world, only a united church can credibly testify to the reconciling power of the gospel. The scandal of Christian disunity then is necessarily a central missiological problem and not some peripheral, second-order issue. Regrettably, the relational unity that Jesus teaches is far from being reflected broadly in the American church today. This reality should lead us to mourn and repent for our apathy toward and complicity in perpetuating disunity.

Unity of the Church in the First Millennium

The unity that Jesus prayed for was not just aspiration; unity is a spiritual reality that we are to express at every opportunity in our life together as one large, diverse family. The apostles and the early church seemed to have taken Jesus's charge for abiding love and unity seriously as the call to express the reality of the indivisibility of Christ's body is given repeatedly throughout the New Testament epistles. And while the early church was certainly not free of strident disputes that threatened unity (1 Cor 1:10; Gal 5:19-21; Jas 4:1-2), the first millennium of church history did at least exhibit oneness in terms of visible, ecclesiastical structure. It was not until the second millennium that the church would eventually become a tree of many branches in the aftermath of major ecclesiastical ruptures like the Great Schism of 1054 and the sixteenth century Protestant Reformation.

In AD 325, a diverse, geographically representative group of about 300 early church fathers gathered in Nicaea for the first universally recognized ecumenical council, resulting in the Nicene Creed, a statement of faith that all three major branches of the Christian faith today affirm. Regarding the church, the Nicene Creed declares, "We believe in one holy catholic and apostolic church" (Burn 1909, 3). The four marks of the church in this phrase—one, holy, catholic, and apostolic—provided the framing for reflections on the church throughout the first millennium and beyond.

The first mark, "one," speaks to her unity and indivisibility. In this sense, oneness is not something that we manufacture or achieve through effort. Rather the oneness of the church refers to an ontological reality. The church is one cosmic organism that God has gathered and so we must aspire to express and manifest the reality of our oneness in relational unity. To use the various images of the church that appear in the New Testament, there is only one body of Christ. Jesus is not returning for multiple brides. We are stones, being built up into one temple, not multiple temples. And we are part of one household whether or not we recognize and honor our common kinship. The church is "holy" in the sense of being set apart by God for his sacred purposes. "Catholic," which means "universal" or "concerning the whole," reflects the vastness of the church that includes all the redeemed people of God through time and space. Finally, the apostolic church is built on the foundation of the apostles and prophets with Christ as the cornerstone (Eph 2:20).

Modern Ecumenical Movement

In the last century we have witnessed a surge of renewed interest in Christian unity in the rise of the modern ecumenical movement. In an attempt to embody greater visible unity, ecclesial structures were formed from global-level bodies like the World Council of Churches (WCC) and the World Evangelical Fellowship (now called the World Evangelical Alliance or WEA), to national-level fellowships in the US like the National Council of Churches (NCC). Also, high-level, intra-Christian dialogue between Roman Catholic, Orthodox, and various Protestant traditions have resulted in statements that clarify and articulate the basis for unity and cooperation. Notably, following the Second Vatican Council, the Roman Catholic Church has been quite active in engaging the Orthodox Church and various Protestant traditions in serious theological dialogue and collaborating to produce ecumenical documents such as *Evangelicals and Catholics Together* in 1994 and *Declaration on the Way*, jointly crafted with Lutherans in 2015.

It is important to note that early in the ecumenical movement, Christian unity was not pursued just as some abstract ecclesiological ideal; the unity of the church was rightly tied to the mission of the church. The modern ecumenical movement grew out from the desire of the missionary movement to address the scandal and hindrance of disunity for Christian witness (World Council of Churches 1999, 109). Under the leadership of John Mackay, who insisted that ecumenicalism must connote "equally the missionary movement and the movement toward unity," the International Missionary Council and the World Council of Churches merged into one organization, rediscovering and affirming the truth that "the *unity* of the Church and the *mission* of the Church both belong, in equal degree, to the *essence* of the Church" (Van Dusen 1959, 327).

By the 1980s, the WCC and the global ecumenical movement experienced a loss of vision and energy (Armstrong 2021, 139–40). Notably there was a conspicuous absence of evangelicals and Pentecostals, who would come to constitute the leading edge of numerical growth in the global church, especially in Africa and Asia. Evangelicals had long disassociated from the WCC over various issues and moved on to other cooperative, evangelical entities like the WEA and the Lausanne movement where they could pursue their missional priorities.

Commenting on the WCC/WEA chasm, Thomas Oden, a longtime observer and participant in the ecumenical movement, asserted that the WCC and WEA quarreled over direction and structural makeup. Evangelicals desired "loose and informal cooperation into joint practical efforts" while others in the WCC emphasized "formal dialogue leading toward visible unity" (Oden 2002, 46). Evangelicals preferred localized governance with minimal bureaucracy, whereas others sought a more hierarchical and centralized structure. Oden also criticized the WCC's strong resistance to evangelical priorities like verbal gospel proclamation and instead strongly promoted agendas that evangelicals viewed with suspicion, like liberation theology and anti-capitalism. There has since been encouraging signs of progress in bridge-building within the global ecumenical movement and the mending of old wounds such as those between the WEA and WCC. Active participants like John Armstrong have expressed hope that a fresh wind is blowing through the global ecumenical movement, coalescing into the emergence of a new, younger, more informal ecumenism (Oden 2021, 138ff).

While I believe that the global ecumenical movement and high level gathering of church leaders plays an important role in advancing relational unity within the global church, intra-Christian reconciliation within the American church also requires radical changes at the grassroots, individual, and congregational level. Fundamentally, American evangelicals must adopt a more biblically informed perception of and attitude toward Christian others and strengthen their chronically anemic understanding of the nature of the church.

The Journey toward a Bigger View of the Church

In talking with and hearing the stories of fellow evangelicals who have undertaken this journey of intra-Christian peacemaking, and in recounting my own journey, I have noticed some commonly cited changes or movements in this process. This observation points to the fact that there are certain cultural assumptions and commitments commonly associated with the way American evangelical faith is constructed that can lead to an intuitive resistance toward even the idea of Christian unity.

In this section, I will share just a few things I had to unlearn and relearn in order to enlarge my heart for Christian others and the church. I would also encourage you to listen to the stories of others who are much further along in this journey than I am. For example, John Armstrong, who has long devoted his life to promoting Christian unity, recounts his inspiring journey toward catholicity in *Your Church Is Too Small* (Armstrong 2010) and *Tear Down These Walls* (Armstrong 2021).

Looking back, I realize I harbored a strong sectarian impulse, which Rex Koivisto aptly describes as "seeking unity in uniformity rather than unity in diversity and expecting other Christians to comply fully with my views before I can have genuine fellowship with them—as well as holding them doctrinally suspicious until they do" (Koivisto 2009, 33). I was quite suspicious of Christian others, like Anglicans, Pentecostals, and especially Catholics. I confess that my prejudices toward Catholics were not based on informed inquiry; I just accepted what I often heard from others about Catholics—that they wrongly worship Mary and promote a works righteousness.

I experienced a major paradigm shift by reading Paul Hiebert's article (1983) on what categorizes a Christian. I encountered this brilliant article during a time where I was wrestling with a cluster of questions like, "Is there a minimum content to the gospel that one must affirm to become a Christian?" and "How much error can one mix in with orthodoxy and still be a Christian?" At the time, this question was especially troubling to me as I would hear public prayers from our church leaders that were clearly modalistic. Would that make them a heretic and therefore outside the orthodox Christian faith?

In short, I came to realize that the questions I was struggling with were reductionistic and formed based on bounded set thinking. Bounded sets, also called well-defined intrinsic sets, refer to categories with clearly defined boundaries (i.e., something can only be in or out of the set) whereby membership within the set is determined by what something is in and of itself. A Christian then, according to this approach, is someone who must possess a certain defined list of criteria like beliefs and behaviors.

Centered sets, or well-defined extrinsic sets, represent an alternative approach to category building and while these sets also have clearly defined boundaries, inclusion in the set is not contingent on intrinsic qualities but rather on how it is related to the center. So, a Christian in this way of thinking is someone who is moving toward Jesus, the center, while recognizing that people moving toward the center start from different levels of proximity from the center. Thus, a centered set is not a static, homogeneous set like a bounded set.

Adopting, as Hiebert advised, a centered-set approach to the category of "Christian" liberated me from the impossible task of coming up with a list of intrinsic criteria for inclusion. I looked for a consensus among evangelical theologians and could find none. Instead, the centered-set approach empowered me to see Christian as a dynamic, relational category that raises a different set of questions from the ones I struggled to answer satisfactorily. Rather than "What do you know?" the more germane question became "Who do you love?" and "Where does your allegiance reside?" (Lee 2007, 29).

This shift had a profound impact on how I began to see Christian others and think theologically about Christian conversion. Whereas I intuitively questioned whether non-evangelicals were Christian because they may not have conformed to my ever-changing set of criteria in my neat bounded set way of thinking, centered-set thinking allowed me to make peace with the reality of real differences in beliefs and practices among professing Christians. The centered-set paradigm also freed me to see that we may very well be part of the same household of God because we are all willing to follow Christ faithfully according to the light we have been given. This necessarily involves a mixture of truth and error as I came to understand that all our versions of the Christian faith reflect the same mixtures of biblical fidelity, idolatry, and distortions. For now, we all see in a mirror dimly, and no theological system has it all right.

Exemplified by evangelicals like John MacArthur (1995), who are strongly critical of *Evangelicals and Catholics Together*, many have questioned if we can really have unity given the reality of what they perceive to be major theological disagreements. A shift away from bounded set thinking about Christians loosened my impulse to feel like we need to settle all our theological differences as a prerequisite to unity and partnership and enabled me to move beyond this impasse.

> What we share in Christ transcends mere social ties like nationality, political affiliation, and even blood relationships.

This does not mean that we ought to downplay our differences or avoid hard conversations for that would be cheap unity that seeks to avoid conflict and settles for the lowest common denominator. Rather we must pursue truth together—graciously and in love as a conversation among family members—while remaining focused on advancing the mission of God's kingdom.

Thanks again to Paul Hiebert (1985), I also experienced an epistemological shift toward what he called "critical realism" and away from a view that placed much more confidence in my ability to comprehend truth objectively. Critical realism affirms that the external world is real and humanly perceivable but that our understanding of reality is partial and mediated by various filters. This view acknowledges that given human inability to understand all there is to know about the universe, a perfect correspondence between human perception and reality is unrealistic. Holding to greater epistemological modesty led me to become a more willing and eager learner that was open to conversation partners outside of my narrow religious tradition.

Accordingly, I began to read more widely which prompted me to check my biases and to actually engage with the ideas of those that I previously dismissed or ignored. For example, through Richard Foster's *Streams of Living Water* (1998) I gained a new appreciation for the different emphases and perspectives that different Christian traditions have on spiritual formation, and it made me more aware of the limitations and blind spots of my own tradition. Reading Alister McGrath's *Iustitia Dei* (2005) led me to realize that the chasm between the Tridentine and Protestant views on justification was not as wide as I thought and that there is in fact common ground concerning the centrality of God's grace.

Getting to know extended family on my wife's side who were committed, God-loving Catholics was also impactful. If disunity is driven by fear and the fundamental absence of mutual trust and regard for the other, then slowly building trust through positive intergroup contact, as Gordon Allport (1958) suggested in his social theory on prejudice reduction, is a necessary path to reconciliation. In spending time with my extended cousins, I was able to witness first-hand the beauty and sincerity of their faith.

Concurrently, the aforementioned shifts also provided a renewed perspective in reading the biblical passages related to our common life in Christ. With my conscience pricked, I started taking more seriously the repeated admonitions in the epistles about living out the reality of our oneness in Christ:

> As a prisoner for the Lord, then, I urge you to live a life worthy of the calling you have received. Be completely humble and gentle; be patient, bearing with one another in love. Make every effort to keep the unity of the Spirit through the bond of peace. There is one body and one Spirit, just as you were called to one hope when you were called; one Lord, one faith, one baptism; one God and Father of all, who is over all and through all and in all. (Eph 4:1–6)

Living our lives in a way that fosters greater Christian unity requires that we fundamentally change how professing Christians see each other. We must recognize that which binds us together is so much stronger and deeper than that which separates us. What we share in Christ transcends mere social ties like nationality, political affiliation, and even blood relationships—a common allegiance to our Lord Jesus, brought into the family by a common Holy Spirit, a common mission, a common hope, a common destiny. This is what I must remind myself of when I sense the spirit of criticism and sectarianism swelling up inside when encountering Christians whose socio-political outlooks I vehemently disagree with.

We must also correct the low, anemic view of the church that is prevalent within the American evangelical church, which commonly sees the church as little more than a voluntary organization that warrants little commitment on our part and that exists to dispense religious goods. The church is not merely a passing sociological phenomenon; it is a living, divinely conceived and preserved entity. The church is inseparably related to and drawn into the life of the triune God. The church is the fulfillment of God's promise to restore and preserve humanity though Christ. The church bears the continuing mission of God to expand the rule of God. The church, more than a mere incidental human institution or appendix, is central to God's redemptive plan—now and forever. God is a missionary God and as the Father has sent the Son into the world to reconcile all things under his authority, the triune God is sending the church into the world as his agents of reconciliation to bring about the kingdom in fullness.

Final Reflections and Practical Steps

For Pastor Scott Chapman, the journey toward expressing Christian unity began with the realization that his church, The Chapel, would never be able to reach their community on their own given the immensity of the task (Chapman 2022). He simply started contacting the pastors of churches in his area to get to know them and potentially partner with them to reach their community. These connections eventually led to the formation of Christ Together,[2] a networking and resourcing ministry that helps local churches partner with other area churches for missional engagement. For Chapman, forging cross-denominational partnerships led to a bigger view of the church and a greater desire to see visible unity within the global church.

As a small practical step forward, I encourage church leaders and congregations to begin praying for area churches to thrive in advancing God's kingdom work, communicating to the congregation that other churches and parachurch groups are not your competitors but co-laborers in God's mission. Pray for the transformation of our hearts so that when we think about and engage with other professing Christians, we do not come from a place of contempt and suspicion but rather love and respect of fellow image bearers.

Leaning into unity in a fractured world takes courage since it will certainly invite criticism from all sides of the divide. Charles Colson and J. I. Packer were both instrumental in producing the collaborative document *Evangelicals and Catholics Together* (ECT) and both predictably endured strong backlash from fellow Christians. Colson's commitment to the ECT came at a high felt cost—radio stations dropped his broadcasts and the Prison Fellowship lost donations of approximately 1.5 million dollars and yet, he remarked, "When all is said and done, and my life is viewed in perspective, ECT is likely to be the most significant project I invested my time and capital into. It has been well worth the struggle, and I think we have yet to see the great things God will do with it" (Aitken 2005, 388).

Faced with what he perceived to be untrue accusations of going theologically soft, betraying the Reformation, abandoning justification by faith alone, and so forth, Packer reflected, "I was surprised at the violence of initial negative Protestant reaction, but I should not have been. Years ago, I came to realize that fear plays a larger part in North American motivation than is ever

---

2 Because the ministry by design is decentralized, exact numbers related to their reach are hard to track but just nine years into the ministry, they have partners in ninety-six cities in the U.S. and Canada and have a distribution list of over three thousand.

acknowledged. The sitting-on-a-volcano feeling is very American and is easily exploited. But fear clouds the mind and generates defensive responses that drive wisdom out of the window" (Packer 1994).

Courageous leadership is not driven by fear of the mob, and it does not pander to the populistic whims of "itching ears" (2 Tim 4:3). Courageous leadership is driven by love for God and others and by a staunch commitment to our God-given mission. In the face of inevitable hostility and resistance, we must remember that our resolve is rooted in our obedience to Jesus. The task of progressively healing the deeply entrenched and rancorous divides that plague the church may seem insurmountable. It will require unrelenting prayer for patience, resilience, and divine wisdom.

The Lausanne Covenant rightly affirms that "evangelization requires the whole church to take the whole gospel to the whole world" (The Lausanne Covenant 1974, sec. 6). Gospel witness that reaches the whole world today requires a diverse but united church, a church that is bound in our common love for our Lord Jesus and one another and united in pursuing God's mission of reconciling all things under Christ. Only a visibly united church can offer a truly credible gospel witness to a fractured and divided world, and a pure, unified church (Rev 7:9) is herself part of the redemptive work of God that will be fully realized in the final eschatological kingdom.

References Cited

Aitken, Jonathan. 2005. *Charles W. Colson: A Life Redeemed.* New York: Doubleday.

Allport, Gordon. 1958. *The Nature of Prejudice.* New York: Doubleday.

Armstrong, John H. 2010. *Your Church Is Too Small: Why Unity in Christ's Mission Is Vital to the Future of the Church.* Grand Rapids, MI: Zondervan.

Armstrong, John H. 2021. *Tear Down These Walls: Following Jesus into Deeper Unity.* Eugene, OR: Cascade Books.

Bishop, Bill. 2008. *The Big Sort: Why the Clustering of Like-Minded America Is Tearing Us Apart.* Boston: Houghton Mifflin Harcourt.

Brooks, David. 2020. "America Is Having a Moral Convulsion." *The Atlantic*, October 5, 2020. https://www.theatlantic.com/ideas/archive/2020/10/collapsing-levels-trust-are-devastating-america/616581/.

Burn, A. E. 1909. *The Nicene Creed.* London: Rivingtons.

Burnett, John. 2022. "Americans Are Fleeing to Places Where Political Views Match Their Own." NPR, February 18, sec. National. https://www.npr.org/2022/02/18/1081295373/the-big-sort-americans-move-to-areas-political-alignment.

Chapman, Scott. 2022. Interview by Michael Hakmin Lee. Video Conference, March 9, 2022.

Dalrymple, Timothy. 2021. "The Splintering of the Evangelical Soul." *Christianity Today*, April 16, 2021. https://www.christianitytoday.com/ct/2021/april-web-only/splintering-of-evangelical-soul.html.

Denker, Angela. 2019. *Red State Christians: Understanding the Voters Who Elected Donald Trump*. Minneapolis, MN: Fortress Press.

Devlin, Kat, and Aidan Connaughton. 2020. "Most Approve of National Response to COVID-19 in 14 Advanced Economies." *Pew Research Center*, August 27, 2020. https://www.pewresearch.org/global/2020/08/27/most-approve-of-national-response-to-covid-19-in-14-advanced-economies/.

Erickson, Millard J. 1998. *Christian Theology*. 2nd ed. Grand Rapids, MI: Baker Book House.

"Evangelicals and Catholics Together: The Christian Mission in the Third Millennium." *First Things*. Accessed March 3, 2022. https://www.firstthings.com/article/1994/05/evangelicals-catholics-together-the-christian-mission-in-the-third-millennium.

Foster, Richard J. 1998. *Streams of Living Water: Celebrating the Great Traditions of Christian Faith*. San Francisco: HarperSanFrancisco.

Gorski, Philip S., and Samuel L. Perry. 2022. *The Flag and the Cross: White Christian Nationalism and the Threat to American Democracy*. New York: Oxford University Press.

Harris, Tristan. 2019. "Our Brains Are No Match for Our Technology." *New York Times*, December 5, 2019, sec. Opinion.

Hiebert, Paul G. 1983. "The Category 'Christian' in the Mission Task." *International Review of Mission* 72, 421–27.

Hiebert, Paul G. 1985. "Epistemological Foundations for Science and Theology." *Theological Students Fellowship Bulletin* 8, no. 4: 5–10.

Huntington, Samuel P. 1983. *American Politics: The Promise of Disharmony*, rev. ed. Cambridge, MA: Belknap Press.

Jones, Robert P. 2020. *White Too Long: The Legacy of White Supremacy in American Christianity*. Illustrated edition. New York: Simon and Schuster.

Koivisto, Rex A. 2009. *One Lord, One Faith, Second Edition: A Theology for Cross-Denominational Renewal*. 2nd ed. Eugene, OR: Wipf and Stock.

The Lausanne Movement. The Lausanne Covenant. 1974. https://www.lausanne.org/content/covenant/lausanne-covenant#cov.

Lee, Michael Hakmin. 2007. "Assessment of Paul Hiebert's Centered-Set Approach to the Category 'Christian.'" Master's thesis, Dallas Theological Seminary.

Lifeway Research. 2018. "Politics in the Church," November 1, 2018. https://research.lifeway.com/2018/11/01/politics-in-the-church/.

MacArthur, John. 1995. "Evangelicals and Catholics Together." *The Master's Seminary Journal* 6, no. 1: 7–37.

McGrath, Alister E. 2005. *Iustitia Dei: A History of the Christian Doctrine of Justification*. Cambridge: Cambridge University Press.

Newbigin, Lesslie. 1961. *Is Christ Divided? A Plea for Christian Unity in a Revolutionary Age*. Grand Rapids, MI: Eerdmans.

Oden, Thomas C. 2002. "Wither Christian Unity?" *Christianity Today* 46, no. 9: 46–48.

Packer, J. I. 1994. "Why I Signed 'Evangelicals and Catholics Together.'" *Christianity Today*, December 12, 1994. https://www.christianitytoday.com/ct/1994/december12/j-i-packer-why-i-signed-evangelical-and-catholics-together.html.

Posner, Sarah. 2020. *Unholy: Why White Evangelicals Worship at the Altar of Donald Trump*. New York: Random House.

Stetzer, Ed. 2018. *Christians in the Age of Outrage: How to Bring Our Best When the World Is at Its Worst*. Carol Stream, IL: Tyndale Momentum.

Van Dusen, Henry P. 1959. "Christian Missions and Christian Unity." *Theology Today* 16, no. 3: 319–28.

World Council of Churches. 1999. "Mission and Evangelism in Unity Today." *International Review of Mission* 88, no. 348/349: 109–27.

Chapter 5

Toward a Theological Account of Christian Forgiveness in Intergenerational Communal Contexts

Kazusa Okaya

"Is there not in the Christian faith yet something other than forgiveness of sins?" (Barth 2006, 150). Forgiveness is at the heart of Christian faith and practice, both as an indicative (God's forgiveness offered through the Son) and an imperative (our obligation as Christians to forgive as we have been forgiven). Jesus taught us to pray "forgive us our debts, as we also have forgiven our debtors" (Matt 6:12 ESV). Paul exhorted Christians in Ephesians 4:32 to "Be kind to one another, tenderhearted, forgiving one another, as God in Christ forgave you." Christians are clearly commanded in Scripture to forgive as those first forgiven by God.

The difficult question is: what makes Christian forgiveness distinctively Christian? In today's polarized and fragmented world, there has been a growing interest in the theology of reconciliation. As a result, books and journal articles exploring the theology of forgiveness have proliferated. Nevertheless, most theological accounts only articulate models of Christian forgiveness in a one-to-one, individual context, while corporate and intergenerational forgiveness is often left unaddressed.[1] Hence the aim of this chapter is to explore the limitations of the existing theological models and propose ways in which Christian forgiveness can be applied to broader communal contexts.

Survey of Philosophical and Theological Landscape

Philosophical interest in forgiveness has risen dramatically since the horrific events of the Second World War. French-Continental philosophers such as Jacques Derrida and Paul Ricoeur focused on the exploration of "pure" forgiveness, to consider the *possibility* of forgiving the unforgivable. Derrida critiqued views of forgiveness which presupposes repentance as a prior condition. For Derrida, such forgiveness is only possible when the offender

---

1 In fact, Anthony Bash explicitly defines forgiveness as a personal enactment that cannot happen beyond the realm of individual one-one situations. See Bash (2007, 123–40).

becomes "forgivable" as a result of repentance, which is not pure forgiveness but is more akin to a social transaction. Therefore, pure forgiveness for Derrida remains an impossible paradox (Derrida 2001, 32).

Ricoeur, on the other hand, sought to locate the difficult possibility of forgiveness in "non-transactional" gift-giving, and argued that forgiveness requires a separation of the offensive act from the moral agent (Ricoeur 2006, 489–93). Ricoeur argues, "Everything, finally, hangs on the possibility of separating the agent from the action. This unbinding would mark the inscription, in the field of the horizontal disparity between power and act, of the vertical disparity between the great height of forgiveness and the abyss of guilt" (Ricoeur 2006, 490).

Compared to the Continental philosophers, North American philosophers were not so much interested in the *possibility* of forgiveness but rather in *conditions* of when it was moral to forgive. Jeffrie Murphy argued that forgiveness is forswearing the emotion of resentment on moral grounds (Murphy 1998, 21). This is possible under the conditions when the offender has "divorced themselves from their own evil act" (Murphy 1998, 25–26). Building on to Murphy's account, Joram Haber analyzes forgiveness not as an emotional change in forswearing of resentment, but as involving a performative utterance (such as "I forgive you") which expresses the *intention* of the forgiver to will-away his resentment (Haber 1991, 39–40).

Space does not allow us to outline the philosophical arguments in detail, yet for our purposes, the important point to note is that: (1) the North American philosophers generally share in common the notion that forgiveness involves eliminating "resentment" of some sort, either by undergoing emotional change or by making a conscious judgment; (2) most agree that some kind of condition, such as prior apology, must exist for forgiveness to be morally justified; and (3) that most consider forgiveness as involving a separation of the *identity* of the offender from the *act* of the offense. This notion of forgiveness as intentional judgment and separation of act with agent, will be echoed in the theological realm.

In the theology of forgiveness, two theologians stand out today as the dominant voices in the discussion. First is Gregory Jones, who, in his seminal book *Embodying Forgiveness* (Jones 1995), harshly criticized therapeutic models of forgiveness. One such example was the pastoral theological approach Lewis B. Smedes laid out in *Forgive and Forget* (Smedes 2007), which Jones critiques as paving the way for "cheap forgiveness." He argues that the biblical notion of forgiveness never ends with individual self-healing but must lead to the reconciliation of two parties. Jones also argues that distinctive Christian forgiveness ought to be modeled after the triune shape of divine forgiveness.

He views God's forgiveness through the Son as a judgment of grace, which is simultaneously a confrontation of our sins and a gracious offer of forgiveness.

Repentance is the proper mode of accepting this judgment of grace (Jones 1995, 145–46). For Jones, God's judgment of grace becomes a paradigmatic pattern for Christian forgiveness, where the offer of forgiveness goes hand in hand with the display of sin and need for justice. A distinctive contribution by Jones is his construal of forgiveness as a habit that must be cultivated within the life of the church, through ecclesial practices such as confession of sin, baptism, and the Lord's Supper (Jones 1995, 163–207).

Second is Miroslav Volf, whose book *Exclusion and Embrace* (Volf 1996), has become a groundbreaking work in the understanding of Christian reconciliation. His most extensive treatment of forgiveness is seen in his later work, *Free of Charge* (Volf 2005). Volf appropriates Luther's reading of Paul to articulate Christian forgiveness in terms of gift-giving. Forgiveness bears a triune shape as the Father forgave humanity by offering his Son as a gift, whereas humans receive the gift of Christ by repentance, enabled by the work of the Holy Spirit. This triune shape of divine forgiveness provides a paradigm for Christian forgiveness where we also offer our gift of self-sacrificial forgiveness. Just as God has forgiven us unconditionally, our offer of forgiveness also ought to be unconditional. Nevertheless, just as gift-giving is not complete until it is received, this gift of forgiveness must be received by the offender in the form of repentance for it to be completed in the act of reconciliation (Volf 2005, 181–86).

Jones and Volf stand as major voices in the theology of forgiveness today. There are some noticeable differences between the two accounts, especially in the role of forgetfulness, where Volf considers forgiveness to involve non-remembrance, while Jones differs from Volf in arguing that forgiveness entails "remembering well." Nevertheless, the two share much in common in their general understanding of Christian forgiveness. They both agree that: (1) Christian forgiveness must be modeled after God's triune shape of forgiveness displayed in the atonement; (2) Christian forgiveness must be motivated by understanding the forgiven-ness that we were first granted by God; (3) forgiveness does not end in an individual act of forswearing resentment, but must lead to the reconciliation of two parties; and (4) Christian forgiveness is unconditional, while repentance is crucial as a means of *receiving* such forgiveness.

Limitations of Existing Models

We will now consider some limitations of the existing Christian forgiveness model, especially in relation to its applicability in communal settings. Jones and Volf both provide eloquent accounts of Christian forgiveness in interpersonal contexts. They also both succeed in articulating a distinctively Christian model, mirroring the divine shape of forgiveness. Nevertheless, neither Jones nor Volf attempt to articulate how Christian forgiveness occurs in inter-communal or intergenerational contexts.[2] This omission is peculiar, considering how the need for reconciliation and forgiveness is most prevalent within the context of communal and intergenerational resentment.

Perhaps they neglected this corporate element of forgiveness due to their understanding of forgiveness as resulting in the expiation of guilt. This notion is most clearly stated by Volf in *The End of Memory*: "when we forgive those who have wronged us, we make our own God's miracle of forgiveness. Echoing God's unfathomable graciousness, we decouple the deed from the offender" (Volf 2006, 208). Here, Volf follows North American philosophers in contending that forgiveness enables separation of the agent from the offense, which translates theologically to the event of the cross where our guilt is expiated by Christ's death.[3] Because our guilt is expiated at the cross as Christ is judged on our behalf, we are considered a "new humanity," a different entity from our past, sinful self. Using Volf's language, by offering forgiveness, we replicate Christ's forgiveness by decoupling the offense from the offender.

Yet, this understanding of forgiveness as involving separation of act and agent is precisely where the difficulty lies in applying this model to communal settings. In many cases of communal resentment, the agent directly responsible for the offense is not the object of forgiveness. This is especially the case in intergenerational contexts where resentment between groups exists in the current generation against those who have not directly committed moral harm. Hence it becomes difficult to apply the "separating the deed from the offender" model to intergenerational settings where the deed does not always belong to a particular individual in the current generation.[4]

Another difficulty of Jones and Volf's model lies in the ambivalent theological grounding for the transformation of the offender. Because both Jones and Volf seek to establish the unconditionality of Christian forgiveness, they deny the view that repentance is a prior condition for Christian forgiveness. To be sure, they emphasize the need for forgiveness to be *received* by the offender in repentance

---

[2] Jones does argue for the importance of an ecclesial community in nurturing the virtue of forgiveness as a craft. Yet, he does not articulate the logic of forgiveness in cases where resentment exists on communal and inter-generational levels.

[3] Although Volf differs in not seeing such separation as prior requirements for forgiveness (the way conditionality is described by many philosophers) but as the act of forgiveness itself.

[4] Jones does not explicitly follow the separation of deed/offender model. Yet, Jones does not have a clear conceptual mechanism of inter-personal forgiveness like Volf, and hence it is difficult to pinpoint what exactly forgiveness "does" in Jones's account when he insists that our forgiveness ought to model God's judgment of grace.

and point to the importance of transformation of the offender within a reconciled relationship. Yet, if forgiveness is construed primarily as gift-giving (Volf) or as judgment of grace (Jones), both metaphors expressing a temporal event, we are left with the impression that the transformation of the offender is not intrinsic to the movement of forgiveness but is rather a result of it.

Recently, Catholic theologian James Voiss, in his *Rethinking Christian Forgiveness* (Voiss 2015), also criticized the models espoused by Jones and Volf in a similar vein. Voiss argues that these Protestant models cannot account for "third-party forgiveness," where forgiveness is offered on behalf of another, as in cases of communal forgiveness. Voiss names one reason for this shortcoming on the theological basis being grounded in substitutionary theories of atonement. He argues that the substitutionary theories of the atonement locate the *loci* of divine forgiveness at the event of the crucifixion, marginalizing the incarnation and the earthly ministry of Jesus as being irrelevant to the act of divine forgiveness itself (Voiss 2015, 301). He also sees the separation of the guilt and agent model as being problematic, for it does not serve as a sufficient ground for the transformation of the offender. For the offender to be transformed in repentance, they must be the same agent who has committed the offense (Voiss 2015, 387). Voiss proposes an alternative model by abandoning the traditional substitutionary atonement theories, grounding his model on sacramental cosmology which places Christ's incarnation as the *loci* of divine forgiveness (Voiss 2015, 324–25). Hence, in forgiving others, Christians participate in Christ's incarnation by becoming mediators of divine grace, where God's forgiveness is offered to the offender through our sacramental mediation (Voiss 2014, 363).

> In forgiving others, Christians participate in Christ's incarnation by becoming mediators of divine grace.

There is much to appreciate in Voiss's critique of the existing model and his salient pastoral concerns. His abandonment of traditional substitutionary theories is also understandable, as he seeks to view forgiveness as essentially a restoration of relationship, which includes space for the transformation of the offender. However, as a student of Protestant evangelical theology, there are certain presuppositions I cannot accept.[5] Hence, I would like to suggest a way in which a model of Christian forgiveness can meet the challenges of the

---

5 Such as the post Vatican II sacramental cosmology, the notion of non-Christians being "unconscious" recipients of God's forgiveness, and the denial of substitutionary theories of the atonement.

existing model without departing from the traditional understanding of the atonement.

For this purpose, I will suggest that the paradigm for Christian forgiveness is better located not only in the *event* of the atonement but in the broader context of *union with Christ*. Putting union with Christ as the broader paradigm for Christian forgiveness would establish a foundation where forgiveness and transformation can both be grounded *intrinsically* within Christian forgiveness. This model will also allow space for accounting for intergenerational forgiveness, where what is required is not so much a forensic expiation of guilt but a remedy for communal shame.

Forgiveness Based on Union with Christ

Theologians agree that distinctive Christian forgiveness must not only be *motivated* by our forgiveness, but also be *modeled* after the pattern of divine forgiveness. Jones uses judgment of grace, and Volf uses the metaphor of *gift-giving* to depict how human forgiveness can echo the shape of God's trinitarian act of forgiveness. Unlike Voiss, we need not deny substitutionary accounts of forgiveness to expand our horizon of Christian forgiveness.

Instead, I propose theologically zooming out as it were, to locate the paradigm of divine forgiveness in the concept of union with Christ. Union with Christ is an important theological motif especially prominent in the Pauline corpus and is recently considered as providing much of the basis of soteriology.[6] The Pauline corpus is saturated with the language of Christians being "in Christ." Especially noteworthy is the use in Romans 5–8, where Paul emphasizes our union with Christ as the basis of our participation in Christ's death and resurrection. I follow Oliver Crisp and others who argue for a logical (but not temporal) primacy of union with Christ in relation to the atonement (Crisp 2020, 163–80).[7]

Hence as Richard Gaffin has noted, justification and sanctification are not two isolated events but are only different facets of union with Christ (Gaffin 1978, 130–31). It is not that Christ's death and resurrection are later applied to believers as some kind of legal fiction (a reputation traditional accounts of atonement often receive). Instead, it is because sinners are united to Christ by

---

[6] For a recent discussion of union with Christ in New Testament studies, see *Paul and Union with Christ* (Campbell 2015).

[7] Some might argue that union with Christ does not relate to a model for the atonement per se but is rather what applies the atonement to believers. Yet, this is precisely the point Crisp takes pains to refute. For Crisp, union with Christ is logically (though not temporally) prior to and intrinsic to the whole work of the atonement.

the Holy Spirit that we partake in his death and resurrection (Rom 6:3–5).[8] We are counted righteous and forgiven not because Christ's righteousness is externally *imputed* upon us apart from Christ, but because we *partake* in his righteousness and sanctification.[9]

If we are to zoom out and locate our paradigm for Christian forgiveness within the larger framework of union with Christ, we will be able to overcome many of the pitfalls associated with the traditional accounts without throwing out the traditional atonement model altogether. It is not that God offered an external gift called "forgiveness" outside of Christ. Rather, God's gift was a self-offering of Christ for the forgiveness of our sins. God's gift to humanity was Christ himself, and not an abstract entity called "forgiveness." Just as God has offered *himself* (in Christ) to humanity and invited us to be united with him, by imitating his way of forgiveness, we do not simply offer an external gift called "forgiveness" but essentially offer *ourselves* to the offender for the purpose of reunion.[10]

Hence Christian forgiveness is not merely a performative speech-act or a one-time transaction between "I forgive you" and "I'm sorry." The gift of forgiveness is a sacrificial self-offering that initiates a reconciling relationship between the two parties. The self-offering of forgiveness allows the offender to accept and *participate* in the judgment of grace made by the forgiver. The decision to forgive is often a difficult and painful one, which involves a certain sense of self-sacrifice. Hence forgiveness as judgment of grace displays the pain and the sacrifice of the forgiver, inviting the other to participate in it. The weight of this judgment is fully felt by the forgiven party as they are united in the reconciled relationship. Just as believers partake in the death of Christ and experience "death to self" by being united to him, the forgiven party also participates in the pain of the forgiver by dying to their former self.[11]

Construing forgiveness within the whole movement of union with Christ also provides grounding for the transformation of the offender. Union with

---

8 It must be noted that Volf also mentions the importance of union with Christ (Volf 2005, 150). Yet, his use of union is to ground the motivation for Christians to forgive, and not as a paradigm of Christian forgiveness.

9 This is not a denial of the doctrine of imputation per se but situating imputation within union with Christ. Kevin Vanhoozer proposes union with Christ as a bridge between the traditional reformed understanding of imputed righteousness and the New Perspective on Paul, suggesting the term "incorporated righteousness" (Perrin 2011, 235–58).

10 I use the term "reunion" to signal how our inter-personal forgiveness is paradigmatically similar to "union" with Christ, but distinct in that it is not a metaphysical union.

11 I am not denying the importance of the cross and the substitutionary models of the atonement (which correlates to the forgiver's judgment of grace) but am locating it within a wider framework of union with Christ.

Christ is the foundation for the dual gratia of justification and sanctification. As John Calvin wrote, one cannot participate in Christ's righteousness while not being sanctified, as that would entail dividing Christ's body in two (Calvin 2008, 523). This is why the fast-food gospel, where forgiveness of sin is declared without transformation of lives, is cheap grace, a promise of forgiveness without costly discipleship (Bonhoeffer 1995, 45). Just as union with Christ entails both forgiveness and sanctification, the "reunion" of the offender and the offended entails not only that the offender is now declared "forgiven" but also grounds the ongoing transformation of the offender.

Forgiveness initiates a relationship where the forgiven party continues to be transformed in repentance through participation in the life and narrative of the forgiver. As philosopher Charles Griswold articulated, the newly established relationship invites a certain "rewriting" of one's personal narrative (Griswold 2007, 104–5). Those united to Christ are baptized into his story, which provides the new perspective for believers to view and discern their own life-narrative. Likewise, the forgiven party is now able to see their own life-narrative through the perspective and narrative of the forgiver.

There is one caveat, however. Although the above model provides an overreaching analogy to divine forgiveness, the analogy must not be conflated with the essence. As part of Christian discipleship, we are called to imitate Christ, not to replace him. In other words, though we may mirror Christ's dynamics of forgiveness and his invitation of union with Christ, we cannot, and should not pretend, that we can offer divine forgiveness, the ultimate forgiveness of sin. This is the point I diverge with Voiss's model, where he considers divine forgiveness to be entrusted to Christians in their sacramental mediation. I worry this approach has a danger in conflating God's forgiveness with our own. An infinite qualitative difference exists between our union with Christ and our "reunion" with others.

Furthermore, while a clear perpetrator-victim relationship exists between humanity and God in the case of divine forgiveness, such is not the case between sinful creatures. There is usually an inter-mixing of the offender and offended relationship, and the gift of forgiveness often goes both ways. Hence unlike Voiss, I take my participatory account of Christian forgiveness not as mediating God's forgiveness per se but as only a fitting parable of divine forgiveness—motivated, modeled, and pointing toward, but not equal to, the true forgiveness found in Christ.

How does this paradigm allow us to speak of Christian forgiveness on a communal and intergenerational level? Because union with Christ includes, but is not exhausted by, the notion of expiation of guilt. As we have previously seen, the dominant theological model tends to understand forgiveness as a way of dealing with the guilt of the offender. As Volf writes, "the removal of guilt is crucial to forgiveness. If guilt remains, forgiveness hasn't happened" (Volf 2006, 195). Expiation of guilt would serve as the proper paradigm for forgiveness within direct victim-perpetrator relationships. Yet, this model loses its applicability when the agent responsible for causing harm is absent from the picture, as in intergenerational contexts.

This is what leads Anthony Bash to conclude that forgiveness can only happen in one-to-one interpersonal settings (Bash 2007, 123–40). Much has been written recently on corporate guilt and the transmission of intergenerational moral responsibility.[12] Although an important area for communal reconciliation, it is beyond the scope of this essay.[13] Yet, even in communal contexts where guilt is difficult to define, I would suggest that there is another factor crucial to forgiveness which is often overlooked in its Western understanding: shame.

The Role of Shame in Communal Forgiveness

A crucial yet often overlooked element in forgiveness is the notion of shame. Shame and honor play an important role in forgiveness, especially in communal and intergenerational contexts. Recently, there has been rising interest among biblical scholars on the topic of shame, exemplified by works such as Ti-Lau's *Defending Shame* (Lau 2020) and DeSilva's *Honor, Patronage, Kinship and Purity* (DeSilva 2000). Yet, perhaps the most noticeable development was seen in the field of missiology, such as contributions by Jason Georges and Mark Baker in *Ministering in Honor-Shame Cultures* (Georges and Baker 2016) and Brad Vaughn in *Saving God's Face* (Vaughn 2013). Missiologists rightly turned to shame as an important and overlooked biblical category for sin, which opens new possibilities in the contextualization of the gospel message.

Although there is not a consensus among scholars as to the proper distinction between shame and guilt, there are areas of broad agreement. Many consider guilt to be associated with specific acts (Smedes 1993, 9). You become guilty when you have committed a moral wrong, and the remedy for guilt is considered to be the removal of guilt. In a judicial system, this is manifested in the shape of punishments, while the biblical paradigm is the expiation of guilt.

---

12 Such as the important work on communal responsibility by Phillip Pettit. See Pettit 2007.

13 My intuition is that even when intergenerational corporate guilt can be established, it would be a qualitatively different kind of guilt and different kind of moral wrongdoing compared to the original guilt (i.e., participation in a racist narrative as opposed to the guilt of slave ownership).

On the other hand, shame occurs with a decrease in social capital, whether real or imaginary (Elshof and Vaughn 2021, 59). Unlike guilt, the remedy for shame is not its removal but restoration of honor. For example, if a murderer is punished by serving his due in prison, his guilt is considered to be expiated by means of punishment (at least legally speaking). Yet this will not change his shameful status in society if his social capital has not been restored.

In most cases, the offender would bear *both* guilt and shame. If a person has committed murder, he would be guilty due to his moral action *and* be put to shame as his social capital is decreased. Herman Bavinck sees the origin of both guilt and shame in the Garden of Eden, where Adam and Eve become guilty of trespass, which led to a newfound emotion of shame when they recognized their nakedness (Bavinck 2006, 173). Since sin involves both guilt and shame, divine forgiveness as a remedy for sin involves not only the removal of guilt but also the restoration of honor.

> Divine forgiveness as a remedy for sin involves not only the removal of guilt but also the restoration of honor.

As Georges and Baker outline, Christ's shameful death on the cross and his vindication at the resurrection enables humanity's honor to be restored by participating in Christ's shameful death and his glorious resurrection (Georges and Baker 2016, 106–13). Hence Christians are said to "put on Christ" (Rom 13:14) and partake in his glory (2 Thess 2:14).

Shame is important in our discussion of communal forgiveness because shame is not essentially about one's actions (what you have done) but about one's social status (what others think of you). And this "other" is mainly the perception of the offended community. Hence the shame incurred by the act of one man/woman can spread communally as described in 2 Samuel 19:5, "You have today covered with shame the faces of all your servants." For example, if your father is imprisoned for murder, you would not be *guilty*, but you and your community would bear the *shame*. This is especially true in collectivist societies where we are said to share a common "face," as Brad Vaughn illustrates in *Saving God's Face* (Vaughn 2013, 151–58).

The point is, although you might not be *guilty* of an act you have not committed, you still bear the *shame* of the community, even across generations. Hence, even in contexts where the current generation may not be *guilty* of what the previous generation has done, they still bear shame from the perspective of the offended community. By extending the gift of forgiveness in these communal intergenerational contexts, the forgiven party can partake in the honor which belongs to the community of the forgiver. For contexts of intergenerational and communal forgiveness where direct guilt is difficult to locate, I propose focusing on shame and restoration of honor, rather than expiation of guilt.

Toward a Model of Communal Forgiveness

I have so far proposed two emendations to the traditional model of Christian forgiveness for it to be intelligible in a communal context: (1) union with Christ as the controlling paradigm; and (2) focusing on communal shame rather than guilt. To illustrate how this plays out, I will present a real-life scenario of what I have witnessed while serving as a campus minister for International Fellowship of Evangelical Students (IFES). At one East Asian Regional Conference, a group of students from different ethnicities were brought together in a small group setting. One day, a Korean delegate Sujin approached a Japanese student Yuki, and confessed her bitterness against Japan and her willingness to forgive the Japanese people.[14] Her bitterness was primarily caused by the horrific stories she heard growing up about the way the Japanese people treated the Koreans during WWII. Yuki was not born at the time of the war, and therefore not directly guilty of the wartime crimes which caused Sujin's resentment.[15] Nevertheless, from Sujin's perspective, Yuki is a member of her moral community (Japan), which she associates with the perpetration and shame.[16] This is a case where one could share in the shame of the moral community without being directly guilty for its moral actions.

Yuki was initially taken back without knowing how to respond. Growing up in Japan, she did not have much knowledge about Japan's wartime crimes and the pain experienced by the Korean people. Yet, Yuki eventually decided to accept Sujin's forgiveness, and their friendship began. For Sujin, the offer of forgiveness was not merely a platitude, but a self-offering, an invitation to a new reconciling relationship. She was opening up her heart in sharing her collective experience of pain, and by offering forgiveness, she was offering herself in judgment of grace. As Yuki received Sujin's forgiveness, she was able to participate in the narrative of her community, the stories of pain and suffering the Korean people have experienced during the war. This newfound relationship led to transformation, as Yuki was now able to see her own identity from the lens of the other.

---

14 Names are changed for reasons of privacy.

15 For our purpose, we will posit that the Japanese student does not share in the guilt of her ancestors. Whether such innocence is possible is open to debate. Yet, our purpose here is to show how communal forgiveness is possible even if guilt cannot be identified.

16 Shame here is defined as a decrease in social capital (Elshof and Vaughn 2021, 59).

Furthermore, as Yuki entered into the reconciled relationship, her shame was covered and vindicated as she participates in the honor of Sujin's community. This case is an example of communal, intergenerational forgiveness where forgiveness happens not as a single event, but as a mutual-transformative process within the reconciling relationship, initiated by the self-offering of forgiveness.

But what if Yuki rejects the offer of forgiveness? Would Sujin's offer of forgiveness be void of meaning? If the offer of forgiveness is rejected by Yuki, she would not be able to participate in the reconciling relationship, which is the basis for forgiveness and transformation. This does not mean Sujin has not forgiven Yuki, since her self-gift of forgiveness has already been offered. What it means is that forgiveness has yet to be completed. To be sure, though incomplete, such forgiveness still has value, especially in terms of healing of the forgiver.[17] Yet, as Jones points out, Christian forgiveness does not end with relinquishing of personal resentment but has its *telos* at restoration of relationships. Hence a gift of forgiveness must be received to complete the cycles of forgiveness and to initiate a reconciling relationship of "reunion."

There are other possibilities of communal forgiveness, such as political forgiveness (political representative pronouncing forgiveness to another community), third-party vicarious forgiveness (forgiving someone on behalf of another), and forgiveness toward abstract communal entities (forgiving a particular ethnicity in general). These cases all require careful and different articulations of collective identity and moral agency, which is beyond the scope of this essay. Nevertheless, each of these cases would be difficult to articulate in traditional models of Christian forgiveness, which centers on the event of the cross and expiation of guilt alone. By utilizing union with Christ as the paradigmatic shape of Christian forgiveness and considering the importance of communal shame, we are better equipped to postulate other difficult cases of communal forgiveness.

Missiological Implications

Finally, this participatory account for Christian forgiveness has important missiological implications. As I have pointed out earlier, the proposed model of Christian forgiveness serves only as an *ectype* of the *archetype* found in divine forgiveness. Christian forgiveness is motivated by divine forgiveness, and follows the pattern of divine forgiveness, but is not a substitute for it. Unlike Voiss, I do not believe we can mediate divine forgiveness on behalf of God.

---

17 Hence Jones's dismissal of Smedes's model as being "therapeutic" could be downplaying the importance of emotional healing of the forgiver.

Nevertheless, there is an important missiological implication to our act of Christian forgiveness modeled after union with Christ. Borrowing the analogy from Kevin Vanhoozer, we *play-out* the drama of forgiveness in Christ through our act of forgiving (Vanhoozer 2005, 397). For Christians, our own life-narrative is deeply embedded with the scriptural narrative of God's forgiveness through the Son. As forgiveness opens up space for the offender to participate in our life-narrative, they will not only participate in our story, but also inevitably encounter the deeper narrative of the gospel.

This reality becomes a powerful witness to the gospel message as the offender experiences the effect of life-transforming forgiveness first-hand through the forgiver. When the forgiven party accepts not only our invitation of forgiveness, but ultimately God's invitation of divine forgiveness, the earthly "reunion" is transposed into an eschatological *communion*. As brothers and sisters mutually united in the same body of Christ, the reconciled relationship is no longer a parable but becomes an eschatological reality. Only then would we not only model Christ's forgiveness but participate together in Christ, together receiving the ultimate forgiveness of sin.

Conclusion

Gaining a theological understanding of forgiveness remains an important task in today's fractured world. Especially urgent is the need for a theology of forgiveness in communal and intergenerational contexts.[18] This chapter has addressed some of the shortcomings of the existing model and proposed a way forward in situating the paradigm for Christian forgiveness within the context of union with Christ. The advantage of the proposed participatory model is its elasticity in incorporating different aspects of soteriology, not only focusing on the moment of the cross/expiation of guilt. Inattentiveness to shame is one example of such shortcomings in the traditional understanding of forgiveness, which has important implications especially in non-Western missional contexts oriented more toward communal identity. Although interpersonal forgiveness is not a substitute for God's ultimate forgiveness of sin, it is motivated by, modeled after, and serves as a powerful testimony to the true forgiveness found in Christ.

---

18 Some areas for further consideration include the theology of Christian apology and repentance, the relationship between forgiveness and power, forgiveness's relationship with justice, and the emotional healing of the forgiver.

References Cited

Barth, Karl. 2006. *The Faith of the Church: A Commentary on the Apostles' Creed According to Calvin's Catechism*. N.p.: Wipf and Stock.

Bash, Anthony. 2007. *Forgiveness and Christian Ethics*. Cambridge: Cambridge University Press.

Bavinck, Herman. 2006. *Reformed Dogmatics: Volume 3: Sin and Salvation in Christ*. Edited by John Bolt. Translated by John Vriend. Grand Rapids, MI: Baker Academic.

Bonhoeffer, Dietrich, and Eric Metaxas. 1995. *The Cost of Discipleship*. New York: Touchstone.

Calvin, John. 2008. *Institutes of the Christian Religion*. Revised edition. Peabody, MA: Hendrickson Publishers.

Campbell, Constantine R. 2015. *Paul and Union with Christ: An Exegetical and Theological Study*. Grand Rapids, MI: Zondervan Academic.

Crisp, Oliver D. 2020. *Approaching the Atonement: The Reconciling Work of Christ*. Downers Grove, IL: IVP Academic.

Derrida, Jacques. 2001. *On Cosmopolitanism and Forgiveness*. London: Routledge.

DeSilva, David A. 2000. *Honor, Patronage, Kinship and Purity: Unlocking New Testament Culture*. Downers Grove, IL: IVP Academic.

Elshof, Gregg Ten, and Brad Vaughn. 2021. *For Shame: Rediscovering the Virtues of a Maligned Emotion*. Grand Rapids, MI: Zondervan.

Gaffin, Richard B. 1978. *The Centrality of the Resurrection: A Study in Paul's Soteriology*. Grand Rapids, MI: Baker Book House.

Georges, Jayson, and Mark D. Baker. 2016. *Ministering in Honor-Shame Cultures: Biblical Foundations and Practical Essentials*. Downers Grove, IL: IVP Academic.

Griswold, Charles. 2007. *Forgiveness: A Philosophical Exploration*. New York: Cambridge University Press.

Haber, Joram Graf. 1991. *Forgiveness*. Savage, MD: Rowman and Littlefield Publishers.

Jones, L. Gregory. 1995. *Embodying Forgiveness: A Theological Analysis*. Grand Rapids, MI: Eerdmans.

Lau, Te-Li. 2020. *Defending Shame: Its Formative Power in Paul's Letters*. Grand Rapids, MI: Baker Academic.

Murphy, Jeffrie G., and Jean Hampton. 1998. *Forgiveness and Mercy*. Reprint edition. Cambridge: Cambridge University Press.

Perrin, Nicholas, and Richard B. Hays, eds. 2011. *Jesus, Paul and the People of God: A Theological Dialogue with N. T. Wright*. Downers Grove, IL: IVP Academic.

Pettit, Philip. 2007. "Responsibility Incorporated." *Ethics* 117, no. 2: 171–201.

Ricoeur, Paul. 2006. *Memory, History, Forgetting*. Translated by Kathleen Blamey and David Pellauer. Chicago: University of Chicago Press.

Smedes, Lewis B. 1993. *Shame and Grace: Healing the Shame We Don't Deserve*. San Francisco: HarperSanFrancisco.

Smedes, Lewis B. 2007. *Forgive and Forget: Healing the Hurts We Don't Deserve*. 2nd edition. New York: HarperOne.

Vanhoozer, Kevin J. 2005. *The Drama of Doctrine: A Canonical Linguistic Approach to Christian Doctrine*. 1st edition. Louisville, KY: Westminster John Knox Press.

Vaughn, Brad. 2013. *Saving God's Face: A Chinese Contextualization of Salvation through Honor and Shame*. Pasadena, CA: William Carey International University Press.

Voiss, James K. 2015. *Rethinking Christian Forgiveness: Theological, Philosophical, and Psychological Explorations*. Collegeville, MN: Liturgical Press.

Volf, Miroslav. 1996. *Exclusion and Embrace: A Theological Exploration of Identity, Otherness, and Reconciliation*. Nashville, TN: Abingdon.

Volf, Miroslav. 2005. *Free of Charge: Giving and Forgiving in a Culture Stripped of Grace*. Grand Rapids, MI: Zondervan. Volf, Miroslav. 2006. *The End of Memory: Remembering Rightly in a Violent World*. The Stob Lectures 2002. Grand Rapids, MI: Eerdmans.

Part 2
Reconciliation Practices

Chapter 6

Reconciling Discipleship
Living as Ecclesia Wherever We Go

Manuel and Jeanette Böhm

Why We Need Reconciling Disciples

The global COVID-19 pandemic and other major crises in recent years have highlighted how believers have lost touch with their communities or are struggling to live out their faith (Nortey 2022). But one can't just argue with a post-COVID reality, since church attendance and growth had been in decline prior to the pandemic.[1] This observation leads to the following questions: Do we know what it means to be a follower of Christ individually and corporately? Has our faith become irrelevant for the societal challenges and therefore our good news is not applicable to real life problems?

Alan Hirsch argues that the church in the West has forgotten how to make disciples. He remarks that disciple making has become an intellectual exercise, a course or program, and that we created a culture of being a consumer, rather than active participant. This mindset stands in the way of being a lively, mature follower of Jesus, whose life is so Spirit-filled, that others want to walk with us to learn what it means to be a disciple of Jesus (Hirsch 2011, 140).

As followers of Jesus, we are called to be reconciling disciples (2 Cor 5:18–21) that "embark on the prophetic journey that leads to reconciliation and transformation around the world" (Salter McNeil 2015, 15) and to live out transformed lives empowered by the love of God (Castro 1978, 87; Yoder 2000, 52; Matt 22:36–40). Through Christ's love, churches are commissioned into their communities and are called to becoming centers of reconciliation (Reimer 2020b, 54).

Proposed is an approach to be *reconciling disciples*, who equip believers to be mature disciples of Jesus. We define *reconciling disciples* as "followers

---

1 See: EFC study on church attendance: https://www.faithtoday.ca/Magazines/2020-Jan-Feb/Not-Christian-anymore_(2022/12/28); The Canadian Census shows: "In 2021, over 19.3 million people reported a Christian religion, representing just over half of the Canadian population (53.3%). However, this proportion is down from 67.3% in 2011 and 77.1% in 2001." https://www150.statcan.gc.ca/n1/daily-quotidien/221026/dq221026b-eng.htm (2022/12/28).

of Jesus who are reconciled with their Creator, their own story of pain and suffering, and walking their journey of healing and restoration with those around them." Through this transformation process, they are then able to lead others to be reconciled with God and people around them—to be agents of transformation in their communities that need the good news of the kingdom of God. Corporately understood as ecclesia, they understand what it means to be called to take responsibility for their communities (Reimer 2017, 47).

Foundations for Reconciling Discipleship

Reconciliation and the Mission of God

Since the 1952 international missionary conference in Willingen, Germany, mission theology has embraced the concept of *missio Dei*, and modern missiologists would not argue against a trinitarian and holistic approach of mission (Nagy 2022, 164). Reconciliation though, still seems to be discussed in either the vertical or horizontal perspective (Bright 1965). Considering David Bosch's understanding of mission, an individual perspective on reconciliation as a salvation of the individual is problematic—almost a separating activity (Bosch 2011a, 403–4). The American Robert Schreiter, through analyzing Pauline theology, points out:

> Reconciliation is a central way of explaining God's work in the world. Through the Son and the Spirit, God is making peace—between God and the world, and thus also within all of creation itself. When this insight is brought together with the concept of the *missio Dei* developed a few decades earlier in missiology, we see the biblical foundations for reconciliation as a paradigm of mission, a paradigm that began taking on a particular poignancy and urgency in the last decade of the twentieth century. (Schreiter 2013, 14)

Johannes Reimer argues for a biblical understanding of reconciliation as the restoration of an active, functioning, peaceful relationship—that is based on an "exchange" (Reimer 2020b, 11–13). His argument builds on his understanding of the noun *catallage* in relation to "the other" and concludes: "The term implies conscious solidarity with the 'other' instead of hostile confrontation" (Reimer 2020b, 11).[2] Similarly, John W. DeGruchy writes: "It involves a process of overcoming alienation through identification and solidarity with the 'other' with the aim of making peace and restoring relationship" (DeGruchy 2002, 51).

Stemming from the negotiation language of the Greeks, this term can also be understood as "something like slipping into the skin of the adversary in order to understand them better and thus find common ground for everyday life

---

2 Translated by authors.

lived" (Reimer 2020b, 11).³ Reconciliation, through empathetic identification with the "other," is an exchange of enmity for friendship, separation for reuniting, hate and anger for love, hurt for healing, brokenness for restoration (Merkel 1990, 261).

Reconciliation is part of the mission of God and therefore a continuation of the relationship between God as Father, Son, and Spirit to all mankind and creation (2 Cor 5:18–21). Reconciliation is the expression of God's love for his people by inviting them into relationship with him to embrace their God-given identity as made in the image of God, living as a child of God (Rom 5:10; Col 1:20–22). Reconciliation occurs when people live in friendship with God that leads to love of self, others, and creation, to bring forth a new humanity (Gal 3:25–29).

> Reconciliation is the expression of God's love for his people.

Our identity as children of God means we also see other people around as created in the image of God. Therefore, they carry the same dignity as we do. Turning toward God and growing closer to him implies that believers move closer to their neighbor, as God has turned toward "those" in similar ways as to "them." Disciples that heard the phrase "your kingdom come" in Jesus's prayer knew from their Jewish background that the coming kingdom would bring healed and restored relationships. When Jesus taught them to pray to "Abba" he showed an immediate access to the Father that was only possible by being truly reconciled with God.

This peace with God for the early church, his *basileia tou theou*,⁴ in one person's life directly translated into the relationships among the people. They understood that they were not only called themselves but were also empowered to forgive even those who would kill them (Sudgen 1983, 23–24; Acts 7:60). This peace with God, following Jesus, immediately leads to reconciliation in all areas of personal life. When Zacchaeus turned to become a disciple, he not only repaid, but sought to even pay further restitutions to those he hurt financially. The early church, touched by the Holy Spirit, started to form a community and began to share their possessions. Reconciliation with God leads to restored relationships among people, cultures, and ethnicities. Thus, church planters, developers, and disciple makers have long rejected the idea that one culture needs to be the leading one, and have also dropped the focus on one, homogenic unit (Tizon 2018, 121).

---

3 Translated by authors.

4 Kingdom of God, or better, the kingly reign of God (lordship), as this represents the impact of *catallasso* (exchange) in one's life.

Discipleship through Church History

Discipleship is not a new phenomenon. The word goes back to the Greek μαθητής which "is understood as a term for someone who stands in relation to another as pupil and is instructed by that person" (Nepper-Christensen 1990–1993, 372).[5]

For the modern mind, a disciple of Jesus could sometimes appear like a servant (e.g., Jesus sends them away to find accommodations and food; see Matt 26:17f; Luke 9:51–52). Thus, being a disciple of Jesus included the duty to "take up his cross" (Matt 16:24–25) and required some to enter persecution, suffering, and death (Matt 10:17–22, 24–25; 20:20–28; 24:9; John 15:20; 16:2). These very practical circumstances were followed by a "μετάνοια (a radical turning around) of lifestyle, world-view, and spiritual orientation, a total transformation of the self, so that Paul is led to claim, 'So if anyone is in Christ, there is a new creation: everything old has passed away; see, everything has become new!' (2 Cor 5:17)" (Kafwanka and Oxbrow 2016, 4).

Nepper-Christensen highlights that this "very radical practice in living conditions distinguished the disciples in several points from the customs of the time. But promises are associated with endurance of the sufferings that accompany discipleship" (Nepper-Christensen 1990–1993, 73; see also Matt 10:22; 19:27–30; 24:13). The disciples of Jesus were promised the help of the Holy Spirit for persecution (Mark 13:11) and to equip them to become witnesses to the ends of the world (Acts 1:8). Embodying the Spirit resulted in gifts intended to build up the church (Rom 12; 1 Cor 12; Eph 4) and to unify them as one global body of Christ. The statement "you will be my witnesses" (Acts 1:8) constitutes the missionary nature of the early church. Disciples of Jesus drew others to the faith, and visible signs followed this multiplication of believers (Acts 2:5).

Our current crisis of disciple making may be a result of the influence that Greek philosophy has had on Christianity since the days of the early church. Placing a high value on right thinking led to the belief that true virtuous behavior would follow virtuous thinking. This notion is based on the concept of the "platonic ideal" that right thinking will influence right action. Our modern pitfall through the Enlightenment became: if there is orthodoxy, orthopraxy will follow.

---

5 Nepper-Christensen further describes how common it was at the time of Jesus for disciples to choose their teacher to learn from him. Jesus turned this model upside down and chose not only men, but also had women who followed him (Matt 4:18–22; 9:9; John 6:70; 15:16). This may have resulted in his "authority that was previously unknown (Matt 7:28–29; Mark 1:22, 27; Luke 4:32; John 7:46). Thus, μαθητής in the context of his ministry took on a meaning that cannot be deduced from the word itself" (372).

Under this framework, a disciple is measured by knowledge, not fruits. Hebrew thinking though, as Jesus taught his disciples, relates everything to God and therefore living wisely is connected to a just relationship with God (Hirsch 2011, 164). Jesus taught how different ways of acting would lead to different thinking—he showed them practically, over and over, how he acted against prominent "right" theology of the time to point to the relationship with the Father. According to this understanding, the early church was meant to be a prolific continuation of walking in the footsteps of the Rabbi Jesus (Bosch 2011b, 75).

If we look at what a disciple was in the first century, Bill Hull believes we can find five key points: (1) Submission to a teacher on learning the ways of Jesus; (2) knowledge of the words of Jesus; (3) knowledge of the works of Jesus's ministry; (4) desire to mirror the life of Jesus; and (5) disciple others to follow Jesus (Hull 2006, 68). This Jesus-like character is well described by John Stott, who explains that disciples of Jesus ought to be like Christ: (1) in his kenotic incarnation, emptying themselves from their own ambitions; (2) in his service—willing to humble themselves down to washing their feet; (3) in his love, willing to give themselves to the fullest; (4) in his patient endurance, even in suffering; and (5) in his mission, incarnationally sent into the world (Stott 2010, 31–35).

Today, Al Tizon defines discipleship as: "following Jesus Christ in love, worship, and community while submitting to the lifelong, Spirit-empowered process of learning the ways of the kingdom of God in all areas of life and all arenas of life, even unto death" (Tizon 2018, 148–49). According to Tizon, this learning of the kingdom lifestyle involves: "(1) a devotional life of worship; (2) a wise life of Bible study and obedience; (3) an interdependent life in Spirit-filled community; (4) an ethical life of personal and social holiness; (5) a peculiar life of contrast and distinction; (6) a missional life of local and global witness; and (7) a reproductive life of mentoring or making disciples (both in the qualitative and quantitative sense)" (Tizon 2018, 151–52).

Against a disproportionate focus on a legalistic obedience, David Bosch states: "Particularly in our contemporary world of violence and counter-violence, of oppression from the right and the left, of the rich getting richer and the poor poorer, it is imperative for the church-in-mission to include the 'superior justice' of the Sermon on the Mount (c.f. Matt 5:20) in its missionary agenda. Its mission cannot concern itself exclusively with the personal, inward, spiritual, and 'vertical' aspects of peoples' lives" (Bosch 2011b, 71). Making disciples means "from the beginning and as matter of course, making new believers sensitive to the needs of others, opening their eyes and hearts to recognize injustice, suffering, oppression, and the plight of those who have fallen by the wayside" (Bosch 2011b, 83). Discipleship in such "isn't just one of the things the church does; it is what the church does. It's not just part of the advancement of God's kingdom; the existence of serious disciples is the most important evidence of God's world on earth" (Hull 2006, 24).

Hull summarizes the three dimensions of being a disciple of Jesus (Hull 2006, 30):

1. Love God with your heart, mind, soul, and strength.
2. Love yourself as you love your neighbors.
3. Even love your enemies.

In these three dimensions, Hull then sees six characteristics that define a disciple of Jesus: "1. Transformed mind, 2. Transformed character, 3. Transformed relationships, 4. Transformed habits, 5. Transformed service, [and] 6. Transformed influence" (Hull 2006, 130).

Dimensions of Reconciling Discipleship

God and Self, Others, and Creation

Discipleship cannot be reduced to an individual, "my Jesus and me"-relationship. Love for God leads directly to a deeper understanding of self and leads toward a restored relationship with the other (Arnold 1996, 17). When Jesus was asked about the greatest commandment, he answered twofold: "Love God, your Lord, with all your heart, with all your soul, and all your mind. ... Love your neighbor as yourself" (Matt 22:37–38). This answer shows that reconciling discipleship demands three dimensions: God, self, others (Sande 2004, 43–47).

Why are we speaking of reconciling self and not a reconciled self? Because reconciliation is always a journey. Romans 12:2 (NIV) speaks of this: "Do not conform to the pattern of this world, but be transformed by the renewing of your mind. Then you will be able to test and approve what God's will is—his good, pleasing and perfect will." Following this verse in conjunction with 2 Corinthians 5 and Matthew 22, a reconciling disciple understands the need for constant reorientation. Constantly following the call of God to be reconciled with himself is the only key to a healthy, healed, and true way of living.

That we still suffer in this world cannot fully be explained, but is somewhat clarified by the words of Neil Anderson: "All of us must experience a certain degree of brokenness before we can fully identify with Christ in his death, burial, and resurrection (in fact, it would be tragic to suffer through personal conflicts and never come to an understanding of the rich inheritance that we all have in Christ)" (Anderson 2008a, 38). Anderson emphasizes that after walking through crisis, finding a way to establish "peace with God is essential if we are to relate to others in a healthy way" (Anderson 2008a, 34). This perspective prevents us from flipping the relationships around into (1) me first—a victim or perpetrator perspective; or (b) a dependency model of losing myself to the other and submitting myself in an unhealthy way (staying a slave to sin of my own or others, or to powers and principalities). We ought to love God in a special way from which self-love and the love of the other derive. All other attempts may lead to unhealthy patterns, which may include even the danger of making reconciliation a project of fixing other people and putting ourselves above others.

A Christian faith without implications on one's lifestyle is only a personal God-relationship with no impact on the inter-personal relationships. Such faith doesn't address structural sin and is not how a reconciling disciple understands their calling. Since Christ is Lord over the whole cosmos disciples are called to follow him into those places where he has conquered evil already (Bosch 2011a, 272). Neil Anderson rightly points out that:

> No society can overcome racism, sexism, classism, or any kind of elitism unless reconciliation has been appropriated on a personal level through genuine repentance, forgiveness and faith in God. That is why secular governments cannot legislate reconciliation, and why the state or any other political authority cannot accomplish the ministry of reconciliation. Non-spiritual authorities can negotiate a truce, but the compliance will only be external and can only be maintained through the rule of law. Reconciliation is a ministry of grace. Apart from the gospel, there is no way to substantially change the nature of fallen humanity. (Anderson 2008a, 13–14)

Becoming a disciple incurs no cost, but being a disciple is costly: one lives not for their own matters anymore but for the causes of Jesus and what he lived and died for (Matt 16:24; Luke 14:25ff. Henrichsen 1989, 72–87). In the same way, the ministry of reconciliation is work; it requires effort and a conscious decision to love God first. Anderson points out, that believers "are to relate to others in the same way that God has related to us. We should never give people what they deserve—we are called to be merciful just as our heavenly Father is merciful to us. But that is not going far enough. We are to be gracious and give people what they need—the gift of love" (Anderson 2008a, 127). This love is not an emotion; it is a conscious decision to go beyond human feelings and to let the Holy Spirit transpire through us a peace that goes beyond our understanding (Phil 4:7; Col 3:15).

Reconciliation often includes dealing with hurt and trauma—it includes a desire for justice. Most people wonder where justice takes place. Hurt people often want to see the wrongdoer experience a sort of punishment: something that realigns them with social norms by imposing a consequence and making reparation if possible. The desire for justice is linked to a very human desire of a closure regarding the hurt/loss experienced. But what type of justice should reconciling disciples pursue? A punitive justice that highlights the wrongdoer and the legal consequences? Or a restorative justice that restores brokenness, redeems what was done wrong by transforming people and whole communities? Gary Chapman notes that "justice may bring some sense of satisfaction to the offended person; justice typically does not restore relationships" (Chapman 2013, 14).

One is advised poorly if asked to "just forgive" the oppressor. Romans 12:18 calls believers to be at peace with others, as far as it depends on us. "But it doesn't fully depend on us and therefore it isn't always possible. If the offending party doesn't want to be reconciled, then it is not possible. To complete the process of reconciliation, the offending party has to assume some degree of responsibility" (Anderson 2008a, 26). On the journey toward reconciliation, forgiveness takes an important place. According to Reimer, forgiveness includes several phases: (1) the readiness and decision to forgive; (2) understanding what truly happened; (3) being able to express what hurt and what emotions are felt; (4) naming the wrongdoing; (5) mourning the injustice before God; (6) seeking the wrongdoer to understand the why; and (7) speaking forgiveness (Reimer 2020a, 47). Thus, it is important to differentiate what forgiveness is for and that it isn't intended to throw the question of justice away. Anderson states: "We do not heal in order to forgive. We forgive in order to heal. The healing process cannot even start, and reconciliation cannot take place, until we face the crisis of forgiveness" (Anderson 2008a, 136).

Instead of staying in the past perspective, one could rather focus on Jesus and how his mission gives a framework for reconciliation, for leaving the past behind, and creating a new future. Jesus says: "You will know the truth, and the truth will set you free" (John 8:32). This includes the past and the future—in Paul's image, the old man (made according to the flesh) is stripped down and a new man (made in the Spirit) is put on (Col 3:5–15). "Thus, restoration is a two-step process: (a) we realize what is old in us and leave it, (b) we understand what God's new creation for us is and put it on" (Reimer 2018b, 104).

This new creation extends into the understanding of the world. Including an environmental, creation-oriented aspect of reconciliation in a missional approach goes beyond the typical vertical and horizontal toward a "circular dimension" or even "triple reconciliation" (Tizon 2018, 174). Environmental stewardship is not just something that the green parties from the 80s or the more recent movement "Fridays for Future" call for (see Paul in Rom 8:19–22).

We have been raping our planet to the extent that the human-induced climate change produces "more frequent and intense extreme events [that] … natural and human systems are pushed beyond their ability to adapt" (IPCC 2022, 9). Many other irreversible developments led the WWF to conclude as early as 2012: "by 2030 even two planets will not be enough" (Du Plessis 2012).[6] Our lifestyles are causing shifts in the seasonal timing and subsequently forcing half of the species assessed globally to shift poleward or to higher elevation to sustain a habitat they can live in—to say nothing of the impacts we humans are experiencing in our cities (IPCC 2022, 9).

A reconciling discipleship movement will therefore ask for more than blaming one or the other but seek to address evil structures and systemic sin that goes beyond the individual (Sudgen 1983, 44). God's creation waits for the return of his children that turn back to their God-given task to take care of creation (Gen 2:15; see also: Gnanakan 2017, 43). Finding our way back to that calling requires a reconciliation with the creator and is followed by repentance from the destructive ways (Stott 2010, 50).

The promotion of socially just structures is not possible without political commitment. The church is called to serve people, and if we abstain from political involvement, we support the existing order between those in power and those who are powerless (Sudgen 1983, 64).

Inter-state reconciliation requires discipled decision makers. Power systems continue to follow the Babylonian myth and narrative of a "redemptive violence" (Wink 2014, 48–53). We strive for peace through war, security through power, and argue for a nation and national security on power systems that suppress the weak and poor (Wink 2014, 59–63). Reconciling disciples understand that the political mission of the church cannot come through violence, but kenotic obedience to a nonviolent way (Cyster 1997, 5).

Furthermore, such an understanding of mission includes reconciliation efforts that lead to peacemaking: "A holistic mission goes beyond the integration of word and deed, it beckons us to take part in a different kind of integration—namely, the mending of cultural, tribal, and national brokenness, reconciling enemies among the nations as integral to the Great Commission. Peacemaking is not the whole of disciple making, but without it, the church is not making disciples of Christ. Peacemaking is disciple making is mission" (Tizon 2018, 173).

---
6 For more facts and figures that make environmental protection an urgent imperative, see: http://www.umweltschutz.de (20.01.2020).

Discipling Others to Be Reconciled Reconcilers

The greatest commandment and the Great Commission are like a compass and a journey. We need the compass first to stay on track during the journey. It is crucial to understand reconciliation with others as the key to discipleship, because discipleship without relationship is just focusing on conversions and numbers. Living as a reconciled disciple happens in the context of real life, a context that determines how we are living our testimony. People can only relate to Christ if they see his disciples living according to their words (Bosch 2011a, 297).

Human life is never conflict free. We as humans are not perfect and that makes us capable of stepping into mission with a "bold humility" (Tizon 2018, 95), knowing that we are broken, but still called. Followers of Jesus are those who are reconciled with their Creator, and their own story of pain, suffering, and restoration. Through this transformation process, they are then able to lead others to be reconciled with God and people around them—they can even be agents of transformation in their communities that need the good news of the kingdom of God.

Therefore, discipling others needs to include building up competencies of not only conflict resolution, but also transformation toward a deeper relationship.[7] If done well, Reimer claims that restored relationships of individuals and agents proclaiming forgiveness can lead to whole reconciled nations (Reimer 2020a, 35). This goal requires a church to teach their members to become true reconciling disciples by establishing a culture of forgiveness (Reimer 2020a, 68–71).

In today's understanding, discipleship is comparable to mentoring, letting another person look deeply in one's own life, but also equipping the one being discipled to show their true life, weaknesses, and faults without judgment. Discipleship enables growth and includes a holistic view of life—wherever others are in need, a discipling mentor is willing to serve (Mark 10:45; Luke 22:24–27; John 13:4–8, 12–17; Phil 2:5–8). Hull suggests three dimensions of disciple making: deliverance, development, and deployment (Hull 2006, 34). You find disciples, develop them, and then send them out. Discipleship is a lifelong journey of following Jesus, not a program. This view is a common error within churches (Hull 2006, 36). Although a disciple is simply one who follows Jesus, Hull argues that for a Christian to maintain accountability and receive support, a disciple must submit to at least one mentor. Discipleship is therefore grown in community and will never bear fruit without an authentic, fruitful lifestyle (Hull 2006, 36).

---

7 The circumstances of organized violence like war, abuse through a stranger, and unwillingness of the other to reconcile are not discussed in this chapter.

As discussed above, reconciliation deals with hurt and brokenness. To disciple others, one must clearly point away from themselves and invite the Holy Spirit as the leader for this journey. Anderson emphasizes: "We cannot think for them, confess for them, believe for them, repent for them or forgive others for them, but we can help them. Discipleship counseling empowers believers to determine their own destiny. If they refuse to accept responsibility for their own attitudes and actions, there is not much anyone can do for them" (Anderson 2008a, 79).

The goal for reconciling disciples is to lead the hurt and broken into the presence of God, inviting them to be reconciled with God, themselves, and one another, and to go beyond peace based on human efforts. Reconciling disciples invite people around them to join and serve God together. This enables victims and perpetrators to leave behind the stigma and identities of the past, and to become fellow servants to the Lord of mission, Jesus the reconciler, and joining him in proclaiming his kingdom in word and deed.

> Reconciling disciples invite people around them to join and serve God together.

The Mission of the Church: A Collective of Disciples

Since people are hurt in relationships, the way toward healing also happens in relationships. Mature Christians are not produced by programs. People heal and grow in their faith in genuine relationships, in true communities that live the gospel of hope and healing, showing the love of God in living letters (Sudgen 1983, 111). Reconciliation in the horizontal and vertical makes a church a reconciled reconciler only if done across divides.

A church can become a place to make disciples that have embraced the model of God's way of establishing peace among humanity and himself (Tizon 2018, 123–28). Church is supposed to be discipleship in a multi-ethnic community—a messianic community and new creation, representing a new humanity in Christ that has reconciled the Jews and the Gentiles "in himself" (Eph 2:14–16). Hull describes community as "the relationships we form to help us live out our beliefs. God never intended us to follow Christ and engage in the disciplines of this life alone. In community, others hold us accountable for our hearts' intentions, they test our words and sentiments, and they rescue us from a life of waste and self-indulgence" (Hull 2006, 189).

The early movement of disciples has been introduced through Matthew as ecclesia (Bosch 2011b, 60). Whether a church congregation is oriented toward the ideal of the ecclesia, or is rather stuck in its own tradition, becomes visible in its vision, mission, and activity. Reimer (Reimer 2009, 221) points out that being ecclesia means the self-understanding of a church as:

1. A sent one: in the continuation of Christ's call, it is called out to take over responsibility.
2. Called to a locality: church is a local agent to take over responsibility in a specific time and space.
3. Called and equipped holistically with a specific set of gifts (material, social, intellectual, spiritual).

Following Bosch one can understand that church as a community of believers is only then an apostolic contrast community, if she is as much *in-the-world* as she is *different-to-the-world* (Bosch 2011a, 284). A follower of Jesus is called to a certain "nonconformity" (Stott 2010, 17), to live in the tension to not become too conformed to the world, but also not to escape it. Bosch asserts: "A missionary community is one that understands itself as being both different from and committed to its environment; it exists within its context in a way which is both winsome and challenging" (Bosch 2011b, 84). So many Christians jump between these poles as "either/or," but don't know how to live in that tension—they live in the world Monday to Friday and don't know how to live their faith in the ordinary, and then fully immerse themselves on the weekend to overcome the stress of the week (Bosch 2011a, 286).

The call to the reconciling disciple is to live in convivence (Sundermeier 1996, 190–91), a life with the people, a community on their way together, shared life, mutual support and celebrating.[8] Bonhoeffer highlighted how "Church is only church when it is there for others ... It must participate in the worldly tasks of community life, not ruling, but helping, serving" (Bonhoeffer 1998, 560). Convivence expresses a community in which people are there for each other which then leads to freedom, since the missional presence of the people of God in the life of others is a living testimony (Faix 2008, 70–71). Hull points out that this is the crucial responsibility of the "mysterious organism called the church ... to show Christ to the world as one" (Hull 2006, 165).

A reconciling discipleship community—a church—must learn that though conflict belongs to the human life, it presents an opportunity to grow and to live according to the sacrifice that Jesus ultimately made on the cross (Lederrach 2014, 123; Sande 2004, 30). Our churches need to learn to truly unveil the roots of conflict, show honest forgiveness and repentance, and live together in a restored relationship.

---

8 See also: Sundermeier, *Mission—Geschenk der Freiheit,* 2005.

Johannes Reimer in his book *Missio Politica* (Reimer 2017, 75–77) describes in a nutshell how believers can not only live with the people but point them toward Jesus in a way that is built on trust and fascination, working through different layers of cultural design—their way of living—toward a life with Christ. This description includes a model of project-oriented Christian Community Development work that tailors a specific project based on a territorial approach of a local church, their giftedness combined with the needs of the community, toward a prayer and Spirit led missional church style (Reimer 2017, 96–99).[9] This so called "society-relevant church wants to see the kingdom of God realized in the life of community" (Reimer 2017, 98). Following this pattern, a reconciling disciple wants to understand the issues at hand. What in the community needs to be reconciled, what level of hurt and healing exists? What are the wounds or gaps in society based on a collective memory that prevent life from flourishing in this particular area? Therefore, a collective of reconciling disciples is called to: (1) Join the wounded; (2) name the wounds; (3) forgive those who harmed; and (4) build a common future (Böhm 2020, 12–13).

A reconciling church is a community of people that understand themselves as being sent (into the mission of God), placed in a specific place and time (locality), and therefore seeks to understand their God-given potential (gifts on all levels: material/physical, social-emotional, intellectual, spiritual). A reconciling church is a prayer-focused, Spirit-informed, prophetic voice in their community, showing people the God-designed alternative to life. With an understanding of who they are, they strive to serve the needs of people and bring them in touch with the "contrast community" of ecclesia, a fellowship of believers that makes a difference in their community by being salt and light. They are willing to address structural sin and advocate for the marginalized. They follow Jesus in calling individuals and groups to live together for a common future, by (1) joining the broken/outcast/hurt; (2) overcoming hurt and trauma through naming wrongdoings in love; (3) releasing repentance, forgiveness, and healing; and (4) establishing systems that enable a flourishing life.

---

9 The model includes several steps described by Bloemberg: (a) The congregation formulates its vision and mission; (b) names its action space; (c) identifies its potential; (d) conducts a context analysis; (e) describes its task and sets goals; (f) engages in the targeted project; and (g) evaluates the work and continues it effectively. The model of a Missional cycle of Christian Community Transformation includes the following phases: Localization, Potential analysis, Context analysis, Visioning, Planning, Acting, Evaluating, Celebrating. See: Reimer, Johannes in: Bloemberg 2019, 114.

Conclusion

Reconciliation is at the heart of the mission of God and therefore a continuation of the relationship between God as Father, Son, and Spirit to all mankind and creation. Reconciliation is the expression of God's love for his people by inviting them into relationship with him to embrace their God-given identity as image bearers and children of God. Reconciliation includes the redeeming act of restoring corrupted minds and destructive behaviors to heal broken relationships between people and their creator, themselves, other people, and all creation.

Therefore, reconciling disciples *embody* the hope of reconciliation. They have realigned their self-image and accepted God's love and peace in their lives. They are centered in their being, longing to live a life that glorifies God and expresses love to people.

They *embrace* the gifts that God gave them to serve people kenoticly (they are willing to humble/empty themselves). They went on the journey to explore the needs of the people around them and put in the work to discover what the good news would look like for the people.

They want to *experience* the peace of Christ with their community. They actively pursue *shalom* on all levels of life and seek partners to bring signs of God's kingdom into reality. They serve the community with other people and enable others to become part of God's mission. They "do" church with, not for people (Bosch 2011b, 384).

Subsequently, a reconciling church follows the embody, embrace, and experience model and thus we conclude: reconciling discipleship is the journey of individuals and groups to live together for a common future by: (1) joining the broken/outcast/hurt; (2) overcoming hurt and trauma through naming wrongdoings in love; (3) releasing repentance, forgiveness, and healing; and (4) establishing systems that enable a flourishing life. Reconciliation occurs when people live in friendship with God that leads to love of self, others, and creation to bring forth a new humanity.

Referenced Cited

Anderson, Neil. 2008a. *Restoring Broken Relationships: The Path to Peace and Forgiveness*. Minneapolis, MN: Bethany House.

Anderson, Neil. 2008b. *The Path to Reconciliation: Connecting People to God and to Each Other*. Ventura, CA: Regal.

Arnold, J. Heinrich. 1996. *Leben in der Nachfolge*. [Living in Discipleship]. Moers, Germany: Brendow.

Bloemberg, Jacob. 2019. *Love [Your City]. 5 Steps to Citywide Movements.* Bloomington, IN: WestBow Press.

Böhm, Manuel. 2020. *Healing of Memories—Reconciling the Church for the Reconciliation of Community.* Forthcoming article, read at the EMS Canada conference. Citation according to personal document of the author.

Bonhoeffer, Dietrich. 1937. *The Cost of Discipleship.* New York: MacMillan.

Bonhoeffer, Dietrich. 1998. *Widerstand und Ergebung: Briefe und Aufzeichnungen aus der Haft.* [Resistance and Surrender: Letters and Notes from Imprisonment]. Volume 8. 2nd edition. Edited by Christian Gremmels, et al. Gütersloh, Germany: Gütersloher Verlagshaus.

Bosch, David. 2011a. *Ganzheitliche Mission: Theologische Perspektiven.* [Witness to the World]. Translated by Reiner Behrens. Marburg an der Lahn, Germany: Francke.

Bosch, David. 2011b. *Transforming Mission: Paradigm Shifts in Theology of Mission.* Twentieth Anniversary Edition, 7th ed. Maryknoll, NY: Orbis Books.

Bright, Bill. 2007. *Four Spiritual Laws: "The Basics" Series.* Peachtree City, GA: Campus Crusade for Christ. Accessed April 14, 2022. https://campusministry.org/docs/tools/FourSpiritualLaws.pdf.

Castro, E. 1978. "Liberation, Development, and Evangelism: Must We Choose in Mission?" In *Occasional Bulletin of Missionary Research* 2, no. 3: 87–90. Overseas Ministries Study Center.

Chapman, Gary, and Jennifer Thomas. 2013. *When Sorry Isn't Enough: Making Things Right with Those You Love.* Chicago: Northfield.

Cyster, Graham. 1997. "Mennonite Discipleship for the Twenty-First Century." In *Discipleship in Context: Papers Read at the Menno Simmons 500 International Symposium, Elspeet, Netherlands, 1996, Occasional Paper #18*, edited by Alle Hoekema et al., 3–9. Elkhart, IL: Institute of Mennonite Studies.

DeGruchy, John. 2002. *Reconciliation: Restoring Justice.* Minneapolis, MN: Fortress Press.

Du Plessis, Morné. "More Than Two Planets Needed by 2030." *World Wildlife Fund,* May 15, 2021. https://www.wwf.org.za/?5960/lpr2012.

Faix, Tobias. 2008. *Würde Jesus bei Ikea Einkaufen? Herausforderungen zur Ganzheitlichen Nachfolge.* [Would Jesus Shop at Ikea?: Challenges to Holistic Discipleship]. 2nd ed. Schwarzenfeld, Germany: Neufeld Verlag.

Gnanakan, Ken. 2017. *Responsible Stewardship of God's Creation.* The WEA Global Issues Series 11, edited by Thomas K. Johnson. Bonn, Germany: Verlag für Kultur und Wissenschaft.

Henrichsen, Walter. 1989. *Machet zu Jüngern. Wie Man Anderen Hilft, In Der Jüngerschaft Zu Wachsen.* [Disciples Are Made—Not Born]. 1974. Translated by Lotte Bormuth. Bielefeld, Germany: Christliche Literatur Verbreitung.

Hirsch, Alan. 2011. *Vergessene Wege. Die Wiederentdeckung Der Missionalen Kraft Der Kirche*. [The Forgotten Ways: Reactivating the Missional Church]. 2006. Translated by Björn Wagner. Schwarzenfeld, Germany: Neufeld Verlag.

Hull, Bill. 2006. *The Complete Book of Discipleship: On Being and Making Followers of Christ*. Colorado Springs, CO: NAVPRESS.

IPCC, 2022: Summary for Policymakers [H. O. Pörtner, D. C. Roberts, E. S. Poloczanska, K. Mintenbeck, M. Tignor, A. Alegría, M. Craig, S. Langsdorf, S. Löschke, V. Möller, A. Okem (eds.)]. In: Climate Change 2022: Impacts, Adaptation and Vulnerability. Contribution of Working Group II to the Sixth Assessment Report of the Intergovernmental Panel on Climate Change [H. O. Pörtner, D. C. Roberts, M. Tignor, E. S. Poloczanska, K. Mintenbeck, A. Alegría, M. Craig, S. Langsdorf, S. Löschke, V. Möller, A. Okem, B. Rama (eds.)]. Cambridge University Press, Cambridge, UK and New York, NY, USA, 3–33, doi:10.1017/9781009325844.001.

Kafwanka, John, and Mark Oxbrow, eds. 2016. *Intentional Discipleship and Disciple-Making: An Anglican Guide for Christian Life and Formation*. London: The Anglican Consultative Council. https://www.anglicancommunion.org/media/220191/intentional-discipleship-and-disciple-making.pdf.

Lederrach, John Paul. 2014. *Reconcile: Conflict Transformation for Ordinary Christians*. Harrisonburg, VA: Herald.

Merkel, H. 1990–1993. "καταλλάσσω." In *Exegetical Dictionary of the New Testament*. Vol. 2. Edited by Horst Balz and Gerhard Schneider, 261–3. Grand Rapids, MI: Eerdmans.

Nagy, Dorottya. 2022. "Behind *Missio Dei*: Reflections on the International Missionary Council's 1952, Willingen, Germany. Conference, One Possible Way of Commemorating after Seventy Years." *V Verbum SVD* 63, no. 2–3 (2022): 161–88.

Nepper-Christensen, P. 1990–1993. "μαθητής." In *Exegetical Dictionary of the New Testament*. Vol. 2. Edited by Horst Balz and Gerhard Schneider, 372–74. Grand Rapids, MI: Eerdmans.

Nortey, Justin. "More Houses of Worship Are Returning to Normal Operations, but in-Person Attendance Is Unchanged since Fall." *Pew Research Center*, March 22, 2022. https://www.pewresearch.org/fact-tank/2022/03/22/more-houses-of-worship-are-returning-to-normal-operations-but-in-person-attendance-is-unchanged-since-fall/.

Reimer, Johannes. 2009. *Die Welt umarmen: Theologie des gesellschaftsrelevanten Gemeindebaus*. [Embracing the World: Theology of Socially Relevant Church Development]. Marburg an der Lahn, Germany: Francke.

Reimer, Johannes. 2017. *Missio Politica: The Mission of Church and Politics*. Carlisle, UK: Langham.

Reimer, Johannes. 2018a. *Gottes Herz Für Deine Stadt. Ideen und Strategien für Gemeinde in der Stadt*. [God's Heart For Your City: Ideas and strategies for church in the city]. Moers, Germany: Brendow and Sohn Verlag.

Reimer, Johannes. 2018b. "Reconciliation as Healing of Memory—A Missionary Task of the Church." In *Reconciliation: Christian Perspectives—Interdisciplinary Approaches.* Edited by Tobias Faix, et al., 100–14. Zürich: LIT.

Reimer, Johannes. 2020a. Vergebung Leben. *Wege Zu Einer Kultur der Versöhnung in der Gemeinde.* [Living Forgiveness. Ways Towards a Culture of Reconciliation in the Church]. Mittenaar-Bicken, Germany: Werdewelt Verlags- und Medienhaus GmbH.

Reimer, Johannes. 2020b *Wo Versöhnung zu Hause ist. Gemeinde als Versöhnungszentrum.* [Where Reconciliation Is at Home: The Church as a Centre of Reconciliation]. Mittenaar-Bicken, Gemany: Werdewelt Verlags- und Medienhaus GmbH.

Salter McNeil, Brenda. 2015. *Roadmap to Reconciliation: Moving Communities into Unity, Wholeness and Justice.* Downers Grove, IL: InterVarsity Press.

Sande, Ken. 2004. *Peace Maker: A Biblical Guide to Resolving Personal Conflict.* 3rd ed. Grand Rapids, MI: Baker Books.

Schreiter, Robert. 2013. "The Emergence of Reconciliation as a Paradigm of Mission: Dimensions, Levels, and Characteristics." In *Mission as Ministry of Reconciliation.* Book 16 of the *Regnum Edinburgh Centenary Series.* Edited by Robert Schreiter and Knud Jørgensen, 9–29. Oxford: Regnum Books International.

Stott, John. 2010. *The Radical Disciple: Some Neglected Aspects of Our Calling.* Downers Grove, IL: InterVarsity Press.

Sudgen, Christopher. 1983. *Radikale Nachfolge: Impulse zu Einem Zeichenhaften Leben.* [Radical Disciple]. 1981. Translated by Ulrike Wettach. Witten, Germany: Bundes Verlag.

Sundermeier, Theo. 1996. *Den Fremden verstehen: Eine praktische Hermeneutik.* [Understanding the Stranger: A Practical Hermeneutics]. Göttingen, Germany: Vandenhoeck and Ruprecht.

Tizon, Al. 2018. *Whole and Reconciled: Gospel, Church, and Mission in a Fractured World.* Grand Rapids, MI: Baker Academic.

Wink, Walter. 2014. *Verwandlung der Mächte: Eine Theologie der Gewaltfreiheit.* [The Powers That Be: Theology For a New Millenium]. 1999. Translated by Anka Schneider and Anja Mehrmann. Edited by Thomas Nauerth and Georg Steins. Regensburg, Germany: Verlag Friedrich Pustet.

Yoder, John Howard. 2000. *Nachfolge Christi als Gestalt Politischer Verantwortung.* [Discipleship As Political Responsibility]. 2nd ed. Weisenheim am Berg, Germany: Agape Verlag.

Chapter 7

Worldview Questions in Mission Training and Praxis

The Unintended Consequences of Comfortable Oppositional Thinking

Annette R. Harrison

One of my husband's seminary professors used to wonder about the unintended damage done by the adversarial nature of the classroom when it pits boys and girls against each other as they grow up. He then remarked that we should not be surprised at the difficulty men and women have in successful cooperation and collaboration in marriage. This reference to unexamined consequences prompted me to consider our use of worldview questions in mission training. I noticed that there are very few, if any, references to other people in the most frequently used worldview training questions. These observations suggest that our training materials either exclude the "other" by focusing so much on us, or they position us in an oppositional stance to the "other." Exclusion and erasure of others sabotages the work of the global Christian community as ambassadors for Christ (2 Cor 5:18–20).[1]

The Framework of Christian Worldview Questions

Christian worldview questions are a valuable tool for exploring epistemological commitments about how the world works—for us as well as for the people we want to engage with the gospel (cf. Allen 2020; Wilkens and Sanford 2009). This training is crucial for cross-cultural workers, as well as for developing strategies for worldview transformation (Hiebert 2008; Kraft 1997, 2008). On the other hand, we must carefully consider the unintended consequences of the current uses of this tool.

There does not seem to be a single coherent set of worldview questions used by today's evangelicals, though many of the worldview questions are concerned with the presentation of God as truth, the creation, fall, and

---

[1] All Scripture references taken from the NIV unless otherwise noted.

redemption (cf. Mulvihill 2019; Smith 2015). These are often called "pillars" of a biblical or Christian worldview used in Christian education as well as in apologetic training. Other presentations include questions closer to the philosophical perspective, examining the nature of reality and our perceptions of it: Who are we? Where are we? These are often used to present a comparison/contrast of worldviews, setting a Christian worldview up against humanism, existentialism, nationalism, consumerism, and other worldviews (cf. Sproul 1985/1996; Wilkens and Sanford 2009).

Even in anthropological models of worldview, self-identity is predicated through contrast. Kearney explains that "other" may begin with impersonal surroundings, such as the physical environment, but eventually the "other" becomes other people who are not like me (or us) (Kearney 1984, 71). Moreover, we also develop stances toward these "others." Kearney lists possibilities such as harmonious equilibrium, subordination, or dominance (Kearney 1984, 73). As we will see below, God's people have adopted some of these possible stances toward the "others" whom they were trying to reach with the gospel.

Beyond the educational, apologetic, or anthropological uses of a worldview framework, there are missiological discussions that probe who the "other" is to me and who I am to the "other." Some examples include discussions of finance (cf. Bonk 2007; Lederleitner 2010; Ngubu 2018), leadership (cf. Handley 2021; Lingenfelter 2008), and theological representation (cf. Adeney et al. 2014; Rah 2009). Scholars in other areas such as intercultural communication (cf. Gudykunst 2004) and religion (cf. Volf 1996) also recognize the challenges in reaching beyond ourselves to the "other." While these scholars intentionally include the "other" in their discussions, strategies to train missionaries and strategies to reconcile "others" to Christ seem to stall in oppositional stance and perspective.

The contribution of this discussion is to re-examine worldview questions often used in mission training and praxis in order to identify unintended consequences. We begin with a review of how previous mission models have conceptualized the "other" before moving on to examine how the "other" is erased, excluded, or opposed in the worldview questions of identity (Who am I?), place or space (Where am I?), power (Who is in charge?), and purpose (Why am I?).[2] An important finding concerns the ways in which worldview questions reify categories of comfort in opposition to the uncomfortably foreign "other." The resulting comfort and opposition unintentionally sabotage efforts of faithful witness and the reconciling power of the gospel.

---

2 These questions were chosen based on Moreau, Campbell, and Greener 2014, 57.

Who Is the "Other"?

Mission thinking has struggled with models of "the other," from the exoticism and romanticism of "the native," to the well-meaning, but misguided "Three C's" model of the nineteenth century. As Kearney would predict, both models rely on a stance toward the "other." The first subordinates the exotic "other" who is kept at a safe distance to be marveled at as in a menagerie. Likewise, the Three C's model relies on a dominant stance toward the "other" who needs our educational system and conversion to our religion and our way of thinking and living.

More recently, missiologists have unintentionally created categories of the "other" in a quest for successful church growth strategies. For example, Donald McGavran's Homogeneous Unit Principle (HUP) in combination with Ralph Winter's Unreached People Group method of assessing the remaining task have both elevated the homogeneous, quantifiable nature of the "other."[3]

Current training models have turned attention from quantifying the remaining task to increasing our motivation to learn, know, and reach out to the "other." These training models include the Cultural Intelligence model (Livermore 2009), Cultural Dimensions models (cf. Hofstede, Hofstede, and Minkov 2010; Meyers 2014), and Cultural Types models (cf. Lanier 2000; Lingenfelter and Myers 2016). Other contributions encourage suspending immediate judgment and evaluation long enough to remain open, accepting, and trusting (cf. Elmer 2006). All of these models have value, but they continue to train through the use of categories of opposition as predicted in Kearney's original explanation of the development of worldview.

The persistent use of the oppositional us and "other" has had unintentional outcomes in missionary stances, theological assumptions, missionary-sending patterns, and relationships within the global Christian community. Statistics of mission going and giving convincingly demonstrate that very few Christians move beyond the comfort of their own Christian community. According to the Traveling Team "Mission Stats" web page, an estimated 95 percent of people in full-time Christian ministry in countries around the world work in a church context ("Christians of the World" section of "Mission Stats" page, accessed at https://www.thetravelingteam.org/stats).[4] Another set of statistics on that same web page shows that an estimated 77.3 percent of missionaries work among reached peoples, while an estimated 22.1 percent of missionaries work among

---

3 It is worth pointing out that the HUP has been rejected by leaders from the Majority church if only because it does not reflect the lived realities in multi-ethnic, multilingual, and pluralistic contexts around the world (cf. Harrison 2015; Tira and Uytanlet 2020).

4 "In ministries, there are 4.19 million full-time Christian workers and 95% are working within the Christian world" [original source, *Frontier Harvest Ministries*, 2007].

unevangelized and unreached peoples.[5] These two sets of statistics indicate that most Christian workers serve within a Christian context, rather than in a non-Christian context.

Also, if our giving reveals our motivations, we are not highly motivated to support work that benefits the religious "other" (cf. Luke 12:34). The Traveling Team estimates that for every $100,000 (USD) earned by Christians, we give $1.70 (USD) to work among those most different from ourselves—unreached people groups ("Missionary Stats," the "Money and Missions" section, https://www.thetravelingteam.org/stats).

> Few Christians move beyond the comfort of their own Christian community.

The current choices of many Christians seem to reflect the same reluctance to engage the "other" as the expert in religious law who asked, "And who is my neighbor?" (Luke 10:29). Jesus's answer demonstrates that this is not quite the right question, not only because it misses the point that God's mercy, compassion, and grace are available to all, but also because the religious expert, like us, may have had a neatly sanitized, objectively distant concept of "neighbor."

This is not a theological treatise on "neighbor," though it is worth a brief consideration of the dramatic shift from the traditional rabbinic understanding of the Leviticus 19 command to "love [your neighbor] as yourself" to the expanded understanding taught by Jesus Christ. There are implications for "neighbor" within the global church and for those who still have not heard of or confessed Christ as Lord.

Who Is My Neighbor?

In the context of the giving of the law in the Old Testament, "neighbor" was a new social category that referred to another member of the emerging Hebrew community. It was necessary to establish God-worshippers from the former Egyptian slave class as members of one, united community, both for their own sociopolitical survival as a new nation and as a key element of God's missional purposes. Doing good to each other and living in merciful solidarity was part of the "city on a hill" centripetal witness of the nation of Israel to the world.

---

5 "If everyone is obeying God's 'calling' to be a missionary wherever they are then God is apparently calling 99.9995% of people to work among the half of the world population that already has the gospel and calling virtually no one (.0005%) to relocate among the other half of the world population that are not Christian. You have a better chance of being in a plane crash than being one of the few missionaries to the unreached." The Traveling Team "Mission Stats" page, the conclusion of the section entitled "Missionaries and Workers," accessed June 13, 2023.

As is clear in missional readings of the Old Testament, God did not intend his blessings and promises to be exclusive to the people of Israel. Thus, Jesus's reply to the expert in religious law unwraps God's original intent. His goodness and grace are not limited to the worthy ones defined by specific social, cultural, religious, or linguistic characteristics. The man who is robbed in Jesus's parable had no clothes, and no belongings that would identify him as part of a specific community. He is also unconscious, so he cannot speak and identify himself through choice of language or an accent. He is any man, and he is Everyman. He is the "other." The Samaritan is called "good" because he accepts the wounded man as a neighbor in need, fully human, and thus of equal value and worth as himself.

Implications

What are the implications for mission training and praxis? First, our worldview may need an update so that our definition of "other" is not so categorically different and distant from ourselves. Our neighbor the "other" is a human being in need of reconciliation to God, just like us (Eph 2:11–22). Next, we also need to remember the necessary and beautiful attraction of unity and harmony in the highly diverse, global Christian community (cf. John 17:6–8, 18, 20–22). Within the "us" are people of many nations, cultures, and languages. This means that someone we may have once regarded as "other" is actually part of "us." Both the centripetal attraction of unity and the centrifugal call to reconcile all people to God involves those whom we once regarded as "other," and whom we now regard as "us." If this is so, how would we answer the first worldview question, "Who am I?"

Who Am I? Myself and the "Other"

Generally, the first question in worldview formation concerns self-identity. Beginning with an examination of ourselves has value. A foundational assumption in cross-cultural training is that when we know ourselves, we can better prepare to engage with people from other cultures (cf. Elmer 2002; Lane 2002; Livermore 2009). But as Hiebert pointed out, we may have so much to say about ourselves that we inadvertently erase the "other" and miss the essential biblical focus of our role in reconciling "others" to Christ (Hiebert 2008, 287–90).[6]

---

[6] The emergence of the self and of self-identity is also a frequent starting point for secular sociologists and anthropologists in the study of other cultures (cf. Cooley 1902; Kearney 1984; Mead 1934). It is pertinent to this discussion that all of these explorations have taken place in the context of individualistic cultures which tend to elevate the individual at the expense of "others."

Turning so much focus on ourselves and erasing the "other" may also cause weakness within the Christian community because it elevates an individualistic perspective over value for community (Rah 2009, 30–31, 33, 35–38, 40). The consequences for the centripetal and centrifugal forces of witness are significant. A poorly functioning Christian community does not attract the nations to it (Matt 5:13–16). Too much focus on ourselves weakens or erases the desire to put God's glory and the good of our neighbor above our own reputation and comfort.

In this context, "go and make disciples" (Matt 28:19) becomes the self-validating "we are all missionaries" (cf. Crider 2015; Hayashi 2017). It is true that God has sent all of us, however in my experience, the effect of the "we are all missionaries" mantra seems to simply excuse the lack of motivation to reach beyond our own nation's socioeconomic barriers to cross-cultural, cross-linguistic witness. Again, this is evidenced in the low rate of sending missionaries to people who have little or no access to the gospel (The Traveling Team 2023).

A rejection of individualism accompanied by an embrace of collectivism does not solve the problem, as tempting as it sounds to many of my Gen Z students. Scripture provides answers to the questions and concerns of individualists and collectivists alike. Embracing one self-identity or another on that continuum will not improve our motivation or ability to recognize our identities or to bring "others" to Christ that they might be reconciled to him.

Instead, Scripture teaches us that when we ask, "Who am I," we discover that we are "strangers and aliens" on earth. Christ's worldview, Christ's culture, and Christ's ways are to be our ways as much as possible (Eph 2:19–22; 1 Pet 2:9–12; Rom 12:1–2). This is the Pilgrim Principle as described by Andrew Walls (1996, 8–9). The more we can take on the renewed identity of a foreigner on earth, the less encumbered we are by the constraints of the worldview and culture that has formed us from birth (cf. Walls 1996, 8–9, 25, 54; See also Volf 1996, 20–21, 36–39).

Recent discussions of hybridity make an important contribution here. Jones comments that the theological implications of hybridity work on our spiritual and theological convictions regarding a Christian's ultimate allegiance and therefore even on our social identities (Jones 2022, 13). In other words, as our allegiance to Christ becomes the very foundation of our self-identity, exclusionary boundaries are weakened. Then we are ready for the appointment as an ambassador for the kingdom of God (2 Cor 5:17–21). An embrace of these renewed self-identities prepares us to approach the "other."

The "other" may be most present in our worldview in issues of power and representation. The metaphor of "the table" is helpful here to evoke the power of ownership in place or in arena. "A seat at the table" references inclusion in important conversations and decisions. Further, Christians from diverse backgrounds should consider implications of "the table" for unity and communion. Whose table are we sitting at?

Where Am I? Whose Table?

Edward R. Murrow is credited with commenting on the challenge of the "last three feet" to meet in personal exchange and connection.[7] It is comparatively easy to cross thousands of miles of ocean and landmass, and much more difficult to move the relatively insignificant last few feet to meet the "other" where they are. This is certainly a temptation for many large missionary communities, especially when the mission organization may establish a "base" of some sort that includes housing.[8] While practical and helpful for many reasons, the unintentional outcome is to comfortably cloister missionaries with those like "us," rather than doing life with the "others."

Tables seclude us from the "other" in a way similar to the mission base. Rah recounts a telling anecdote about Korean and Anglo groups in a US seminary cafeteria. Well-intentioned Anglo students invited Korean students to join the Anglos at "their" table. When the Korean students responded with an invitation to the Anglo students to sit at "Korean tables," the Anglos responded that they would not feel comfortable (Rah 2009, 120–21). This reality is tragic and revealing, especially because it is not an unusual situation. The university where I teach struggles with a similar cafeteria segregation. Choosing to sit with people "like us" or those who are already in our friend group is a normal and comfortable human tendency. Homophily is a powerful social dynamic.

The Power of Homophily

The insidious nature of homophily is exposed when it highlights racial or ethnic inequities or socioeconomic differences. In his 2015 TED talk, social scientist and cultural critic Dr. Rich Benjamin claims that the United States is as residentially segregated today as it was in the 1970s. This is not necessarily because of laws or explicit policy, but as he discovered in his research, people prefer to live with people "like us." The unintentional outcome is racially segregated communities (Benjamin 2009, Loc. 123, 189, 2653, 4272; 2015, minute 10:51).

I have seen this dynamic where I live. When my husband and I first relocated to Salem, Oregon, we were told that it was a "very white" city. While

---

[7] Edward R. Murrow, Director, United States Information Agency 1961–1964 on ABC TV, "Issues and Answers," August 4, 1963.

[8] Examples from my former organization include the SIL bases of Ukarumpa in Papua New Guinea and Yaoundé in Cameroon.

there is certainly a majority Anglo population, in our first year in Salem I counted connections with people from at least fourteen different ethnicities. But at that time, we lived in an apartment complex with relatively low-income renters. A few years ago, when we were able to purchase a home in a modest neighborhood, we discovered that only a few of our neighbors are non-white. Most likely, this is homophily based on socioeconomics rather than race or ethnicity. But the outcome is the same: we prefer to sit in comfort at our own table, with people like us, not with the "other" at "their table."[9]

Enlarging the Table

In seeking a solution to the power of homophily, we face the temptation to address the imbalance of privilege and power. But homophily is about comfort, not about power. Have we, like the teacher of the law, become too comfortable in our own skin and forgotten that the "other" is our neighbor?

This is where, once again, the centripetal and centrifugal forces of Christian community and of mission intersect in mission as reconciliation. When the Christian community is openly accepting of and delighting in its multicultural and hybrid identities, the "others" may be drawn to the light of the unity of Christ in diversity. At the same time, the multicultural nature of the Christian community may train Christians to be open and accepting of the "other" even before they are sent out into the world.

But even in a multicultural church, the challenge of "the table" remains. Elsewhere I have described the ingenious solution to include diverse peoples in one community practiced by churches in the Republic of Congo (Brazzaville) (Harrison 2015, 3, 5). The churches stressed the true and universal nature of Christianity through the choice of an international language and a language of wider communication for Scripture reading and teaching. At the same time, the churches affirmed the diversity of the local cultural backgrounds of congregants through the weekly sharing of songs and testimonies in local languages tied to ethnic identity. They enlarged the table of the Christian community through the use of both local and international languages in church services and other activities.

Study abroad programs and short-term mission trips provide additional examples of ways to enlarge the table. Though the history of exchanges and close contact between peoples has not always brought brotherly unity, the history of study abroad programs demonstrates the underlying belief that "walking a mile" in someone else's shoes can be a transformative experience

---

9 All of these examples are limited to the United States, yet they illustrate the powerful human tendency toward "tribalism" (cf. Kougoum 2009; Pohor 2010, 699–701).

that results in changed attitudes toward the "other" (Lee 2012). Some short-term mission trips operate in this vein as "vision trips" that purport to sow a vision for ministering cross-culturally. If done well, these opportunities may also help culturally isolated Christians draw near to the "other."

In the context of global migration there are more and more opportunities to get to know the "other" on our doorstep and to offer hospitality (cf. Fancher 2022; Jenkins 2002; Payne 2013). Various statistics concerning how many international students are ever invited into an American home demonstrate both the tremendous opportunities on our doorstep, and the twin powers of comfort and homophily that inhibit hospitality to strangers. Most of the more than one million international students each year in the United States never see the inside of an American home (InterVarsity 2017). On the other hand, ShortTermMissions.com says that "upward of two million" people participate each year in short-term mission trips (Short Term Missions 2022). Once again, there is a disturbing trend that we are willing to make the journey of thousands of miles, but not necessarily to go the last three feet.

Readjusting Our Identities

The key question remains how to leave our own table and go sit with the "other." Volf describes this work as "readjust[ing] our identities to make space" for the "other" (Volf 1996, 29). Tactics for approaching this readjustment are many. They include reducing the depersonalization of the "other" (Escobar 2003, 156); lowering the anxieties associated with approaching strangers (Gudykunst 2002, 185–86); asking forgiveness (Crossman 2009, 287); working toward "mutuality" (Slimbach 2005, 220); and checking our own motivations (Van Dyne, Ang and Livermore 2010, 134–35, 138). But the most insightful discussion may be from Duane Elmer, who turns the focus on our own characters, encouraging the development of crucial personal characteristics like openness, acceptance, willingness to trust, to learn, etc. (Elmer 2006, 37–88). Though these are characteristics to develop in our own lives, they are the qualities that make us most effective when meeting and building relationships with the "other." There are many tools available for training cross-cultural workers. What remains is a personal commitment to make space in our lives in order to "do life" with the "other"—something Jesus modeled for us when eating with tax collectors and sinners.

As we join the "other" at an enlarged table, disagreements or tensions are bound to arise. These disagreements often center on power and control. What are the implications for mission training and for strategic models of mission as reconciliation?

Who Is in Charge? Power and Conflict

Ambassadors live in arenas of conflict and tension. When countries are at peace, the tension for the ambassador is between competing values and allegiances, between the immediate local context and the far-away source of the ambassador's authority. "Who is in charge" is at once the easiest worldview question, but also the one that presents tremendous challenge in our relationships with others.

Christians, people from other Abrahamic religions, and even some of our Hindu and Buddhist neighbors may answer that "God" is in charge; however, there is inevitable and inherent conflict in worldviews grounded in different religions (cf. Slimbach 2005, 215; Wilkens and Sanford 2009). Moreover, even global Christianity lacks universal agreement on how God's authority may be communicated and discerned. Some communities look primarily to the traditional head of the church, others to experiences of the community of believers; some adhere to *sola scriptura*, while other communities seek personal revelation from the Holy Spirit. The key issue for this discussion does not concern whether God is in charge or not, or how we can know revealed truth, but rather what we do as faithful ambassadors in the face of inevitable conflict? An approach to mission as reconciliation hinges on this convergence of disagreement with the "other," as well as the "other's" estrangement from God.

There is no "culture neutral" approach to a clash of positions (cf. Augsberger 1992; Hammer 2005; Ting-Toomey and Oetzel 2002). This insight is as vital for missionary training as it is for missiological strategies of reconciliation. An initial reflex in Western cultures when faced with a conflict is to persuade the "other" that there is one right position (usually ours). This makes knowledge and argumentation a weapon of conquest rather than an opportunity for wisdom (cf. Jas 3:13–18). The limited choice of right or wrong in an argument is based on the assumption that it is necessary to defeat the weak idea before proposing the "right" solution. It is also based on a conceptualization of knowledge as impersonal statements of facts.

The Two-Sided Approach

The propositional argumentation approach is exemplified by various ministries which train Christians to use worldview as an apologetic device.[10] In a similar way, Wilkens and Sanford (2009) demonstrate how to tease apart worldviews commonly encountered in Western societies, such as individualism, consumerism, moral relativism, and postmodern tribalism. The purpose of their informative presentation is ultimately an apologetic one based on the

---

10 See R. C. Sproul's introductory talk on the concept of worldview, at minute 16:47 (Sproul 1985/1996) and "Why we started Worldview Academy" (https://www.worldview.org/about).

assumption of a conflict with only two sides, a clash of propositional statements objectively removed from the subjective experiences of life and applied belief.

Nabeel Qureshi's journey to faith is a striking example of the blind spot of an apologetic approach to reconciliation with Christ. While *Seeking Allah, Finding Jesus* is an excellent instruction in many points of debate between Muslims and Christians, even Qureshi himself seems to overlook the many comments he makes concerning the faithful, long-term, truthful, and reconciling relationship of the friend who first introduced him to Christ (Qureshi 2016).[11] There would have been no argument and no opportunity to wrestle with opposing belief without the presence of the faithful friend. Reconciliation to God does not turn on winning the argument, but on our willingness to engage and to be present to the "other."

Furthermore, persuasive argumentation may work in a culture that prizes the logic and rationality of an argument. But this approach is fatal to the credentials of the ambassador in cultures that privilege harmony and cooperation above argumentation, in Japan, for example, or Indonesia. Additionally, in the current American ideological climate that claims the authority of personal truth, it is once again evident that an adversarial approach to the clash of positions turns claims of authority into a weapon. Not only would the relationship between the self and "other" be strained or damaged, but the possibility of reconciliation to God would likely be strained or damaged as well.

Making the Two Sides One

One creative alternative to a two-sided approach is to make the two sides into one. "If you want the window open, and I want it shut, and if we keep phrasing our desires in terms of competition, then one of us must win, the 'other' lose" writes Augsberger. "But if we discover that what you really want is fresh air, and what I am concerned about is avoiding a draft, we may find a new and creative way to meet both desires" (Augsberger 1992, 57–58).

> An important way to win over your "enemy" is to make him your friend.

Reconciliation aims for all parties to begin working toward a common objective. An important way to win over your "enemy" is to make him your friend. My husband and I learned this tactic from Halidou Lompo in Niger,[12]

---

11 Nabeel's friend David is used in part as a storytelling device to bring up various topics of faith. See Part 3, Chapters 20–23, Part 4, Chapters 24–26, Part 7, Chapter 39, Part 8, Chapter 43, Part 9, Chapter 44, Part 10, Chapter 48, and the Expanded Epilogue, pages 284–86 and 288–90.

12 Margaret Thatcher is also credited with "turning an enemy into a friend" in her eulogy of former President Ronald Reagan.

and it seems to be a principle behind Jesus's instructions about how to respond to aggressors (Matt 5:40–42). By anticipating the "other's" needs or desires and seeking to meet them before we are asked, we demonstrate our willingness to work toward a common objective and connection.

The Power of Common Connection for Reconciliation

One could argue that Christ's desire for reconciliation was so fierce that he consistently overturned oppositional situations defined by social, political, cultural, and linguistic boundaries. Consider his admonitions regarding revenge and enemies, charged within the context of a politically subdued people (Matt 5:41, 43–46) and his proclamations concerning faith found among Gentiles like the Roman officer (Matt 8:10–13) and the Syrophoenician woman (Mark 7:26–29). He even went so far as to transform the definition of family (Matt 12:46–50). He violated Jewish laws concerning ceremonial purity by touching someone with a skin disease (Matt 8:3) and by touching a corpse (Luke 7:14–15). Rather than accept the status quo of boundaries that kept people on opposing sides, Christ united the two sides in "one new humanity" (Eph 2:14–16).

Miroslav Volf noted that Paul recognized the way in which Christ resolved the division between two sides of a conflict and applied it in his letter to the Ephesians. He urges the Ephesians to leave behind the two-sided tension between Jew and Gentile and to emphasize Christ as their—and our—common footing (cf. Eph 2:13–19).

> Paul's solution to the tension between universality and particularity is ingenious. Its logic is simple: the oneness of God requires God's universality; God's universality entails human equality; human equality implies equal access by all to the blessings of the one God; equal access is incompatible with ascription of religious significance to genealogy; Christ, the seed of Abraham, is both the fulfillment of the genealogical promise to Abraham and the end of genealogy as a privileged locus of access to God; faith in Christ replaces birth into a people. As a consequence, all peoples can have access to the one God of Abraham and Sarah on equal terms. (Volf 1996, 44)

Mission as reconciliation seeks unity and equal access for all people on God's terms and under his authority. We cannot perceive or treat the "other" as an enemy in this endeavor, but as a fellow human, a neighbor, who also needs reconciliation with God in Christ. "The Scriptures lead us to a startling conclusion: *at the deepest level of identity as humans, there are no others—there is only us*" (Hiebert 2008, 289, emphasis in the original).

Reconciliation as the universal need of humanity points to the final worldview question: "Why am I?"

Why Am I?

Observations made earlier in this discussion come together here. Once again, it is pertinent that these worldview questions were developed in the context of individualistic cultures which tend to elevate the individual at the expense of "other." In the case of the "Why am I?" question, the "other" is erased. Just as significantly, the rest of the Christian community, the "us," also is ignored or omitted. These erasures weaken the impact of this worldview question for mission training and mission as reconciliation at best and serve theological misinterpretation at worst.

First, people were not created in isolation. Adam was created first, but when God saw that his uniqueness and thus his isolation as the only human was not good, God created a helpmate (Gen 2). Furthermore, Eve was not created in opposition to Adam as an "other," but to accompany and partner with him. We cannot overlook these fundamental points of human existence because they speak to human purpose in a profound way.

Next, humans were created to be fruitful. While the Genesis account points to fruitfulness in terms of biological reproduction (Gen 1:28), subtle alterations are introduced throughout the arc of the Old Testament and into the New Testament.[13] Abraham's biological fruitfulness is tied to the concept of blessing (Gen 12:2–3; 17:1–8). Blessing for one people or nation is tied to the concept of blessing for all peoples and nations (cf. Gen 28:3; 35:11–12; Deut 4:5–8; Ps 67; Jer 4:1–2). As the separation caused by the original and continuing sin of humans becomes more and more profoundly illustrated in the nation of Israel, the final solution of God incarnate comes to fruition in the ultimate act of reconciliation. Even in that context, Jesus ties fruitfulness to blessing to reconciliation between God and people, and between individuals (cf. John 15:1–17; 17:3, 22–24; 20:22–23). Pentecost and the subsequent story of the replication and growth of communities of believers demonstrates the combination of fruitfulness, blessing, and reconciliation to God. We cannot truly understand our purpose apart from the arc of Scripture, nor from our relative position in that arc.

---

13 In the Genesis account, all reproducing creatures are commanded to be fruitful. First the birds, animals, fish, and other creatures are given the command (Gen 1:22; Gen 8:17), and then the humans (Gen 1:28; Gen 9:1, 7). But the extension from fruitfulness to blessing is only given to Abraham and his descendants (Gen 12:2–3; 17:1–8).

Third, the "other" is integral to our purpose of fruitfulness and blessing. As much as I appreciate the "blessed to be a blessing" phrase, it implies the subject and erases the object. Who is to receive the blessing? The "other." And who is the "other?" As discussed earlier, there are no boundaries, no specific defining social, cultural, or linguistic characteristics of the "other," our neighbor. He or she is the fellow human being also loved and called by God into reconciled union.

Our purpose should always point to Christ, who points us to the "other," our neighbor (Luke 10:25–37). It is significant that Christ's perspective of the unknown man attacked by bandits is not that he is "other," but that he is a member of our human community, our neighbor. This perspective becomes even more noteworthy when we consider Jesus's response to the teacher of the law who had answered well to the question about the most important commandment.

> "Well said, teacher," the man replied. "You are right in saying that God is one and there is no other but him. To love him with all your heart, with all your understanding and with all your strength, and to love your neighbor as yourself is more important than all burnt offerings and sacrifices." When Jesus saw that he had answered wisely, he said to him, "You are not far from the kingdom of God." And from then on no one dared to ask him any more questions. (Mark 12:32–34)

When we love our neighbor as ourselves by making the same blessing of reconciliation with God that we enjoy available to our neighbor, we are fulfilling our purpose in the kingdom of God through obedience to God's greatest desire.

From Comfortable Opposition to Reconciliation

From the beginning of this discussion, the pattern of oppositional categories in mission strategy and in models used for cross-cultural training has been clear. In questions of identity (who am I?), place or space (where am I?), conflict (who is in charge?) and purpose (why am I?), the worldview framework inadvertently puts us in an oppositional category and stance to the "other" or even erases the "other." Moreover, we are most likely not aware of our worldview as oppositional, only as "normal" and even "right." And, as noted above, the power of being with other people who have the same "normal" as we do, homophily, is difficult to resist. It is comfortable and therefore desirable, whereas taking steps to meet an unknown person on their terms may seem threatening, strange, and isolating when the thrill of the exotic wears off.

I have also pointed out that we have tools at our disposal to "enlarge our tent" (Isa 54:2) thus weakening boundaries of our own human construction. By embracing our pilgrim identity and our ambassadorial role, we can weaken the attraction of social, cultural, and linguistic aspects of identity and become "150 percent persons" (Lingenfelter and Mayers 2016, 114): wider and more inclusive than we are now. Being 150 percent persons allows us to be familiar with more contexts and to enjoy fellowship at more tables. Most importantly, we can engage creatively in the search for common footing with the "other," effectively turning the oppositional character of the relationship on its head. Reconciliation with God and with others is a blessing that is intended for fruitful reproduction.

Pointing out the oppositional categories and stances of worldview questions does not diminish their value for training any more than a co-ed classroom diminishes the value of general education (or of marriage). Instead, let us become aware of the unintended consequences of comfortable oppositional thinking for mission training and mission strategy.

References Cited

Adeney, Miriam, with Boon Chayavichitsilp, Jodi Gatlin, Jennifer Gebhart, Megan Hamshar, and Kevin Moxon. 2014. "Seeking Asian-American Theologies." *Evangelical Missions Quarterly* 50, no. 2 (April): 148–55.

Allen, Scott David. 2020. *Why Social Justice Is Not Biblical Justice: An Urgent Appeal to Fellow Christians in a Time of Social Crisis*. Grand Rapids, MI: Credo House Publishers.

Augsberger, David. 1992. *Conflict Mediation across Cultures: Pathways and Patterns*. Louisville, KY: Westminster John Knox Publishers.

Benjamin, Rich. 2009. *Searching for Whitopia: An Improbable Journey to the Heart of White America*. New York: Hachette Books.

Bonk, Jonathan. 2007. "Missions and Money: Affluence as a Western Missionary Problem Revisited." *International Bulletin of Missionary Research* 31, no. 4 (October): 171–74.

Cooley, Charles Horton. 1902. *Human Nature and the Social Order*. New York: Scribner.

Crider, Caleb. 2015. "Who Are You Calling a Missionary?" *For the Church on Mission: Missionary Skills for All of God's People* (blog), March 24, 2015. http://www.calebcrider.com/blog/2015/3/10/who-are-you-calling-a-missionary.

Crossman, Meg. 2009. "Minority Groups in China: Can Han Christians Reach Them?" In *Missions from the Majority World: Progress, Challenges and Case Studies*, edited by Enoch Wan and Michael Pocock, 283–95. Pasadena, CA: William Carey Library.

Elmer, Duane. 2002. *Cross-Cultural Connections: Stepping Out and Fitting in Around the World*. Downers Grove, IL: IVP Academic.

Elmer, Duane. 2006. *Cross-Cultural Servanthood: Serving the World in Christlike Humility*. Downers Grove, IL: IVP Books.

Escobar, Samuel. 2003. *The New Global Mission: The Gospel from Everywhere to Everyone*. Downers Grove, IL: IVP Academic.

Fancher, Karen. 2022. "The Transformational Work of Building Peace." Presentation at Evangelical Missiological Society, Northwest Region, Beaverton, Oregon.

Gudykunst, William B. 2002. "Intercultural Communication Theories." In *Handbook of International and Intercultural Communication*. 2nd ed. Edited by William B. Gudykunst and Bela Mody, 183–205. Thousand Oaks, CA: Sage Publications.

Gudykunst, William B. 2004. *Bridging Differences: Effective Intergroup Communication*. 4th edition. Thousand Oaks, CA: Sage Publications.

Hammer, Mitchell R. 2005. "The Intercultural Conflict Style Inventory: A Conceptual Framework and Measure of Intercultural Conflict Resolution Approaches." *International Journal of Intercultural Relations* 29, no. 6 (November): 675–95.

Handley, Joseph W. 2021a. "Polycentrism as the New Leadership Paradigm." *Lausanne Global Analysis* 10, no. 3 (May): https://lausanne.org/content/lga/2021-05/polycentrism-as-the-new-leadership-paradigm.

Handley, Joseph W. 2021b. "Polycentric Leadership for Kingdom Movements." Preprint. https://www.researchgate.net/publication/355168262_polycentric_leadership_for_kingdom_movements.

Harrison, Annette R. 2015. "Using Scripture in Multilingual Churches." *Evangelical Missions Quarterly* 51, no. 2 (April): 190–95.

Hayashi, Jonathan. 2017. "Not Everyone Is a Missionary." *Evangelica Sola* (blog), May 2, 2017. https://jonathanhayashi.com/not-everyone-is-a-missionary/.

Hiebert, Paul G. 2008. *Transforming Worldviews: An Anthropological Understanding of How People Change*. Grand Rapids, MI: Baker Academic.

Hofstede, Geert, Gert Jan Hofstede, and Michael Minkov. 2010. *Cultures and Organizations: Software of the Mind*. 3rd ed. New York: McGraw Hill.

InterVarsity. 2017. "ISM Integration Toolkit." Accessed March 21, 2022. https://ism.intervarsity.org/sites/ism/files/resource/file/Integration_Stats_Facts_Vision.pdf.

Jenkins, Philip. 2002. *The Next Christendom: The Coming of Global Christianity*. Oxford: Oxford University Press.

Jones, Arun W. 2022. "Hybridity and Christian Identity." *Missiology: An International Review* 50, no. 1: 7–16.

Kearney, Michael. 1984. *World View*. Novato, CA: Chandler and Sharp Publishers.

Kougoum, Galbert. 2009. *Pour une Église-Communauté-de-Paix dans un Contexte Multiethnique Conflictuel. Le Cas du Cameroun*. [For a Community-of-Peace Church in a Multiethnic Context of Conflict: The Case of Cameroon]. PhD diss., University of Montréal.

Kraft, Charles H. 1997. *Anthropology for Christian Witness*. Maryknoll, NY: Orbis Books.

Kraft, Charles H. 2008. *Worldview for Christian Witness*. Pasadena, CA: William Carey Library.

Lane, Patty. 2002. *A Beginner's Guide to Crossing Cultures: Making Friends in a Multicultural World*. Downers Grove, IL: IVP Books.

Lanier, Sarah. 2000. *Foreign to Familiar: A Guide to Understanding Hot and Cold Climate Cultures*. Hagerstown, MD: McDougal Publishing Company.

Lederleitner, Mary T. 2010. *Cross-Cultural Partnerships: Navigating the Complexities of Money and Missions*. Downers Grove, IL: IVP Books.

Lee, Megan. 2012. "The Complete History of Study Abroad." *GO Overseas* (blog), updated July 7, 2015. https://www.gooverseas.com/blog/history-study-abroad.

Lingenfelter, Sherwood. 2008. *Leading Cross-Culturally: Covenant Relationships for Effective Christian Leadership*. Grand Rapids, MI: Baker Academic.

Lingenfelter, Sherwood G., and Marvin K. Mayers. 2016. *Ministering Cross-Culturally: A Model for Effective Personal Relationships*. 3rd edition. Grand Rapids, MI: Baker Academic.

Mead, George Herbert. 1934. *Mind, Self and Society: From the Standpoint of a Social Behaviorist*. Chicago: University of Chicago Press.

Moreau, A. Scott, Evvy Hay Campbell, and Susan Greener. 2014. *Effective Intercultural Communication*. Grand Rapids, MI: Baker Academic.

Mulvihill, Josh. 2019. *Biblical Worldview: What It Is, Why It Matters, and How to Shape the Worldview of the Next Generation*. Roanoke, VA: Renewanation.

Ngumbu, Rémy. 2018. *Le Missionnaire Noir: Les défis de la culture financière des associations confessionnelles en République Démocratique du Congo*. [The Black Missionary: The challenges of the financial culture of religious organizations in the Democratic Republic of Congo]. Independently Published.

Payne, J. D. 2013. *Pressure Points: Twelve Global Issues Shaping the Face of the Church*. Nashville, TN: Thomas Nelson Publishers.

Pohor, Rubin. 2010. "Tribalism, Ethnicity and Race." In *Africa Bible Commentary*, edited by Tokunboh Adeyemo et al., 699–701. Grand Rapids, MI: Zondervan.

Putnam, Robert D. 2020. *Bowling Alone: The Collapse and Revival of American Community*, rev. ed. New York: Simon and Schuster.

Qureshi, Nabeel. 2016. *Seeking Allah, Finding Jesus: A Devout Muslim Encounters Christianity*. Grand Rapids, MI: Zondervan.

Rah, Soong-Chan. 2009. *The Next Evangelicalism: Freeing the Church from Western Cultural Captivity*. Downers Grove, IL: IVP Books.

Short Term Missions. 2022. Mission Guide, Accessed March 21, 2022. ShortTermMissions.com is now missionguide.global. https://missionguide.global/articles/mission-trip-research.

Slimbach, Richard. 2005. "The Transcultural Journey." *Frontiers: The Interdisciplinary Journal of Study Abroad* 11, no. 1 (August): 205–30.

Smith, C. Fred. 2015. *Developing a Biblical Worldview: Seeing Things God's Way.* Nashville, TN: B&H Publishing Group.

Sproul, R. C. (1985/1996). "Secularism." In *Christian Worldviews*, a cassette and video teaching series accessed through Ligonier Ministries, https://www.ligonier.org/learn/series/christian-worldview.

"Status of Global Christianity, 2023, in the Context of 1900–2050." 2023. Center for the Study of Global Christianity at Gordon-Conwell Theological Seminary. Accessed February 24, 2023. https://www.gordonconwell.edu/center-for-global-christianity/resources/status-of-global-christianity/.

The Traveling Team. 2023. "Mission Stats: The Current State of the World." *The Traveling Team*, Mission Statistics. https://www.thetravelingteam.org/stats. Accessed multiple times between March–September 2022 and June 2023.

Ting-Toomey, Stella, and John G. Oetzel. 2002. "Cross-Cultural Face Concerns and Conflict Styles." In *Handbook of International and Intercultural Communication.* 2nd edition. Edited by William B. Gudykunst and Bela Mody, 143–63. Thousand Oaks, CA: Sage Publications.

Tira, Sadiri Joy, and Juliet Lee Uytanlet. 2020. *A Hybrid World: Diaspora, Hybridity and Missio Dei.* Littleton, CO: William Carey Publishing.

Van Dyne, Linn, Soon Ang, and David Livermore. 2010. "Cultural Intelligence: A Pathway for Leading in a Rapidly Globalizing World." In *Leading Across Differences: Cases and Perspectives*, edited by Kelly M. Hannum and Belinda B. McFeeters, 131–38. San Francisco, CA: Pfeiffer.

Volf, Miroslav. 1996. *Exclusion and Embrace: A Theological Exploration of Identity, Otherness and Reconciliation.* Nashville, TN: Abingdon Press.

Walls, Andrew. 1996. *The Missionary Movement in Christian History: Studies in the Transmission of Faith.* Maryknoll, NY: Orbis Books.

Wilkens, Steve, and Mark L. Sanford. 2009. *Hidden Worldviews: Eight Cultural Stories That Shape Our Lives.* Downers Grove, IL: IVP Academic.

Chapter 8

Welcomed at God's Table

Moving from Abstraction to Embodied Reconciliation through Hospitality

Aubry G. Smith

Hiebert's Bounded and Centered Sets

In the late twentieth century, anthropologist Paul Hiebert proposed an application of intrinsic and extrinsic mathematical sets to missiological concepts of Christian identity and community formation (Hiebert 1978, 24–29; 1994, 107–36). American society, Hiebert claimed, primarily bases its ontological systems on bounded, binary sets in which an object is intrinsically "A" or "not-A" (Hiebert 1994, 114).[1] In a "bounded set," a clear boundary separates objects inside the category and those outside the category. Objects within the category must meet certain criteria for entry by possessing certain intrinsic characteristics. In addition to being intrinsically homogeneous, bounded sets are also static because of the intrinsic, essential characteristics its members possess: the object is either in or out of the set, with clear boundaries separating the two categories (Hiebert 1994, 113). An apple is an apple because of its intrinsic properties; a banana is not an apple and is not part of the categorical set of "apple."

Applied to human communities, bounded sets require essential and definitive characteristics to be present in order for a person to be included in the set. Skin color, tribal affiliation, political allegiance, or denominational membership could all potentially comprise tight boundaries based on intrinsic properties. The bounded set promotes the image of a single fixed identity with its particular characteristics, and people who do not display that identity through those identity markers are outside the boundaries of the group.

---

[1] American society has likely since shifted significantly in its ontological categories since the time of Hiebert's writing. Among younger generations, fuzzy sets and hybridity are more highly favored than clearly defined categories. An exploration of this shift falls outside the scope of this chapter.

In contrast, extrinsic sets are formed on the basis of relationships to a common reference point, rather than a shared internal essence.[2] In a "centered-set," belonging in a group is defined not by intrinsic characteristics, but by the relationship of the objects to the center. Some objects may be near the center, but moving away from the center, and are therefore not part of the set. Some objects may be far away from the center, but moving toward it, and therefore are part of the set.

Hiebert writes, "While centered sets are not created by drawing boundaries, they do have sharp boundaries that separate things inside the set from those outside it—between things related to or moving toward the center and those that are not" (Hiebert 1994, 124). While the boundary exists, the focus is on the relationship to the center, rather than maintaining a clear boundary or essential characteristics to maintain the purity of the set. Thus, the set is a diverse dynamic of relationships that defies uniformity and homogeneity. When applied to human communities, centered sets allow for significant diversity among members of a group, because they are united not by intrinsic characteristics or behaviors but by their relationship or allegiance to a center. Those in a dynamic relationship of drawing closer to the center belong to the group.

Hiebert's conceptual model is consistent with movement away from cultural essentialism in anthropology since the mid-twentieth century. The essentialist view of identity is appealing because of its rigidity and bounded nature. Essentialism is easier to grasp and conceptualize, to know who shares a particular identity and who does not. The signals of membership and belonging are clearer: blood relation, skin color, nationality, or a particular behavior. Group identity in essentialism or a bounded set is surrounded by a solid boundary. The group is assumed to be a single fixed, homogeneous identity (Brubaker 2002, 164).

The impermeable boundaries, formed around membership signals, define who must be excluded and relegated to the out-group. Essentialism reduces human existence to static categories that are easier to manage and maintain, and often leads to stereotyping. Modern anthropological models, however, acknowledge the fluidity and processual nature of identities, which shift and are reconfigured over time. Hiebert's centered sets allow for a group to form around a new allegiance and identity, allowing diversity to exist, but redistributes allegiances and signals of belonging based on the center.

---

2 Hiebert wrote of four basic sets based on two variables: intrinsic well-formed (bounded), extrinsic well-formed (centered), intrinsic fuzzy, and extrinsic fuzzy. This chapter focuses on bounded and centered sets only for the sake of clarity and brevity.

This chapter explores identity politics and ministry realities in Belfast, Northern Ireland through Hiebert's model of bounded and centered sets. Reconciliation in Belfast has been pursued by maintaining strong identity boundaries between conflicting groups, leading to reconciliation that is not embodied in everyday life. This chapter also describes a centered-set approach to ministry among refugees and other "outsiders" in Northern Ireland through the relational practices of hospitality, in which reconciliation can be embodied in space and time.

Case Study: Belfast Sectarian Identity

In Northern Ireland, the political rhetoric and local narrative proclaims two reified, homogeneous identities: Catholic and Protestant. In Hiebert's terms, Catholic and Protestant form bounded sets with highly essentialized characteristics. Northern Irish typically use the terms "Catholic" and "Protestant" primarily as ethnonationalist alignments, rather than as religious terms defined by the Reformation.[3] Most Catholics identify as "Irish," and most Catholics would desire a unified Ireland. Most Protestant Northern Irish identify as "British," and desire to maintain the political affiliation with the United Kingdom that it has had officially since 1921.[4]

These competing identities and political goals go back hundreds of years, to 1690, when the Protestant William of Orange conquered the Catholic King James II in the Battle of the Boyne. "The Troubles" was the understated name of the violent sectarian conflict that began in 1969 and officially ended April 1998 with the Good Friday Agreement. The Troubles resulted in over 3,500 deaths and 47,500 injuries (Murtagh and Boland 2019, 8). Shirlow and Murtagh argue that while the Northern Irish conflict is not based on religion, "religion acts as a boundary marker with regard to competing aspirations regarding forms of Britishness and Irishness" (Shirlow and Murtagh 2006, 15). Essentialist notions of group identity prevail especially among the working class, promulgated by political rhetoric, murals and memorials, and symbols of identity that maintain clear boundaries between the two groups.

While much of the violence of the Troubles ended in 1998, sectarianism continues to affect the city, clearly demonstrated in the use of urban space to denote ethnonational identity. In 2017, 93 percent of children in Northern Ireland attended a school segregated along Catholic-Protestant lines (Ulster

---

3 Throughout this chapter, the terms "Catholic" and "Protestant" will assume the Northern Irish connotations of political and ethnic allegiances and identity, rather than as primarily religious terms.

4 As in any complex human culture, these statements about Catholic and Protestant identity and loyalty are generally true but not universally so.

University 2021). Segregated housing remains a defining feature of identity in Belfast, particularly among the working class. The emotive power of spatial memory remains strong in Northern Ireland for those who remember the Troubles. One Protestant Northern Irish woman remarked on a walk up Divis Mountain, a historically Catholic area, "I could just *feel* it on the drive. We would have never come up here twenty years ago; this was 'bandit country.'"

"Bandit country" is a common Northern Irish Protestant phrase denoting a predominantly Catholic territory, connoting danger and fear of attack. This same woman has never told her elderly parents where she works on the Falls Road in West Belfast, an area known as a stronghold for the Irish Republican Army (IRA) during the Troubles. Two decades after the end of the Troubles, Belfast residents avoid particular neighborhoods and streets occupied by the "other" as a protective strategy. The spatial and territorial memory still carries significant emotive strength in Northern Ireland.

> Two decades after the end of the Troubles, Belfast residents avoid particular neighborhoods and streets.

Violence, though much reduced since the Troubles, continues along the city's "flashpoints," where Protestant and Catholic neighborhoods interface. The government first constructed Peace Walls in 1969 at the beginning of the Troubles to separate the communities at these interfaces. The entry points of the walls are closed down every evening and during eruptions of conflict or protests. In 2017, the Belfast Interface Project identified ninety-seven Peace Wall structures in Belfast, many of them constructed or made higher or longer since the end of the Troubles (Belfast Interface Project 2017).

Boulton writes, "Whilst the barriers were originally intended to stop violence, in fact they have served to formalize, symbolize, and in some respects heighten, the differences between each side" (Boulton 2014, 105). While the local government plans the removal of the Peace Walls by 2023 to increase mobility and intergroup contact in the city, residents near the Peace Walls strongly oppose the removal of the walls (Dixon et al. 2020, 926). Residents perceive that wall removal will not only increase interface violence but would also symbolize the surrender of identity and memory among two groups proclaiming the mantra, "Not an Inch!" (Herrault and Murtagh 2019, 252).

Within these segregated spaces and on the very Peace Walls themselves, symbols of ethnonational identity are ubiquitous, maintaining clear boundaries, shaping identity, and bringing the past into the present through the senses. Sectarian murals depict both martyrs and soldiers throughout the working-class areas of the city, and signal the allegiances of particular neighborhoods. Flags are important group identity symbols in Northern Ireland; Protestants fly the British Union Jack, while Catholics fly the Irish Tricolor, and both sides also have a plethora of paramilitary flags (Mastors and Drumhiller 2014, 495). Protests and violence frequently arise over these symbols of either British or Irish identity. The summer months are known locally as "parade season," in which dozens of Catholic and Protestant groups display their cultural and political allegiance through flute and drum bands marching throughout the country, but especially in Belfast. In these ways and more, urban spaces provide a platform for ethnic identity to territorialize a particular geographical area, absconding the space for sectarian memory and symbols of belonging (Nagle 2020, 384).

Language also reinforces the boundaries between the two group identities in Belfast, providing unity among the in-group and heightening the differences with the out-group. Catholic political parties such as Sinn Fein spearhead efforts to keep the Irish language and distinct culture alive through Irish street signs and Irish language schools. Collective identity and allegiance is embedded within the use of a particular language; the Irish language has become a symbol of resistance against colonial British powers (Goldenberg 2002, 88).

In a 2019 study examining an Irish language school in a Protestant area of Belfast, many participants admitted that they kept their learning of the Irish language a secret from their friends and family, who would interpret this as disloyalty to their British identity (Mitchell and Miller 2019, 247–48). Sectarian groups even disagree on the country's name: Protestants call the country "Northern Ireland," denoting its official unity with the UK since 1921, while Catholics refer to it as "the north of Ireland" or simply "the North," rejecting the legal British sovereignty.

The spatial and linguistic markers of reified group identity in Northern Ireland have made reconciliation between sectarian groups complex. The peace process in Northern Ireland has taken shape through an "accommodationist" framework (Nagle 2020, 383). Both ethnic groups are maintained as separate and distinct cultural identities, with city center space shared between the two (McEvoy 2011, 57). The political narrative proclaims "partnership, equality, and mutual respect," but both groups maintain a high sensitivity to marginalization and discrimination (Belfast Agreement 1998). Everything must be carefully and equally drawn out so that one side does not gain an upper hand. However, the crystallized identities of "Catholic" and "Protestant" remain, for the most part, rigid constructions of identity with competing aspirations. Ultimately, the Catholics hold out hope for a united Ireland, while Protestants work to maintain British sovereignty over Northern Ireland.[5]

While significant efforts have been made toward peace and reconciliation in Belfast, the lived reality continues to be one of suspicion, separation, and

---

[5] The 1998 Belfast/Good Friday Agreement allows for the right of self-determination based on a majority consensus for Northern Ireland, so it is entirely possible that Northern Ireland may one day secede from the UK and rejoin the Republic of Ireland.

deep-seated traumatic memory. Traumatic memory is inscribed in the people themselves—in the remaining scars of pipe bomb injuries, in the empty seats around the kitchen table, and in the retelling of stories of the hateful and evil "other" passed down through the generations. Sectarian paramilitary leaders and politicians maintain a political rhetoric of a single, fixed identity to reinforce the homogeneous unity of "Catholic" or "Protestant," an ethnopolitical strategy often employed in group-making strategies (Brubaker 2002, 176).

Catholic and Protestant communities in Northern Ireland epitomize Hiebert's bounded sets. The center of the conflict between the two communities revolves around the maintenance of clear and hardened boundaries of "groupness," of who is "us" and who is "them," in order to maintain a clear group identity (Volf 2019, xvi). As long as the public narratives, spatial reality, embodied experiences, and symbolic identity markers testify to an impermeable "us" and "them," sectarianism will remain. Contact with the "other" will remain a threat to safety and to the loss of identity; for some, violence is an acceptable method of defending that identity. Thus, reconciliation in sectarian Northern Irish communities remains an abstract concept divorced from the lived reality.

Hospitality: Permeating the Boundaries for Embodied Reconciliation

At the core of the *missio Dei* lies God's initiative to enact reconciliation between himself and humanity, culminating in the life, death, and resurrection of Jesus Christ. Repentance and forgiveness form the foundation of this story, and are to be encoded in the relationships and patterns of behavior among followers of Jesus. In addition, a new identity in Christ acts as the impetus for a new code of ethics, breaking down barriers between human enemies and allowing them to be unified in Christ. In Hiebert's model, both "Catholic" and "Protestant" Northern Irish would need to turn toward a new center: from ethnonationalist allegiances and symbols of group belonging, to Christ and his kingdom. This would involve a radical reconfiguration of identity, values, and the boundaries between "us" and "them." Reconciliation must be embodied in the shared spaces and in symbols of belonging and identity. Hospitality is one practice that moves toward embodied reconciliation.

The biblical practice of hospitality—of welcoming the stranger and the outsider—deliberately and radically breaches the barriers of group membership. Hospitality is more than inviting others for dinner or coffee. Hospitality is the opening of lives and boundaries—our physical spaces, food and resources, our full attention, and our very selves, in order to welcome the "other." Christine Pohl writes, "For most of Christian history, hospitality was understood to encompass physical, social, and spiritual dimensions of human existence and relationships. It meant response to the physical needs of strangers for food, shelter, and protection, but also a recognition of their worth and common humanity" (Pohl 1999, 6). Hospitality reaches across reified boundaries and perceived intrinsic differences to invite the "other" to the table.

The New Testament beckons the church back to her exemplar in relationships: the triune God, who at the greatest cost, welcomed his enemies to his table and into his own family as co-heirs. Miroslav Volf argues that the Trinity—the self-giving and other-receiving relationship between Father, Son, and Spirit—acts as a "social vision" for our own communities in conflict (Volf 2019, 347). The *perichoresis* of the Trinity is the divine communion and inherence as one God, and yet the distinct identity of each member is both maintained and permeated among the three. In his divine hospitality, God welcomes his enemies into this embrace, giving them a new collective identity in Christ (Volf 2019, 138).

With this new center, belonging in the group is defined only by a member's relationship to Christ—not ethnic identity, language, or cultural behaviors. This identity must transform all other allegiances and boundaries, all murals painted, and flags flown. Paul describes Christians as now members of Christ's own body, and as having the mind of Christ, with a new connectivity not only to the Godhead but also to one another (1 Cor 2:16; 12:12–27; Eph 4:12–25; 5:30; Col 1:24; 2:19; 3:15). Having been received by God into this communion, the people of God are to make space for the "other" in real space and time, not as an abstracted principle (Volf 2019, 129–30).

When the people of God practice hospitality, they reflect the hospitable God. God showed generous hospitality to humanity by setting the first humans in Eden: a life-giving space of beauty, abundant food, and true intimacy with God. Sin disrupted this relationship, scorning God's hospitality to humanity through creation. Sin's effects resound at every level of human existence—in a lack of internal peace or the formation of hardened pride, in physical sickness and pain or desperate hunger, in disconnected and broken relationships, in systemic oppression and societal evil. Sin is holistic, so must be the cure.

God's welcoming of his enemies into his family through Christ involved both incarnation and physical torture and death, so that humanity might be reconciled to God through Christ's physical body (Col 1:22). Believers have been welcomed into the sphere of God's very presence, and now together are being formed into a new temple to embody his own presence in the world (1 Cor 6:9–20; Eph 2:21). Reconciliation to God is not only an abstract truth, but it has also been dramatically enacted through space and time, in Christ's body and in our bodies among the Christian community.

Sharing food, spaces, and resources combats the tendency to relegate people to an agonistic category of "other." Christine Pohl remarks, "The practice of hospitality forces abstract commitments to loving the neighbor, stranger, and enemy into practical and personal expressions of respect and care for actual neighbors, strangers, and enemies. ... Claims of loving all humankind, of welcoming 'the Other,' have to be accompanied by the hard work of actually welcoming a human being into a real place" (Pohl 1999, 75).

Hospitality is an experience of integrated, embodied spirituality. In a disconnected world marked by virtual meetings, tribalism fostered through social media, and the isolation caused by a global pandemic, the world needs the biblical practice of hospitality to connect our whole selves with the whole selves of others.

Connectivity and Shared Space in Hospitality

Janine Clark studied reconciliation in former war zones, with particular attention to the concept of the "connectivity" of bodies. Rather than an independent, "self-contained entity," Clark's phenomenological interviews describe the body as connected to others through corporeal experiences. Clark argues that "bodies represent important sites of functional connectivity that can bring together communities fractured by war and armed conflict" (Clark 2019, 269).

Sensing the physical experiences of other bodies—such as seeing open wounds or hearing another wailing in grief—triggered empathy and embodied connection in their own physical experiences and formed the basis of reconciliation between fractured parties. Humans are not mere individuals but are embedded within a complex web of social relationships. Bodies affect one another deeply through shared space and empathy (Kelly et al. 2020, 400–7).

True reconciliation must be an integrated, psychosomatic experience because sin is an integrated, psychosomatic experience. Relationships, specifically in proximity to other bodies, are crucial in nurturing healing, wholeness, and spirituality (Hall 2010, 174). In the church, the embodied practices of meeting together, eating and drinking the Eucharist together, encouraging one another, hearing the prayers of others, forgiving and being forgiven, speaking kindly, and confronting sin all involve embeddedness in an environment that connects believers to other bodies (Hall 2010, 175).

Discipleship and spiritual practices do not arise *ex nihilo*, but by watching and imitating the externalized faith of fellow Christians. The biblical commands for living in community are difficult precisely because humans are embedded within these structures in a physical way. The senses are confronted with loud noises, annoying habits, unwashed smells, selfish attitudes, and demanding needs. Commands to love neighbors cannot remain abstracted to the interior world of ideals but must be embodied and externalized in the physical world. Reconciliation that keeps distance, that bars the entrance to our doors and our lives, is an abstracted concept of reconciliation empty of meaning. Abstracted reconciliation maintains deep divisions and "peace walls" with self-protective, rather than self-giving, mechanisms.

Reconfigured Boundaries: Hospitality as Mission among Refugees in Belfast

In response to the humanitarian crises emerging from the Syrian War, the United Kingdom introduced the Vulnerable Persons Resettlement Scheme (VPRS) in 2014, promising refuge for over twenty thousand victims of the Syrian crisis (UNHCR 2017). The UK government resettled approximately 17 percent of the Syrian refugees accepted through the VPRS program in Northern Ireland, resulting in a greater proportion of Syrian refugees in Northern Ireland than in the rest of the UK by population (Lippard and McNamee 2021, 3092; Meredith 2019).

Brexit, the "British Exit" from the European Union also unintentionally triggered a significant increase in asylum claims in Northern Ireland. Belfast has become a backdoor into the UK for asylum seekers in the wake of Brexit, leading to a substantial increase in asylum claims since 2021. Before Brexit, asylum seekers entering the UK could legally be sent back to their first point of entry into the EU. After Brexit came into effect in 2020, asylum claims made in the UK had to be processed in the UK. As a result, increasing numbers of asylum seekers have flown into Dublin from elsewhere in the EU. In the absence of a hard border between the Republic of Ireland and Northern Ireland, asylum seekers travel to Belfast to claim asylum. The UK recorded a 56 percent increase in asylum claims between March 2020 and March 2022, the highest number in over two decades (UK Government 2022).

The sudden influx of refugees and asylum seekers into Belfast since 2015 has created a new divisive dynamic. Northern Irish Catholics, who often resonate with the oppressed and persecuted, often receive refugees and asylum seekers into their neighborhoods with less resistance (Lippard and McNamee 2021, 3106). The Protestant working class, however, generally feel more threatened by the presence of migrants, and it is not uncommon for refugees in Protestant neighborhoods to have their windows broken, their doors graffitied, or to be physically threatened. As a result, the media have identified Northern Ireland as the "race hate capital of Europe" (Doebler, McAreavey, and Shortfall 2018, 2427).

In a 2021 study, low socio-economic status and alignment with Loyalist political agendas correlated with a negative reception to foreigners in Northern Ireland (Lippard and McNamee 2021, 3106–7).[6] For many, the presence of immigrants competing for limited resources represents an intensified threat to Protestant British identity. Mission to the forcibly displaced in Belfast requires a painful and sacrificial reconfiguration of ethnonational boundaries, identities, and cultural values for Northern Irish Christians. Only an embodied approach to mission that embraces the "other" can move reconciliation from an abstract notion to a lived reality.

Mission among refugees and asylum seekers is concerned with not only reconciling them to God in Christ Jesus, but also reconciling their whole selves with their humanity and reestablishing connectivity with others. The embodied experiences of refugees and asylum seekers often include verbal and physical abuse, sexual exploitation, poverty, hunger, war injury, disease, separation from family, exposure to extreme weather, and much more. Refugees feel displacement from their homeland on a visceral level; their identity is often tied up with the land.

The experiences of the body in seeking asylum have a tremendous impact on the whole self, resulting in shame and a sense of disconnection from the rest of humanity (Zeno 2017, 285). Many refugees and asylum seekers are renegotiating their identities as their personal, social, and cultural belonging and rootedness have been profoundly ruptured (Jarrah 2018, 47). Through his research into trauma recovery, Bessel van der Kolk argues that human brains function not merely as single entities, but in connection with other humans. He concludes, "Safe connections are fundamental to meaningful and satisfying lives" (van der Kolk 2014, 79). Hospitality facilitates connectivity between whole human persons, allowing for the safety required to heal from trauma and move toward full reconciliation toward the self and others. For those whose bodies have experienced tremendous abuse and degradation, the power of physical nearness, a caring hand on the arm, and active play, all create connectivity in a powerful way when trust has been established (Vimalasekaran 2020, 128–29).

My husband is the co-director of Acacia Path, a nonprofit connecting local churches and volunteers in Northern Ireland to asylum seekers residing in hotels as they await the outcome of their asylum claim. Acacia Path provides English classes, simple children's programs, and donations of toiletries and clothing provided by local churches as an act of welcome to Belfast. In addition, the members of Acacia Path provide advocacy and social connections for

---

6 The term "Loyalist" denotes a particularly extreme "Protestant," pro-British view of political alignment with the UK.

medical and legal issues and visit refugees and asylum seekers in their homes and elsewhere.

Asylum seekers often comment on how Christian volunteers with Acacia Path treat them, compared to secular and government organizations. For some, it is the first time in many years that they have been treated as human, rather than as a problem to be solved or a blight to be removed. For those from collectivistic societies where honor is mediated by the community and is of higher value than even wealth or food, the extension of hospitality is an expression of humanizing honor and acts as an exchange of honor between host and guest (Georges and Baker 2016, 58).

Dawood,[7] a stateless Muslim asylum seeker from the Middle East, exclaimed, "I love the church. My family lived in a refugee camp in Greece, and then Holland, before coming to Belfast. Christians sat with us, prayed for us, fed my children, and gave us warm clothes. I love the church." Dawood's testimony poignantly describes the holistic power of hospitality to connect with displaced people as whole persons rather than as a crisis to be solved. As a result of these physical experiences of care and welcome, Dawood's prior resistance to the gospel has fallen away.

Hospitality requires the sharing of space, which risks violation of cultural values of quiet, order, and privacy. Opening boundaries up to the "other" necessitates the reconfiguration of our own identities and cultural values. Tolerating the presence of the "other" in our midst is not enough; Jesus welcomed his enemies into his own family with his *blood*. Boisterous children and differences in parenting practices will grate against a love of order and quiet. Christians risk others taking advantage of them. Opening our spaces and selves to communicate belonging to the "other" will assault our values of time and relational boundaries. A confrontation with deep need may expose our inner avarice—a tendency not only to hoard money and resources for the future, but also of time, energy, and our very selves. Many refugees and asylum seekers come from cultures where physical affection is more readily expressed, and hospitality may involve a sacrifice of personal space.

Mission as hospitality shifts the church from mission as controlled strategy to a vulnerable, "faithful presence," expressed through opening the whole self to the "other" through time and shared space (Smither 2021, 10). Mission through hospitality thus becomes mutually transformative, rather than a hegemonic act done by one to another.

For refugees from collectivistic cultures, trauma is most keenly felt in the disruption of belonging, which has been fractured by war, persecution, and

---

[7] His name has been changed to protect his identity.

displacement (Marlowe 2017, 71-83). Belonging entails connectivity with others and shared material and immaterial experiences—geography, history, time, food, traditions, celebrations, clothing, values and ideas. Belonging is symbolized in the sensory experiences of hospitality. For many Arabs, the billowing smoke and smell of *bukhoor* (Arabian incense) is deeply connected with hospitality and belonging. Eating familiar spices or dishes from home conveys comfort that no words can. Many Syrian and Yemeni refugees turn on YouTube videos wherein the videographer simply roams the streets of Syria or Yemen. The sounds of impassioned Arabic haggling in the *souk*, the call to prayer ringing through the air, and the cars honking recall their memory of home. Belonging and safety are experienced immensely through the senses.

Language and words communicate the embrace of the "other" in tremendous ways. Learning phrases in the "other's" native tongue, and also generously allowing them to fumble through their broken English while waiting patiently and kindly is an act of profound space-making. Using words to honor their identity *as they identify themselves* is another expression of hospitality. Many Kurds want to be known as Kurds, not as Syrians or Iraqis, for example. Few people want to be characterized as the most traumatic thing that ever happened to them, and the label of "refugee" or "asylum seeker" given by the government doesn't have to be the label we give them (Marlowe 2017, 36). One Syrian characterized his own identity as *daif*, the Arabic word for guest, rather than refugee, as it connotes greater dignity and implies hospitality on the part of his host nation (Zeno 2017, 290-91).

Hospitality, like reconciliation, must not remain theoretical or abstract; it must invade physical space and be expressed in tangible ways. Hospitality allows for a process of the "other" to move toward belonging not because of nationality, behavior, language, social standing, or other external symbols or intrinsic characteristics. Mission through hospitality draws "outsiders" of great diversity toward a relationship with a new center—Jesus Christ.

Reciprocity: Crossing Identity Boundaries

Just as reconciliation and embrace have reciprocal movements, so too does the practice of hospitality. Guest and host engage in a relational dance of opening up space and self and giving up space and self. A lack of reciprocity in hospitality is not hospitality, but a paternalistic donor-recipient paradigm that requires no relationship. This paradigm is not what God offers to his people. God's lavish grace to humanity in Christ is offered in a covenant, a relationship of uneven reciprocity between God and humanity. He gives salvation and all the attendant riches through his Son. In response, we relate to him with thanksgiving, prayer, praise, and offering our lives for his service and glory. The reciprocal relationship Christians have with God should transform Christian relationships with the "other" into a reciprocity of grace.

Refugees and asylum seekers are not just people with deep needs. As image-bearers of God, they have something that supplies our own lack. Hospitality shown *by* refugees and asylum seekers to the Northern Irish is proving deeply transformative. A Kurdish asylum seeker hosted Martin and Ruth, a Northern Irish couple, with extravagant hospitality in his small, shared apartment. He carefully saved his meager government stipend for weeks in order to provide a generous spread of food in gratitude for things they had helped him with. Martin and Ruth felt embarrassed and uncomfortable as recipients of such generosity, knowing what limited resources this man possessed, but they found that receiving his hospitality strengthened their relationship and lessened the power dynamic between them.

Many displaced people identify the ability to form reciprocal relationships in which they provide for the needs of others as an extremely important factor of mental health and wellbeing (Strang and Quinn 2021, 331–32). One aspect of Christian mission is fostering wholeness. Giving and receiving hospitality facilitates the formation of reciprocal relationships. Hospitality confers honor on those the world degrades with shame and brings wholeness through connectivity with others.

Western Christians, who often experience loneliness and isolation, have much to gain from the migrants in their midst who reflect God's own hospitality as image-bearers. They remind us that material resources are not the only resources (Dean 2013, 283). A group of Yemeni asylum seekers welcomed my husband into their group with humbling hospitality. They get together on weekends, sharing food, smoking, dancing, and telling stories of Yemen before the war. When a man arrived with a mobile phone to sell to the newest member of the group—a man from Chad, not Yemen—money came out from every shallow pocket until this newcomer had enough money to purchase the phone. The tiny chicken in the center of the plate of rice served as a visceral reminder that by giving this man money for a phone, many in the group might not eat tomorrow or even the next day.

> Western Christians, who often experience loneliness and isolation, have much to gain from the migrants in their midst.

An hour later, the group waved farewell to two Yemeni men who were leaving for Scotland. They were not part of the group but had been wandering around the city center that morning, waiting for their ferry which would leave in nine hours. The Yemeni group had invited these strangers to their modest apartment for a shower, a nap, and a meal. This communal sharing and generosity for strangers impacted my husband deeply. The boundaries between the in-group and the out-group were not hardened and crystallized for these Yemeni men; through radically generous hospitality, they drew their guests and themselves toward a relational center. Hospitality is not mere contact and toleration but a willingness to cross cultural and linguistic barriers, ethnic or socio-economic identity markers, and allowing the self to be impacted and given over to the "other."

Being a guest is a passive position with less control than hosting, and can be awkward, particularly if a power or status differential exists between guest and host. Being a guest is a direct challenge to Western hegemonic tendencies and opens the receiver up to deep vulnerability and risk. Being a guest, especially cross-culturally, often means not knowing what to expect or how to behave. When I lived in the Arabian Peninsula, the scorching heat, the cultural lack of concern for food temperature safety, and the relational expectations of being a good guest led to food poisoning many times.

Being a guest means risking a plate full of goat liver or a headache from being doused with perfume. Expectations of how much time should be spent on a visit differ across cultures, and guests risk the embarrassment of missing the social cues and staying either not long enough or too long. The lavish meal beyond the means of the host may make frugal Westerners extremely uncomfortable. Developing a true sense of mutuality by becoming a guest can significantly challenge a sense of superiority.

Conclusion

Hiebert's bounded and centered sets were originally applied to Christian conversion and to Christian communities to articulate how people who do not exhibit the same characteristics and behaviors can be included in the category of "Christian." True embodied reconciliation with the "other" requires a rejection of the personal and political rhetorical narratives of sharp, reified boundaries and homogeneous groups with a single fixed group identity. An application of Hiebert's model to the mission of reconciliation doesn't require the total dissolution of group identities, but a reorientation toward a new center and a focus on the processual and relational nature of mission rather than the defining characteristics of who is "us" and who is "them."

True reconciliation involves reconfiguring boundaries in order to truly embrace the "other." God's own existence in Trinity, of self-giving and other-receiving, offers a pattern for our own embodied living. The Father giving his Son for his enemies, Jesus's example of self-giving to the point of death even for those who tortured his body, and the abiding presence of the Holy Spirit among the members of his body are the foundation of the program of reconciliation Christians are to follow.

God drew near to those who were far off, offering a new center for belonging and identity in Christ. As God was the first reconciler whom we imitate in our relationships with the "other," so too is God the first host. As guests graciously received by God, we welcome others not only into our own space, but into his very life. The self-protecting boundaries and identity markers must fall, at risk to our own selves. We open ourselves with vulnerability to the "other" through hospitality, as we call others to join us at God's table with a new identity and belonging.

References Cited

Belfast Agreement. 1998. "The Belfast Agreement: An Agreement Reached at the Multi-Party Talks on Northern Ireland." https://assets.publishing.service.gov.uk/government/uploads/system/uploads/attachment_data/file/1034123/The_Belfast_Agreement_An_Agreement_Reached_at_the_Multi-Party_Talks_on_Northern_Ireland.pdf.

Belfast Interface Project. 2017. "Interface barriers, peace lines and defensive architecture." Belfast Interface Project, Belfast, UK. http://belfastinterfaceproject.org. Accessed March 27, 2022.

Boulton, J. 2014. "Frontier Wars: Violence and Space in Belfast, Northern Ireland." *Totem: The University of West Ontario Journal of Anthropology* 22, no. 1: 100–13.

Brubaker, Rogers. 2002. "Ethnicity without Groups." *European Journal of Sociology* 43 no. 2: 163–89.

Clark, Janine Natalya. 2019. "'Leaky' Bodies, Connectivity and Embodied Transitional Justice." *International Journal of Transitional Justice* 13, no. 2 (July): 268–89.

Dean, Marcus W. 2013. "Mutuality and Missions: The Western Christian in Global Ministry." *Missiology* 41, no. 3 (July): 273–85.

Dixon, John, Colin Tredoux, Brendan Sturgeon, Bree Hocking, Gemma Davies, Jonny Huck, Duncan Whyatt, Neil Jarman, and Dominic Bryan. 2020. "'When the Walls Come Tumbling Down': The Role of Intergroup Proximity, Threat, and Contact in Shaping Attitudes towards the Removal of Northern Ireland's Peace Walls." *The British Journal of Social Psychology* 59, no. 4 (October): 922–44.

Doebler, Stefanie, Ruth McAreavey, and Sally Shortall. 2018. "Is Racism the New Sectarianism? Negativity towards Immigrants and Ethnic Minorities in Northern Ireland from 2004 to 2015." *Ethnic and Racial Studies* 41, no. 14 (November): 2426–44.

Georges, Jayson, and Mark D. Baker. 2016. *Ministering in Honor-Shame Cultures: Biblical Foundations and Practical Essentials.* Downers Grove, IL: IVP Academic.

Goldenberg, Lisa. 2002. *The Symbolic Significance of the Irish Language in the Northern Ireland Conflict.* Dublin: The Columba Press.

Hall, Elizabeth Lewis. 2010. "What Are Bodies for? An Integrative Examination of Embodiment." *Christian Scholar's Review* 39, no. 2 (Winter): 159–75.

Herrault, Hadrien, and Brendan Murtagh. 2019. "Shared Space in Post-Conflict Belfast." *Space and Polity* 23, no. 3 (December): 251–64.

Hiebert, Paul G. 1978. "Conversion, Culture, and Cognitive Categories." *Gospel in Context* 1, no. 4: 24–29.

Hiebert, Paul G. 1994. "The Category Christian in the Mission Task." In *Anthropological Reflections on Missiological Issues*, 107–36. Grand Rapids, MI: Baker.

Jarrah, Mohaymen. 2018. "Making It in America: A Phenomenological Study of the Identity Reformation of Syrian Refugees." EdD Diss., George Washington University. ProQuest 10785201.

Kelly, Martina, Clark Svrcek, Nigel King, Albert Scherpbier, and Tim Dornan. 2020. "Embodying Empathy: A Phenomenological Study of Physician Touch." *Medical Education* 54, no. 5 (May): 400–7.

Lippard Cameron D., and Catherine McNamee. 2021. "Are Refugees Really Welcome? Understanding Northern Ireland Attitudes towards Syrian Refugees." *Journal of Refugee Studies* 34, no. 3: 3091–112.

Marlowe, Jay. 2017. *Belonging and Transnational Refugee Settlement: Unsettling the Everyday and the Extraordinary.* Studies in Migration and Diaspora. London: Routledge.

Mastors, Elena, and Nicole Drumhiller. 2014. "What's in a Flag? The Protestant Community's Identity, Symbols, and Protests in Belfast." *Peace and Change* 39, no. 4 (October): 495–518.

McEvoy, Joanne. 2011. "Managing Culture in Post-Conflict Societies." *Contemporary Social Science* 6, no. 1: 55–71.

Meredith, Robbie. 2019. "Syrian Refugees: Highest Proportion Resettled in Northern Ireland." BBC News, November 12, 2019. https://www.bbc.co.uk/news/uk-northern-ireland-50391731.

Mitchell, David, and Megan Miller. 2019. "Reconciliation through Language Learning? A Case Study of the Turas Irish Language Project in East Belfast." *Ethnic and Racial Studies* 42, no. 2 (February): 235–53.

Murtagh, Brendan, and Philip Boland. 2019. "Community Asset Transfer and Strategies of Local Accumulation." *Social and Cultural Geography* 20, no. 1 (January): 4–23.

Nagle, John. 2020. "Defying State Amnesia and Memorywars: Non-Sectarian Memory Activism in Beirut and Belfast City Centres." *Social and Cultural Geography* 21, no. 3: 380–401.

Pohl, Christine D. 1999. *Making Room: Recovering Hospitality as a Christian Tradition*. Grand Rapids, MI: Eerdmans.

Shirlow, Peter, and Brendan Murtagh. 2006. *Belfast: Segregation, Violence and the City*. Contemporary Irish Studies. London: Pluto Press.

Smither, Edward L. 2021. *Mission as Hospitality: Imitating the Hospitable God in Mission*. Eugene, Oregon: Cascade Books.

Strang, Alison B., and Neil Quinn. 2021. "Integration or Isolation? Refugees' Social Connections and Wellbeing." *Journal of Refugee Studies* 34, no. 1: 328–53.

UK Government. 2022. "UK Government Immigration Statistics, Year Ending March 2022." Gov.UK, May 26, 2022. https://www.gov.uk/government/statistics/immigration-statistics-year-ending-march-2022/how-many-people-do-we-grant-asylum-or-protection-to.

Ulster University. 2021. "Same Difference? Shared Education and Integrated Education," Education Briefing Paper 13. https://www.ulster.ac.uk/__data/assets/pdf_file/0016/1028320/TEUU-Report-13-Integrated-and-Shared-Education.pdf.

UNHCR. 2017. "UNHCR Study: Integration Efforts Advancing in UK Syria Refugee Settlement." United Nations, November 9, 2017. https://www.unhcr.org/uk/news/press/2017/11/5a0074234/unhcr-study-integration-efforts-advancing-in-uk-syria-refugee-resettlement.html.

Van der Kolk, Bessel. 2014. *The Body Keeps the Score: Brain, Mind, and Body in the Healing of Trauma*. New York: Penguin Random House.

Vimalasekaran, Peter. 2020. "Strategies for Reaching Refugees." In *Scattered and Gathered: A Global Compendium of Diaspora Missiology*, edited by Sadiri Joy Tira and Tetsunao Yamamori, 126–33. Carlisle, UK: Langham Global Library.

Volf, Miroslav. 2019. *Exclusion and Embrace: A Theological Exploration of Identity, Otherness, and Reconciliation*. Revised and Updated. Nashville: Abingdon Press.

Zeno, Basileus. 2017. "Dignity and Humiliation: Identity Formation among Syrian Refugees." *Middle East Law and Governance* 9, no. 3 (September): 282–97.

Chapter 9

Marked by Suffering

Discipleship, Sovereignty, and Suffering in the Gospel of Mark and in Mozambique

Alan Howell

Uhuva (to suffer) was one of the first words I learned when we began studying the Makua-Metto language. As a new resident in Mozambique, it took me a while to overcome my surprise at hearing this word used so often. Our friends and neighbors used it to describe a variety of physical ailments as well as to name the impact of brokenness and hardship in the world around them. *Uhuva* was used often in both personal conversations and public gatherings. To talk about the reconciling work of God then, would require addressing the reality and complexity of pain, separation, distress, and suffering. When we were learning the language and beginning our work of making disciples of Jesus for his kingdom in that part of Africa, the Gospel of Mark was the only Gospel that had been translated into their dialect. Over time, I began to appreciate the deep connections in Mark's Gospel between discipleship, suffering, and the sovereignty of Christ and the deep resonance it had within the African Folk-Islamic context of the Makua-Metto people.[1]

N. T. Wright says:

> Mark's Gospel functions as a little manual for Jesus's followers. It is structured very simply in two halves. The first eight chapters introduce us to the first secret: this Jesus of Nazareth is in fact the Messiah. The second eight chapters introduce us to the second secret: this Messiah is not the mighty warrior, but the Servant King. And at every point, Mark has told the story so as to say to us, his readers: do you get the point? Do you understand? And, if you do, are you prepared to follow this Jesus? Are you ready for a life of discipleship? (Wright 1995, 48)

---

1 Or Makhuwa-Meetto. While a label like "Folk Islam" can be problematic, it seems to be the most common descriptor for a context like this one that has been shaped by the historical influence of Islam as well as continued traditional religious practices. Catholicism also has been influential in this region of Mozambique.

At the center of this Gospel, we find an important intersection of these themes of sovereignty, suffering, and discipleship. In Mark 8:27-30, we have Peter's great confession or declaration that Jesus is the Messiah or King. Then in the following story (Mark 8:31-33), Jesus explains how his crown will come with a cross. Peter pulls him aside and tries to get him to stop talking about the ways his kingdom is linked to his death, but Jesus refuses to give in to that satanic way of thinking, saying that Peter has merely human concerns in mind. Jesus then links this way of suffering in his kingdom with discipleship (Mark 8:34-38). These three threads of discipleship, sovereignty, and suffering are beautifully woven together in this turning point in the narrative and recognizing that helps us notice them throughout Mark's Gospel.[2] This chapter will have two parts: first, we will explore the themes of discipleship, sovereignty, and suffering in the Gospel of Mark; second, we will look at those same themes in the context of northern Mozambique.

Discipleship, Sovereignty, and Suffering in the Gospel of Mark

Early Christian tradition suggests that Mark wrote his Gospel based on the testimony of the Apostle Peter and that they both were connected to the city of Rome.[3] While much remains unknown about the influences that shaped Mark as a writer, there are ancient resources that link him to the continent of Africa at the beginning and end of his life, as well as a significant historical precedent for recognizing that the African memory of Mark has been an important source of inspiration and courage for many.[4]

---

2 For other examples of these three themes in episodes outside of the passion narrative in Mark's Gospel see: 1:9-20; 2:1-17; 4:1-20; 5:1-20; 9:2-13; 10:32-52.

3 See Irenaeus, *Against Heresies* 3.1.1 (ca. 180) and Eusebius, *Eccl. Hist.* 3.39.13-15 (quoting Papias, ca. 110-140), 6.14.5-7 (referencing Clement of Alexandria, ca. 180). For a summary of the testimonies about Mark's Gospel from the early church fathers, see Oden and Hall (1998, xxi-xxix). Also, for more on "The Date and Provenance of Mark's Gospel" including a look at the Anti-Marcionite Prologue (ca. 160-180) as an additional early reference to Mark, see Ellis (1999, 357-76). While my paper is following the proposal that Mark's Gospel is linked to Rome, other scholars who doubt the Papias tradition "locate this Gospel in or near Palestine, usually in a rural context, perhaps Galilee or Syria. They date the Gospel during or just after the Roman-Judean War of 66 to 70 CE." (Rhoads 2012, 2). *Mark as Story* follows that proposal, assuming that the Gospel was originally created and performed "in northern Galilee or southern Syria, to a predominantly peasant audience of mostly Judeans and some Gentiles" (Rhoads 2012, 147).

4 Thomas Oden summarizes the testimony of sources "that Mark was born in Africa, wrote the Gospel of Mark in Rome, preached in Egypt, established the church in Alexandria, where he was imprisoned and suffered, and was comforted by an angel" (2011, 64-65; 178-79). Oden suggests that the memory of Mark could be a source of unity and reconciliation for Christians in Africa as different church traditions honor him "in explicit annual Catholic and ecumenical liturgical recollections of Mark as the first Christian martyr of Africa." He believes that "those who are

While taking seriously Mark's connections to Africa is helpful for our purposes, paying attention to the early witness that the Gospel was written with the church in Rome in mind is significant, as well.[5] Brian Incigneri makes a compelling case for reading Mark's Gospel as having "its origin in Rome" and being "composed in the latter months of 71CE in response to the stressful situation that existed for the Christians of that city" (Incigneri 2003, 2).[6] After having endured the persecution under Nero just a few years earlier, news of the destruction of the Temple in Jerusalem reaches them. That is then followed by witnessing Vespasian and Titus's triumphal entry into Rome which included, among other things, the parading of a torn Temple curtain as part of Rome's display of dominance over the Jewish people (Incigneri 2003, 202–7). That trauma would naturally provoke another crisis of belief and would seem like an ominous sign of things to come (Incigneri, 362–66). We can easily imagine them wondering: Will Christians in Rome once again suffer as scapegoats? (Incigneri 2003, 208).

Incigneri states that Mark's "Gospel reflects the deep religious anxiety of people who had suffered for years. In doubting the power and presence of God, the Christians in Rome faced the same questions that suffering people everywhere face, a prime reason for the ongoing power of this Gospel" (Incigneri 2003, 206). While this book certainly resonates because of the common, human experience of suffering, it also is rooted in specifics that the early disciples would be familiar with. In Mark's telling of Jesus's story, we find references to the forms of capital punishment that Christians in Rome could expect to experience: wild beasts, beheading, crucifixion, and fire, as well as torture and imprisonment (Incigneri 2003, 242).[7]

> Christians in Rome faced the same questions that suffering people everywhere face.

---

looking for an ecumenical beginning point for bringing together diverse Christian viewpoints of African Christianity will naturally turn to Mark. Mark's life and mission embodied the unity of the body of Christ. Mark remains a fixed point of reference for virtually all Christian believers in Africa today" (2011, 29). While this statement and others from Oden may be overly optimistic and lack the necessary nuance for speaking about the continent as a whole, I certainly agree that Mark's memory is a powerful potential resource for the church in Africa.

5 For a helpful overview of the authorship and audience of Mark see, Witherington (2001, 20–31).

6 While the reader may not be convinced by all the examples in Incigneri's argument, the overall picture he paints of the background of Mark's Gospel is impressive and compelling. Even if one sees a different setting as the background or timing of Mark's Gospel, the themes of suffering, sovereignty, and discipleship still remain extremely relevant.

7 Mark's comment that Jesus was "with the wild animals" in 1:13 has varying interpretations. Incigneri believes translating it as "with the beasts" helps us appreciate that it would have been read by Christians under Nero in Rome, following Tacitus (*Annals* 15.44), as linked to the torture and execution that members of the community had experienced (Incigneri 2003, 108–15).

Following this reading, Mark's Gospel, at least partially, functions to prepare disciples for suffering and martyrdom (Incigneri 2003, 82).[8] The shorter version of Mark ends, for example, with the followers of Jesus being afraid (Mark 16:8). If we understand that as the original ending, it can help us appreciate the big questions that the early disciples of Jesus were wrestling with: How will they respond to Jesus as King, in light of their own suffering? Will they be quiet, or will they share the good news? These questions related to sovereignty and suffering that hang in the air in Mark 16:8 are a provocative way to call readers to discipleship. An appreciation for the background of Mark sets the stage for this section of the chapter.

The first thread we will highlight is discipleship. To do so we will need to add another social location that shapes our reading of Mark's Gospel. In addition to what has been mentioned briefly about Africa and Rome, we will also need to consider how the context of Palestine shapes Christ's story. Jesus's role as Rabbi and his calling of disciples, while certainly having parallels in the Greco-Roman context, is significantly shaped by the Jewish context.[9] We will note five observations about the Rabbi-Disciple relationship that are relevant to our topic:[10]

1. In the New Testament, the terms for Rabbi appear seventeen times, while the Greek equivalent for teacher occurs fifty-nine times. In Mark's Gospel, Jesus is called Rabbi (9:5; 11:21; 10:15; 14:45) by disciples. He is called teacher (Διδάσκαλος) by crowds (9:17; 10:1), a scribe (12:32), Pharisees (12:14), Sadducees (12:18), and disciples (4:38; 10:35; 13:1) (Wenthe 2006, 167, 168).
2. Jesus had a surprisingly open admissions policy for disciples, allowing all who expressed a desire to become disciples. While "sharing the more open attitude of the school of Hillel," Jesus seems to have extended that

---

8 Also see Incigneri (2003, 120, 224–25, 238–39, 263–65, 289, 347–49, 366). For those who reject the path of martyrdom initially, Incigneri sees Peter as an archetype for disciples who disowned Jesus because of pressure or persecution (2003, 321).

9 Dean Wenthe notes historical Jewish influences shaping the role of Rabbi in Jesus's day like Ezra and Ben Sira as representatives of the scribal office (Wenthe 2006, 148–50), but believes that "it is more probable that the Rabbi-Disciple relationship's educational antecedents" come from Hellenistic influence more than precedence in the Hebrew Scriptures (143, ft 2). Wenthe argues that "the Rabbi-disciple relationship was a distinctive synthesis of various antecedents. From the Greek and Hellenic world, it derived its distinctive form—a teacher attended by a circle of pupils. From the heritage of Israel, and especially that priestly piety which focused on Torah—explicated by scribe and wise man—it received its content" (Wenthe 2006, 171).

10 For a broad introduction to understanding Jesus as Rabbi in comparison with other Rabbis, see Brad Young (2007). One complication for this topic is "that rabbinic sources were compiled or redacted at later dates than the New Testament" although that does not necessarily "rule out their relevancy" (Neudecker 1999, 246).

approach "by calling fishermen (Mark 1:16) and even tax collectors" (Mark 2:13–17) (Neudecker 1999, 249, ft. 11).

3. The serious commitment between master and disciple meant that if a disciple was sent into exile, then it was "expected that the master would go with him in order to provide the disciple with spiritual guidance. If the master has to go into exile they accompany him" (Neudecker 1999, 251–52).
4. "The death of a rabbi was a major trauma for the circle of disciples" (Wenthe 2006, 160).[11]
5. "The Rabbi-Disciple relationship ... would have occupied a most significant and strategic position in first century Palestine ... as they possessed the potential and actual means to foster social change" (Wenthe 2006, 172).[12]

Discipleship provided a framework that Jesus leveraged to spread the message of his kingdom in a way that was contextually appropriate and significant.[13] Jesus's role as Rabbi meant that he was the authoritative teacher for the community of disciples, and that authority mattered more than the disciples' own backgrounds or qualifications. That connection also meant that disciples would share their master's fate—even in suffering, exile, and death. In Mark's Gospel we also see Jesus's authoritative example in his compassion as he used his power to impact both individuals and institutions, living in the tension between God's goodness, God's power, and human suffering. Discipleship to Jesus, then, following his authoritative example, even at great personal cost, is the best way to navigate that tension.

That leads us to the second thread or theme we will explore: Sovereignty. While the language of kingdom and "standing before kings" occurs throughout the Gospel of Mark,[14] "king" as a title appears only in chapters 6 and 15. Herod is referred to as king in the story of his role in the lead up to the death of John the Baptist (6:14, 22, 25–26). For Mark's purposes, we can see this used in an ironic sense as Herod is the antithesis, the anti-king, in contrast to Jesus.

---

11 In synthesizing the extensive work of Jacob Neusner, Dean Wenthe names this as one of seventeen observations in his "composite of what the Rabbi-Disciple relationship was like in the first century CE" (Wenthe 2006, 158).

12 For more on the background and implications of seeing Jesus as a Rabbi, see Köstenberger (1998).

13 The seriousness and flexibility of this category gave it much potential power for shaping others. Being disciples, around the time of the New Testament, meant being "committed to a recognized leader or teacher or movement, and the relationships ran the spectrum from philosophical (in Philo, *Sacrifices* 7.4; 64.10; 79.10) to technical (rabbinical scribes; *Aboth* 1.1; Shabbat 31a) to sectarian (Pharisees in Josephus, *Antiq.* 13.289; 15.3,370) to revolutionary (zealotlike nationalists in Midrash *Shir Hashirim Zuta*)" (Wilkins 1992, 82).

14 "Kingdom" references in Mark: 1:15; 3:24 (x2); 4:11, 26, 30; 6:23; 9:1, 47; 10:14–15, 23–25; 11:10; 12:34; 13:8 (x2); "standing before kings" in 13:9; 14:25; 15:43.

Jesus is then referred to as King of the Jews in the lead up to his own death (15:2, 9, 12, 18, 26, 32). In that section, Pilate uses this title multiple times and we also have royal symbols like the purple robe and a crown of thorns being placed on Jesus (15:17–18). And in case the reader has somehow missed the messaging, there is a placard with Christ's regal title placed above him (15:26) as he suffers on the cross and dies. Mark wants to show us that Jesus is the true King and that this is what being a king really looks like. Suffering is a part of this story—not suffering inflicted on others but suffering as part of the story of the Sovereign himself. The King is enthroned by being killed; there is no crown without the cross.

Another way that the theme of sovereignty plays a role is in the scenes where we see Jesus's authority on display. In Mark 4:35–6:56, Jesus is the master over nature, demons, sickness and death. He is also a compassionate lord—he has compassion for his followers, the crowds, and those who are hurting and suffering. All kinds of people are asking who Jesus is (disciples, people from his hometown, King Herod), but surprisingly only a demon possessed man seems to know his "secret" identity ("Son of God"). In this encounter, the man known for the legion of demons inside of him throws himself at Jesus's feet. This opposing army is surrendering to Jesus's authority. Legion waves the white flag and requests terms of peace where Christ would send the demonic army into a herd of pigs.[15] In the following story as well, we see other people who, in the face of their own sickness and suffering, surrender and throw themselves at Jesus's feet (Mark 5:22, 33).

Jesus is certainly seen as the powerful king and rabbi who calls people to follow him, and those concepts of sovereignty and discipleship are linked to the third theme or thread we will explore: Suffering. Throughout Mark's Gospel we see him both expelling suffering (using his power and authority to address the pain in the world around him; ex. Mark 5:26, 29, 34) and expecting suffering (he names and predicts that he, the "Son of Man," will also suffer and be rejected; Mark 8:31; 9:12).

While suffering is a crucial part of any hero's journey, Jesus's encounters with suffering and his own experience of suffering is extreme.[16] Mark portrays

---

15 For a thoughtful summary of the Post-Colonial perspective on this story and the potential political layers of meaning linking the demoniac with the Roman tenth legion, which "was based in Syria-Palestine and had a wild boar as the insignia on its standards and seal," see Bird (2018, 81).

16 Dennis MacDonald notes that suffering is a "dominant theme" in Homer's epic tale and suggests that Mark is borrowing or repurposing the story of Odysseus, the suffering hero, to shape the story of Jesus to show that he is "more virtuous and powerful than Odysseus and Hector" (McDonald 2000, 2–3, 16–17, 42). While there may be some echoes of Homer in Mark's Gospel, I believe the similarities in the narratives are rooted in the common human

Jesus as the Suffering Servant of God throughout the Gospel, one who is willing to give up his life (10:45), and then "only in the closing verses," Mark 16:6, "is the suffering of Jesus given titular expression" as he is called the Crucified One (Broadhead 1999, 107).[17] So, his identity is ultimately linked to his crucifixion. While questions may be posed about why exactly Jesus needed to suffer (Stevens 1987), Mark seems to skip past those queries to deal with the reality of Jesus's suffering and its resonance for the disciples' own experience of suffering (Vilijoen 2002). Jesus's experience of suffering gives expression to our own experience of suffering in three meaningful ways.

Lament Psalms and the Passion of the Lord—Ahearne-Kroll argues that five psalms of lament (21, 40, 41, 42, and 68) are evoked in Mark 14–15 and these quotations serve to "foreground the voice of the suffering" King David as our way of interpreting Jesus's own suffering (Ahearne-Kroll 2007, 1, 169, 213). This approach, instead of the more typical Isaiah 53 influenced reading, gives us a narrative connection between their experiences of betrayal (Judas in Mark 14:43–50; Ahithophel in 2 Sam 17:23) and helps "define Jesus as the suffering Davidic Messiah" (Ahearne-Kroll 38, 167).

By tapping into the lament psalms in Mark's Gospel, disciples of Jesus find within the Scriptures the capacity to push back against unsatisfying answers to the reasons for Jesus's suffering (such as, "as it is written" or "because it is God's will") (Ahearne-Kroll 2007, 188), or even pointing to the resurrection as the way to resolve the tension. Instead of explaining it away, in Mark's Gospel we find a reconciling Lord who is willing to inhabit human suffering and trauma with us.[18]

---

experience of suffering and the common quest for heroes to respond well to those challenges. One key difference between the heroes, that MacDonald also notes is that, "When Homer's hero returned to Ithaca he slew his opponents; when Jesus returned to Judea his opponents slew *him*" (McDonald 2000, 17).

17 Edwin Broadhead notes that the "Servant of God" title has an ambiguous and broad background in the Hebrew Scriptures and an enigmatic role in the New Testament (Broadhead 1999, 101). Ultimately, though, he sees this as a "passion metaphor which moves out from the scenes of Jesus' death to encompass the whole of his story" (Broadhead 1999, 107). Broadhead concludes, "Despite the ambiguity of its historical content, the servant image is endowed by the scheme of this Gospel with persuasive descriptive power. It is Jesus' story which provides the standards by which to interpret this title, and not the reverse. In the faithful suffering of Jesus, the mission of the Servant is realized" (Broadhead 1999, 108).

18 "This is not a linear story where resurrection solves the problem of suffering. It is a circular story where suffering and resurrection seem equally and inseparably important to Mark; therefore, we cannot think of the resurrection as the last word in Mark. ... The cross is what makes the story of Jesus so compelling in Mark. Anything that sidesteps the horror or glorifies the suffering distorts Mark's presentation of Jesus' death." Mark appeals to the Psalms of Lament "to make sense of Jesus' suffering" is not a way to "explain away or sidestep the horror by claiming that it is okay because God willed it or by making it the first episode in a divine plan of eschatological vindication of the Righteous Sufferer. But inclusion of these

Prayer as a way to embody the will of God in the tension between God's sovereignty and our suffering—In Jesus's teaching about prayer and his practice of prayer in Mark's Gospel, he chooses to follow not the way of "power *or* suffering, but the will of God" (Dowd 1988, 33). Even in the midst of persecution and martyrdom, "prayer functions in the gospel to remind the community that the power they experience comes from God and is accessible only through prayer (9:29) and that in losing their lives for Jesus' sake and for the sake of the gospel they are the faithful who 'do the will of God.' The community is influenced to prayer, expecting power and accepting suffering" (Dowd 1988, 33).

Prayer, then is better than "a rational solution to the problem of theodicy." In Mark, it is instead "the practice in which the tension between power and suffering is faithfully maintained" (Dowd 1988, 164). That tension is linked to the other tension that Jesus ultimately embraces and embodies, as in the course of Mark's narrative the tension between his suffering and sovereignty is dramatically displayed through his body hanging on the cross.

Solidarity in Suffering and in (Mis)understanding—The persecuted church is in good company when it stands with Jesus. In the face of meaningless suffering, when the people of God feel the weight of their trauma or their own apparent abandonment by God, they can find solidarity in a story of their Lord's suffering, where in his own final moment "(15:37), Jesus just screams" (Incigneri 2003, 252). Disciples of Jesus can experience terrible grief and even death at the hands of Roman authorities. Their martyrdom, as faithful witnesses unto death, turns their persecutors into witnesses, as well. In Mark 15:39, the centurion, after seeing how Jesus cried and died, stated that he was a "Son of God." While we may debate whether this comment is an honest assessment, sarcasm, or an ironic mix of both, "perhaps we should simply say the centurion says more than he knows" (Witherington 2001, 400, ft. 170). Suffering reveals Jesus and his disciples' identities as true children of God and makes the powers and people of this world witnesses to it, whether they fully understand what it is they are witnessing or not.

Mark's Gospel is a tapestry, offering a narrative that is a word of encouragement and challenge to a church facing a variety of pressures.[19] These

---

psalms in the story of Jesus' suffering weaves into the story an ancient tradition of endurance, crying out to God in the midst of suffering, and faithful dissent. It seems that Mark's attempt at understanding Jesus' suffering and death is just as much about Mark's appreciation of the horror of human suffering as it is about the hope that belief in Jesus' resurrection can generate for Mark's readers" (Ahearne-Kroll 2007, 225–26).

19 While this chapter has focused on external pressures, Michael Trainor notes that internal divisions were also a factor. "It seems clear that all was not well and happy in Mark's community. The romantic picture often painted by some of a 'golden age' of the first century CE Christian community is far from the truth. If there is any veracity in Tacitus' account of the Roman Christians, it seems that Mark's household was torn by internal divisions, betrayal,

three themes of discipleship, sovereignty and suffering are woven together in the Gospel of Mark in such a way that pulling on any one of them reveals connections to the other threads as well.

Suffering, Sovereignty and Discipleship in Mozambique

In this section, we will look at our three themes from the perspective of the Makua-Metto culture. We will briefly survey how Islam shapes an understanding of suffering, how the authority structures of traditional kings frames the concept of sovereignty, and then how discipleship is viewed through the lived experience of apprenticeships in northern Mozambique.

"*Pare de Sofrer!*" This slogan ("Stop Suffering!") appears on signs used to promote certain churches in Mozambique.[20] It seems surprising that gatherings ostensibly organized to point people to the person of Jesus lead with a message about freedom from suffering. While we can surely appreciate how Christianity is a liberation from certain kinds of suffering, the fact that Jesus is the "Suffering Servant" who calls us to follow him in taking up our crosses, should indicate that suffering will be a significant part of a disciple's story.

> Promoting Christianity as an end to suffering does not reflect a robust reading of the Gospel of Mark.

Promoting Christianity as an end to suffering does not reflect a robust reading of the Gospel of Mark, and it does not equip disciples of Jesus with resources or responses for suffering.[21] Jesus himself suffered, and as the other synoptic Gospels make clear, a student is not above his teacher (Matt 10:24; Luke 6:40). Since suffering is part of the path to glory for Christ, it is also part of our journey in discipleship.

Promoting Christianity as an end to suffering does not reflect a robust reading of our African context either. The introduction to this chapter referenced how *uhuva* (suffering) was a key word among the Makua-Metto people and how that provided a natural connection point to the Gospel of Mark. Suffering is a major theme in this African Folk-Islamic Context (Howell 2012), but it is also a significant theme for Muslims across the globe. Lawson

---

and power struggles. The evangelist wrote the gospel as a way to address the confusion and strife that was being experienced. Mark was able to recognize the seriousness of the division in the gospel household and sought to respond to it" (2001, 185–86). So, reconciliation is something that is needed both inside and outside the community of faith.

20 For an example sign from Brazil, see Peniponte (2012).

21 While this chapter's focus is Christological, a related topic that is beyond the scope of this study, would be to explore further the connections between suffering, sovereignty, and discipleship in relation to a robust Pneumatology (not the extreme "name it and claim it" of certain forms of Pentecostalism, but the way the Spirit is linked to possession, presence, and power).

notes that, "Muslims are suffering. In most cases where Muslims are turning to Christ, it has had something to do with suffering" (Lawson 2012, 92).[22] It is a topic that must be addressed as part of holistic reconciliation.

When we look to the Qur'an to see what internal resources or responses Muslims have for dealing with suffering from their main religious text, we find multiple references to suffering (e.g., Q 29:10; 64:11). John Bowker notes that the Qur'an focuses on actual experience of suffering, not suffering as a theoretical problem (Bowker 1969, 185). The Qur'an approaches suffering as punishment for sin, as a trial or test, and in some ways as a "necessary part of the purposes of God" in forming human character and revealing a person's "true worth" (Bowker 1969, 190, 192, 194). Because of the strong emphasis on God's omnipotence and compassion, suffering is "almost dissolved as a problem" (Bowker 1969, 186). That version of omnipotence shapes the qur'anic approach to the story of Jesus, assuming that "the crucifixion cannot be true because that would mean the defeat of God: it would mean that he had failed to rescue one of his faithful servants" (Bowker 1969, 202).

In three passages (Q 3:55; 4:156–59; 5:117), we find a rejection of Jesus's death by crucifixion. Ayman Ibrahim notes that "while some of these texts are ambiguous, the point is that Jesus never died on the cross. … The Koranic Jesus is honored and highly esteemed but was not crucified" and someone else was crucified in his place (Ibrahim 2020, 114–15). While the Qur'an's focus on suffering is formed by an attitude of "acceptance that God is in control," "advocating positive action against particular instances of suffering" and prayer, Christianity has more space for trauma as it, "allows for a greater awareness of the genuine nature of tragedy and defeat. … When Jesus was crucified … there was darkness over all the land" (Bowker 1969, 199, 202).

The picture of the reconciling work of Jesus in Mark's Gospel is one of embracing suffering in the passion as well as embracing human suffering through his compassion. Diane Stinton notes that "the meaning of Christ's death and resurrection in relation to the African experience of suffering is absolutely central" (Stinton 2004, 37). "The Qur'an cuts through the problem of suffering by saying that it is within the control of God, and that in a sense, therefore, it comes from him. … But this raises serious questions about the character of God: to think of God as having created suffering to be an inherent fact of creation might be impressive in terms of omnipotence but not in terms of compassion" (Bowker 1969, 189).[23]

---

22 This quote appears among comments about suffering because of cruelty at the hands of other Muslims.

23 For a very helpful work, addressed to the North American context on the topic of suffering and the tension between omnipotence and omnibenevolence in different schools of Islam, see Jackson (2009, 17, 18). Also see, Watt (1979) and Ayoub (1978).

This connection between control (omnipotence) and compassion (omnibenevolence) is a helpful link to the second thread we will explore in this section: the concept of sovereignty. From a Christian perspective, if we want to understand the sovereignty of God, we need to look at the sovereignty of Jesus. Contextualizing that doctrine will require awareness of Mozambican conceptions of sovereignty.

Among the Makua-Metto people, the default traditional leadership structure is a system of kings and chiefs.[24] As I have interacted with kings (and even kings of kings) over the years, I have come to appreciate the way that their authority is both strong and weak—an interesting mix of positional and relational authority. The national government has tended to swing between extremes in their relationship with traditional kings, sometimes downplaying their role and other times leaning on them to assist in governance and to legitimize their own authority. In interviews, I learned that at times their positions of authority caused traditional kings to be targets for violence, and sometimes people with leadership abilities would find creative ways to resist being chosen as leaders.[25] The potential suffering that could come because of even a very limited type of sovereignty or authority would often cause talented people not to lead. In Jesus, though, we see a King who accepts both sovereignty and suffering as part of his story.[26]

Finally, let's consider the connections between Jesus's story and our stories in our third theme: discipleship. In Makua-Metto, the word for *apprentice* is the same word that is commonly used for *disciple*. There is a strong cultural assumption that a person needs to go through an apprenticeship to do any kind of task or profession.[27] That dynamic was helpful in talking about discipleship because it emphasized the process involved in learning and growing in any way of life. One interviewee shared the story of his son who apprenticed to become a mechanic. This interviewee's son had to pay the master to be accepted as an apprentice and then needed to make a final payment to be confirmed by him

---

24 For more on the authority of kings among the Makua-Metto people and particularly how that relates to Christology, see Howell and Best (2021).

25 I did individual interviews on this topic and then discussed these findings with small groups or classes of mostly men (over one hundred participants total at different stages in the development of these ideas).

26 John Bowker notes "the different attitudes of Jesus and Muhammad when facing the possibility of their own defeat and death: Jesus in Gethsemane opted for the way to the cross, Muhammad at the *hijra* opted for the way of success, for the way of co-operating with the power of God, and of becoming God's agent in the elimination of evil and injustice" (Bowker 1970, 123).

27 In conversations and classes on this topic in Mozambique, we would talk through the variety of informal and formal apprenticeship relationships in that context like carpenter, soldier, nurse, and even becoming a thief. In each case, the apprentice needed to take on the posture of learner as they submitted to formation in their new vocation.

or "graduate." The family threw a party to celebrate, and the master presented him with some tools to mark his new status. This mix of formal and informal symbols in the master-apprentice relationship provided layers of meaning that were relevant to compare and contrast with the process of becoming disciples of Jesus as well.

Devaka Premawardhana tells a story of something that happened among a neighboring Makua people living in the Province of Niassa. For years, the Mozambican government had encouraged them to move from near the rivers to the roads, promising that moving from the bush would provide access to schools and medical care, and protect them from dangerous wildlife. Many of the people in the villages though felt deceived as the threat from elephants increased. One day, a man was tragically killed by an elephant in the village of Lioma. When the governor of Niassa Province passed through the village for a pre-arranged visit a few days later, he did not address the attack or listen to their concerns. He merely stepped out of his Land Cruiser and gave a short speech before speeding away to the district capital.

The village had been awaiting this honored guest but the visit "left everyone dispirited, more than the elephant attack already had." The chief of the village told Premawardhana that he was disappointed that the governor had not taken time to listen and that a good leader would abide by the proverb: to be chief or king, "is to walk among the people (*Okhala mwene wettá n'atthu*). The governor's willingness to drive up to, but not walk among, the inhabitants of Lioma, was further proof that the state does not care to notice them, to understand their problems or to bother with their solutions" (Premawardhana 2018, 59–60).

Jesus is a Chief/King and Rabbi who walks with his students and willingly bears the yoke that he calls his disciples to wear (Howell and Montgomery 2018). His commitment to walk with them through all kinds of suffering to bring about reconciliation is a powerful connection point for the Makua-Metto people. Metto or Meetto means "leg" and while interviewees have given different reasons for the application of that term to this people group,[28] leveraging that connection in their name to walking as a metaphor for discipleship has been useful. Discipleship is walking with the Master as he reveals the ways of the living God in the world (Wilkins 1992, 18, 58–59). Discipleship to Jesus as the new Israel links us corporately to a forefather (Jacob) who wrestled with God and then walks with a limp because of it (Gen 32:22–32). Jesus goes before us and models how to prayerfully walk through the valley of suffering and exist in that tension between the power and goodness of God.

---

28 Some say it comes from their tendency to walk long distances and be very mobile, while others believe its origin is in the old practice of appealing to traditional kings by stating that they are "grabbing their leg" to make a request or appeal.

The cross then is what makes Jesus so compelling. In a world full of "gods" who are powerful and victorious, we need a God who willingly suffers (and walks) with us. Jesus does not suffer so we will not have to—instead he shows us how God's sovereignty is at work even amid martyrdom and death and paves the way for us to be reconciled to him and to follow him in that path of discipleship even as it leads us through suffering. That perspective, found in the Gospel of Mark, resonates with significant themes in this African Folk-Islamic context, especially in light of the authority structures of traditional kings and how discipleship is viewed through the lived experience of apprenticeships.

Conclusion

I was one of the last passengers to climb into the back of a large truck carrying people from the district of Chiure back to our home in the town of Montepuez. By the time I arrived, all the seats on benches around the sides of the vehicle were occupied, so I sat down on the floor of the truck bed. As the automobile started down the road, someone commented in Makua-Metto about this White Westerner who had joined them in the bus and how it was odd that I had not leveraged my perceived status to try to claim a seat on a bench. No one knew who I was or realized that I could speak their language. So, as we moved along the road, I listened to a lively conversation about their interpretation of my suffering and suffering in general, with reference to both Islam and Christianity. At a lull in the discussion, I spoke up and noted that I found it significant that the story of Jesus makes it clear that God also knows about suffering. God knows what it is like to lose a child, to suffer unjustly, to experience betrayal and death, even death on a humiliating cross. After getting over their surprise at my awareness and ability to participate in the conversation in Makua-Metto, the discussion continued as we considered the way Jesus speaks to the reality of human suffering.

Suffering is a key connection point for interreligious dialogue with people from a Muslim background in Mozambique and other contexts as well.[29] This topic can serve to highlight the ways that God is involved in the work of reconciliation. In this chapter, we have been reading the Gospel of Mark as a "little manual for disciples" (Wright 1995, 48). We have seen how the connections between the themes or threads of discipleship, suffering, and sovereignty can help us frame pain and trauma appropriately (both personally and collectively).[30]

---

29 For many who come from a background of privilege, the central question is "Does God Exist?" But for those who have experienced deep suffering, a more relevant question often is "Does God care?" (Jackson 2009, 13–18; Jones 1998, 151).

30 Two works that I am convinced are essential resources in this regard are Van der Kolk (2014) and Cone (2011).

We can even find a way to be reconciled to one another by following the path laid out for us by Christ. It is not that Jesus suffers so we won't have to—instead Jesus suffers and shows us how to suffer well. This King is a suffering servant, and the Gospel of Mark ends with important question marks. How will we respond to this suffering king? Will we take up our crosses and follow him? Will we follow him as our Rabbi and King and allow his way of responding to suffering to be our own? By leaning into these questions and living in the tensions that they bring, we can walk with others down a robust path of discipleship even when our common lived experience is marked by suffering.

References Cited

Ahearne-Kroll, Stephen P. 2007. *The Psalms of Lament in Mark's Passion: Jesus' Davidic Suffering.* New York: Cambridge University Press.

Ayoub, Mahmoud Mustafa. 1978. *Redemptive Suffering in Islam.* London: Brill.

Bird, Michael F. 2018. "The Testament of Solomon and Mark 5:1-20: Exorcism and Power over Evil Spirits." In *Reading Mark in Context: Jesus and Second Temple Judaism*, edited by Ben C. Blackwell, John C. Goodrich, and Jason Maston, 77–83. Grand Rapids, MI: Zondervan.

Bowker, John. 1969. "The Problem of Suffering in the Qur'an." *Religious Studies* 4, no. 2: 183–202.

Bowker, John. 1970. *Problems of Suffering in Religions of the World.* New York: Cambridge University Press.

Broadhead, Edwin K. 1999. *Naming Jesus: Titular Christology in the Gospel of Mark.* Journal for the Study of the New Testament Supplement Series, no. 175. Sheffield, UK: Sheffield Academic Press.

Cone, James H. 2011. *The Cross and the Lynching Tree.* Maryknoll, NY: Orbis Books.

Dowd, Sharyn E. 1988. *Prayer, Power, and the Problem of Suffering: Mark 11:22–25 in the Context of Markan Theology.* SBL Dissertation Series, no. 105. Atlanta: Scholars Press.

Ellis, E. Earle. 1999. *The Making of the New Testament Documents.* Biblical Interpretation Series, no. 39. Leiden, Netherlands: Brill.

Eusebius, and Hugh Jackson Lawlor. 1926. *The Ecclesiastical History.* Translated by Kirsopp Lake and J. E. L. Oulton. The Loeb Classical Library. Cambridge, MA: Harvard University Press.

Howell, Alan. 2012. "Turning It Beautiful: Divination, Discernment and a Theology of Suffering." *International Journal of Frontier Missiology* 29, no. 3: 129–37.

Howell, Alan, and R. Andrew Montgomery. 2018. "Jesus as Mwalimu: Christology and the Gospel of Matthew in an African Folk Islamic Context." *International Journal of Frontier Missiology* 35, no. 2: 79–87.

Howell, Alan, and Garrett Best. 2021. "Apocalypse, Authority, and Allegiance: Interpreting Symbols and Revelation in Mozambique." *Transformation: An International Journal of Holistic Mission Studies* 38, no. 2: 124–37.

Ibrahim, Ayman S. 2020. *A Concise Guide to the Quran*. Grand Rapids, MI: Baker Academic.

Incigneri, Brian J. 2003. *The Gospel to the Romans: The Setting and Rhetoric of Mark's Gospel*. Biblical Interpretation Series, no. 65. Boston: Brill.

Irenaeus. 2012. "Against the Heresies." Edited by M. C. Steenberg. Translated by Dominic J. Unger. *Ancient Christian Writers*, no. 64. New York: Newman Press.

Jackson, Sherman A. 2009. *Islam and the Problem of Black Suffering*. New York: Oxford University Press.

Jones, William R. 1998. *Is God a White Racist?: A Preamble to Black Theology*. Boston: Beacon Press.

Köstenberger, Andreas J. 1998. "Jesus as Rabbi in the Fourth Gospel." *Bulletin for Biblical Research* 8: 97–128.

Lawson, Warren F. 2012. "Current Trends in Islam and Christian Mission." In *Toward Respectful Understanding and Witness among Muslims: Essays in Honor of J. Dudley Woodberry*, edited by Evelyne A. Reisacher, 87–94. Pasadena, CA: William Carey Library.

MacDonald, Dennis R. 2000. *The Homeric Epics and the Gospel of Mark*. New Haven, CT: Yale University Press.

Neudecker, Reinhard. 1999. "Master-Disciple/Disciple-Master Relationship in Rabbinic Judaism and in the Gospels." *Gregorianum* 80, no. 2: 245–61.

Oden, Thomas, and C. A. Hall, eds. 1998. *Mark*. The Ancient Christian Commentary on Scripture, vol 2. Downers Grove, IL: InterVarsity Press.

Oden, Thomas. 2011. *The African Memory of Mark: Reassessing Early Church Tradition*. Downers Grove, IL: IVP Academic.

Peniponte. 2012. "Sobre a companha publicitária 'Pare de Sofrer.'" ["About the Advertising Campaign 'Stop Suffering'"] *Sobre O* (blog), December 12, 2012. https://penipotente.wordpress.com/2012/12/12/sobre-a-companha-publicitaria-pare-de-sofrer/.

Premawardhana, Devaka. 2018. *Faith in Flux: Pentecostalism and Mobility in Northern Mozambique*. Philadelphia: University of Pennsylvania Press.

Rhoads, David M. 2012. *Mark as Story: An Introduction to the Narrative of a Gospel*. Edited by Joanna Dewy and Donald Michie. 3rd ed. Minneapolis, MN: Fortress Press.

Stevens, Bruce A. 1987. "'Why Must the Son of Man Suffer?': The Divine Warrior in the Gospel of Mark." *Biblische Zeitschrift* 31, no. 1: 101–10.

Stinton, Diane B. 2004. *Jesus of Africa: Voices of Contemporary African Christology*. Maryknoll, NY: Orbis Books.

Tacitus, Cornelius, Clifford Herschel Moore, and John Jackson. 1925. *Annals*. The Loeb Classical Library. Cambridge, MA: Harvard University Press.

Trainor, Michael F. 2001. *The Quest for Home: The Household in Mark's Community*. Collegeville, MN: The Liturgical Press.

Van der Kolk, Bessel A. 2014. *The Body Keeps the Score: Brain, Mind, and Body in the Healing of Trauma*. New York: Viking.

Viljoen, F. P. 2002. "Mark, the Gospel of the Suffering Son of Man: An Encouragement Directed to a Despondent Religious Minority in the City of Rome." *Die Skriflig* 36, no. 3: 455–74.

Watt, W. Montgomery. 1979. "Suffering in Sunnite Islam." *Studia Islamica* 50: 5–19.

Wenthe, Dean O. 2006. "The social configuration of the Rabbi-disciple relationship: evidence and implications for First Century Palestine." In *Studies in the Hebrew Bible, Qumran, and the Septuagint presented to Eugene Ulrich*, edited by Peter W. Flint, Emanuel Tov, and James C. VanderKam, 143–74. Vestus Testamentum, vol. 101. Leiden, Netherlands: Brill.

Wilkins, Michael J. 1992. *Following the Master: A Biblical Theology of Discipleship*. Grand Rapids, MI: Zondervan.

Witherington III, Ben. 2001. *The Gospel of Mark: A Socio-Rhetorical Commentary*. Grand Rapids, MI: Eerdmans.

Wright, N. T. 1995. *Following Jesus: Biblical Reflections on Discipleship*. Grand Rapids, MI: Eerdmans.

Young, Brad H. 2007. *Meet the Rabbis: Rabbinic Thought and the Teachings of Jesus*. Grand Rapids, MI: Baker Academic.

Part 3
Reconciliation Case Studies

Chapter 10

Ethnicity, Reconciliation, and the Church in Myanmar

Arend A. C. Van Dorp

Missionary work in Myanmar has seen only limited response among the Bamar (ethnic Burmese) people, while the Karen and other minorities have shown much greater openness and receptivity (Maung Shwe Wa 1963, 67–70). Thus, the churches in Myanmar are overwhelmingly made up of ethnic minority people. Moreover, many churches are ethno-culturally defined and predominantly consist of a single ethnic group. This ethnolinguistic demarcation between Myanmar churches creates a significant obstacle for others outside these ethnolinguistic groups to join (Thant Myint-U 2007, 210–11). It also clashes with an understanding of the church as a universal body of believers from diverse ethnic, social, and cultural backgrounds.

The monocultural makeup of many churches makes it extremely difficult for Bamar converts to integrate into a church. Whereas in the larger society they occupy a dominant and privileged position, in the church they often find themselves marginalized, or at least in a minority position (Ngun Ling 2014, 45–51). In order for Christians in Myanmar to break out of this isolation and make a significant impact in this largely Buddhist country, the church will need to abandon its strong ethnic identity and embrace a more inclusive ecclesiology.

Bamar Pride and Prejudice

The Republic of the Union of Myanmar is not a homogeneous society. The history of Burma has long been characterized by the struggle of the Burmans to control the non-Burman segments of the population, and non-Burman resistance to these efforts. During British colonial rule the Burmans lost some of their dominant role, as the colonial powers favored other ethnic groups with preferential treatment. However, after independence, the old inter-ethnic tensions re-emerged. These continue to pose some of the most significant problems for the country today, even after more than seventy years of independence (Osborne 2004, 228).

For hundreds of years, Buddhism has been at the heart of Burmese society. The revered monkhood touches virtually every segment of society. It might be said that Buddhism has held together the religious, cultural, and even political civilization of ancient Burma. It was the bond that connected the Bamar with the Rakhine, Mon, and Shan populations. It is therefore unsurprising that the arrival of Christian missionaries was seen as a threat to national identity and unity. While government authorities occasionally acknowledge the country's ethnic diversity, generally the Buddhist Bamar are considered the backbone of national identity (Walton 2012, 6).

The continuing struggle between the Bamar-dominated army on the one hand and the various ethnic minorities on the other is a clear demonstration of the ideological and existential battle to impose the Bamar vision of the world and to confirm their superior identity and cultural legacy. Social, religious, and historical dynamics, such as the damaging legacy of colonialism, the pervasive influence of Buddhism, the dominant position of the Bamar, and the lasting impact of ethnic rivalries, have created formidable barriers for the reception of the gospel among the people of Myanmar. They reveal the daunting task awaiting the church in its missional calling in this context.

Buddhism has dominated Myanmar for more than fifteen centuries, while Christianity appeared only some three hundred years ago with the arrival of Portuguese and other traders (Duh Kam 1997, 50). Roman Catholic missionaries established themselves in Burma and expanded the Christian community during the seventeenth and eighteenth centuries. By 1778 there were allegedly over three thousand Christians in Rangoon (Kawl Thang Vuta 1983, 39). Among the earliest Protestant missionaries were Adoniram and Ann Judson, who arrived in Burma in 1813, before the military engagements with the British army. Their progress and setbacks were to a large extent connected with the advance of the colonial powers. While the staunchly nationalistic Burmans (the Bamar people) strongly resented the foreign domination of their country, some of the minorities were much less antagonistic, possibly due to the better conditions they experienced under the British.

According to the historian Thant Myint-U, "many Karens came to associate British rule and their cooperation with the British with a better life and future" (Thant Myint-U 2007, 211). Their relative openness to the gospel resulted in numerous conversions and the establishment of a multitude of churches, both in the delta region and in the hill country. This created the perception among the Burmans that the Christians had somehow sold their Burmese heritage to the foreigners. It is therefore no exaggeration to say that colonization has been a mixed blessing for the church. While it opened the

> Colonization has been a mixed blessing for the church.

door for missionaries to proclaim the gospel, it also attached a foreign stigma to Christianity that continues to the present.

The Church as Religious Minority in Myanmar

Whereas Bamar Buddhist ideology is closely linked with national identity, the vast majority of Christians belong to the country's ethnic minorities, predominantly the Karen, Kachin, and Chin. This places Christians in a vulnerable position. They often experience serious disadvantages in social, educational, and professional arenas (Zam Khat Kham 2015, 108). In rural areas, churches regularly face opposition and harassment from Buddhist monks seeking to curb or restrict Christian activities in their area (Fleming 2016, 9–20). Besides a general and widespread dislike toward Christianity as a foreign religion, there is also a disdain for Christians as members of "ethnic minority groups whom the Burmans regard as ethically inferior to them" (Ngun Ling 2014, 51).

These external challenges are compounded by internal hurdles, such as the attitude of Christians toward Buddhists and adherents of other religions. It is not uncommon to hear Christians expressing strongly negative feelings toward Buddhists in particular, which is not surprising given the prejudices and treatment they have faced in this Bamar-dominated society. Many Christians have suffered deeply for their faith at the hands of Burmese Buddhists (Zam Khat Kham 2015, 96, 97; Gravers 2006, 10). Their intense pain transcends their desire to reach out with the gospel message of reconciliation.

The Church and the Challenge of Reconciliation

Ever since gaining independence from British rule Myanmar has been plagued by internal strife. Despite seventy years since independence, the Myanmar army is still engaged in armed conflict with several ethnic organizations, especially in the north and east of the country (Cho Cho Myaing 2013, 51). Mikael Gravers suggests that the conflict is not primarily ethnic, but a prolonged post-colonial conflict between the military seeking to maintain the unity of the nation and minorities fighting for ethnic autonomy. Elsewhere however, he acknowledges that frictions over ethnic identity and nationalism have also been major drivers of the hostility, challenging unity and harmony in the country (Gravers 2006, 8).

Decades of ethnic strife have created an atmosphere of mistrust and bitterness toward the dominant Bamar Buddhists (Gravers 2006, 161, 251). Many Karen and Kachin believers in particular have strong feelings of bitterness toward the Bamar ethnic majority (Cockett 2015, 84, 85). This strong resentment creates major obstacles to the church's missional impact among their Buddhist fellow citizens. In the words of one Myanmar pastor, "we need to acknowledge that these people need the gospel, and we need to love them. But it took a long time for me to love them. I was honestly thinking, they don't go to heaven, praise the Lord! A lot of people are thinking that way" (Go Chin Zam, interview with the author, November 12, 2014). Another pastor heard a Karen Christian announce, "When I go to heaven, I will look around, and if I find any Bamar people there, I would prefer to go to hell." Obviously, reconciliation—not only with God, but also with other people—is deeply needed, even among Christians.

The association of the church with the colonial administration, the pressure of "Burmanization" on the Christian community, and the ethnic diversity of the church in a divided society, have all affected the position and conditions facing the church in Myanmar. Given the plurality of religions in its society, how can the church in Myanmar be committed both to the proclamation of the gospel and to reconciliation in a divided country? In order to engage the schisms in society at large, the church will need to address its own divisions and partitions, which separate and isolate various ethnicities and faith traditions from one another. While it is undoubtedly easier for people from similar backgrounds to come together and build faith communities, there is beauty and fragrance in seeing Christians from different cultures and ethnicities meeting together to worship the one God and Creator of all humankind.

Biblical Reflection on the Church in a Pluralist Society

The Church Is One Body in Christ (Rom 12:3-8; 1 Cor 12:12-31)

One of the most powerful of all New Testament images of the church is Paul's portrayal of the church as the body of Christ (Rom 12:5 ESV). While the idea of a community of people as a body was not unknown in the apostolic era, it was Paul who applied it specifically to the church (Van Gelder 2000, 110; Keener 2009, 145). In Romans 12, Paul employs the image of a body to contend for unity within the church in all its diversity. While composed of different members with individual functions, together they form one body in Christ, and "individually [they are] members one of another" (Rom 12:5 ESV).

Paul further develops this concept of unity in diversity by connecting it with the gifts of the Spirit, which are apportioned "according to the grace given to each of us" (Rom 12:6).[1] Craig Van Gelder affirms this, saying "the nature of the church entails an interdependence among all the members. This interdependence is a function of the diversity of spiritual gifts that have

---
[1] Scripture references are NIV unless noted otherwise.

been given by the Spirit for ministry by members" (Van Gelder 2000, 110). It seems significant that Paul repeatedly underlines the unity of the body in the face of diversity within congregations. Here in Romans, he urges each believer to "not think of yourself more highly than you ought" (Rom 12:3), obviously because some members were tempted to look down on others.

In 1 Corinthians 12, Paul addresses the same issue from two additional angles. First, he speaks to those who feel overlooked, as if they do not belong to the body (1 Cor 12:15, 16). Then, he confronts those who consider themselves superior and want to exclude others who are deemed less important or valuable (1 Cor 12:17). He then makes it clear that "God has placed the parts in the body, every one of them, just as he wanted them to be" (1 Cor 12:18). There is, therefore, in Paul's opinion, no excuse for either excluding oneself or others from the body of Christ. Clearly the church as the body of Christ is not a uniform, homogeneous group of people. However, there is a basic foundational unity, which is organic and integrated, a unity in diversity. This heterogeneous, or composite, unity enables the church to display "the manifold wisdom of God" (Eph 3:10) to this world. Through reconciled relationships and mutual submission church members can experience true oneness within the body of Christ without losing their uniqueness.

Christ Has Removed the Barriers (Eph 2:11–22)

At first glance it may seem that Ephesians 2 addresses similar themes to those found in Romans 12, namely the unity of believers in the church. However, Paul here approaches the subject from a different perspective. In Ephesians he emphasizes the image of "one new humanity out of the two" (Eph 2:15), of coming together in one household (Eph 2:19), and being built into a temple (2:21).

First however, Paul notes that non-Jews used to be "separate from Christ, excluded from citizenship in Israel and foreigners to the covenants of the promise, without hope and without God in the world" (Eph 2:12). Uncircumcised people were outsiders and had no prospect of fellowship with God. Verses 14–18 describe Jesus as the peacemaker, who has broken down the dividing wall of hostility that stood between Jews and Gentiles (Eph 2:14). Some commentators argue that this dividing wall was a reference to the division that existed in the temple between the temple proper and the Court of the Gentiles (Foulkes 2008).

However, according to Leslie Mitton, this wall of hostility should be interpreted metaphorically, as an attitude of the heart "which holds apart whole communities of people in suspicion and hatred of one another … It was this hostility, firmly implanted in human hearts, which Christ had melted away, so that Christians, whether Jewish or Gentile, found themselves knit together in a new and unbelievable friendship" (Mitton 1989, 105). The result is that Christ created "one new humanity out of the two," thus reconciling the two to God and to one another, thereby removing the hostility (Eph 2:15–16). In God's new humanity there is full equality among believers, whatever their background.

In verse 19 Paul announces to the gentile believers "you are no longer foreigners and strangers, but fellow citizens with God's people and also members of his household." From now on they belong together in one house of which Jesus Christ is the cornerstone, a building that "rises to become a holy temple" (Eph 2:21). In verse 20 Paul develops the image even further. Not only do the believers together form a temple, but in Christ they are also "built on the foundation of the apostles and prophets, with Christ Jesus himself as the chief cornerstone."

Paul establishes that God has expanded his covenant with Israel to include all nations, regardless of ethnic origin, circumcision, or non-circumcision, and even without regard to prior compliance with the law, as asserted in verse 15. By the blood of Christ, God has established a new humanity, a spiritual community. Instead of an exclusive single ethnicity, the church is to be an open, inclusive, welcoming, multiethnic community, held together by Christ, its head and cornerstone.

A Message of Unity to the World (John 13:34–35)

Turning to how Jesus describes the church, it is noteworthy that he is not primarily concerned with the nature of the church, but more specifically with how it should function in everyday life. Shortly before his arrest and trial, Jesus spent the last few hours among his disciples, preparing them for a new kind of community that was to have a profound impact in the world (John 13–17). After telling his disciples that he would not be with them much longer, he said, "A new command I give you: Love one another. As I have loved you, so you must love one another. By this everyone will know that you are my disciples, if you love one another" (John 13:34–35).

In the Old Testament the people of Israel had received the command to "love your neighbor as yourself" (Lev 19:18), but here the disciples were told, "As I have loved you, you must love one another." This added a new dimension to the old commandment, and thus it is a "new" commandment. This love led Jesus to lay down his life for them, and he commanded them to love one another in the same way. Their love for one another would bring the outside world to recognize them as true followers of Jesus.

Christians need to take Jesus's command to heart, laying aside petty squabbles and obeying his exhortation to love one another unconditionally. Nothing but a deep desire to follow Jesus in sacrificial love can cultivate a life-changing unity that will send a message to the world. Such love must embrace and include people from every ethnicity, language, culture, and nation. It must include those who are despised and rejected by society, as well as those who have caused suffering for others. Only then will the church be the inclusive community God intended it to be, and only then will the church be able to draw in those who are hungering and thirsting for authentic love and life.

Recognizing the Importance of Reconciliation

One significant outcome from examining the nature of the church within a biblical perspective is to recognize its intrinsic unity within vast diversity. The church brought together Jews and Gentiles, slave and free, male and female (Gal 3:28), yet in spite of this formidable diversity the church serves to display a unique oneness. Reconciliation with God has implications for relationships with others, both within the body of Christ and beyond.

A Unified Body of Believers

Craig Van Gelder highlights the church as a community of people reconciled both with God and with one another (Van Gelder 2000, 108). Christ has brought people together in one body, not merely to worship God and enjoy the privilege of communion with him. Rather, they are called into community, as they now belong together within one family. It is simply incomprehensible for Christians to remain separated from fellow believers, merely on the grounds of ethnic or clan affiliation, social class, educational background, or other identity markers. Allowing any such distinctions to split Christians into separate congregations or communities is incompatible with the reconciling power of Christ, whose purpose it was "to create in himself one new humanity out of the two [Jews and Gentiles], thus making peace, and in one body to reconcile both of them to God through the cross, by which he put to death their hostility" (Eph 2:15, 16). Throughout the New Testament believers are exhorted to strive for unity and mutual love as the natural outgrowth of the fact that "there is one body and one Spirit, just as you were called to one hope when you were called; one Lord, one faith, one baptism; one God and Father of all, who is over all and through all and in all" (Eph 4:4–6).

A Called Community

The church is not only a unified body; it is also a community with a specific calling. When the Apostle Peter addresses his readers as "a chosen people, a royal priesthood, a holy nation, God's special possession" (1 Pet 2:9), he accentuates that they were "called out of darkness." Thus, the church is a called-out community, separated from darkness, from evil, and from the world. As the people of Israel were led out of Egypt, the followers of Christ are called to move out of darkness and into God's presence, toward "his eternal glory in Christ" (1 Pet 5:10).

The church is not only a called-out community, it is also called to be the church together. Like Peter, the Apostle Paul addresses the members of the church in Corinth as "those sanctified in Christ Jesus and *called to be his holy people, together with all* those everywhere who call on the name of our Lord Jesus Christ" (1 Cor 1:2; italics added). The concept of the church as community is essential if the church is to function as missional community. The church does not exist in and for itself but is called both out of and into the world. As church members live and serve together, they are equipped to impact the society around them. John Woodward points out the missional hermeneutic of Ephesians 4, where "leaders learn to lead from the margins as priests ministering to fellow priests, with Christ drawing all of us toward himself at the center" (Woodward 2013, 75).

As a called community the church today has an obligation to live out its calling in the particular context in which it finds itself. Christians face the challenge of demonstrating their faith in an indifferent or even antagonistic environment. Closing themselves off from the outside world is not an option for those who take the clear commands of Scripture to heart. Following these commands requires the courage to explore the intersection between faith and societal values. If reconciliation has any significance beyond the relationship between an individual believer and God, it must have implications both within the Christian community and in society at large.

Christians have a responsibility as agents of reconciliation, as peacemakers, in situations characterized by brokenness and suffering. Peter Rowan has addressed similar challenges for the church in Malaysia. He argues, "In the midst of the brokenness and suffering of the world, the church exists as a community of reconciliation, pointing back to the unique reconciling work of God in Christ on the cross, and pointing forward, by its work and witness, to the ultimate reconciliation of 'all things'" (Rowan 2010, 49).

> Christians have a responsibility as agents of reconciliation, as peacemakers, in situations characterized by brokenness and suffering.

A Multiethnic Mosaic

Having established the essential unity of the church, it is necessary to emphasize the organic diversity within the body of Christ, both locally and worldwide. Diversity within the Christian community is not incompatible with its fundamental unity, as both are rooted in the unity of the Trinity (Van Gelder 2000, 122). Therefore, diversity should not be equated with disunity or seen as a sign of brokenness. There is no inconsistency between the church's unity and its diversity, just as there is no incongruity between the oneness of God and his existence in three Persons. Diversity expresses as much of the church's essence as does its oneness. Paul says that "through the church, the manifold wisdom of God should be made known to the rulers and authorities in the heavenly realms" (Eph 3:10). Aubrey Sequeira contends that "establishing multiethnic churches is not only more faithful to scripture, but … multiethnic churches more fully display the glorious gospel of Jesus Christ" (Sequeira 2015, 30).

Diversity may be expressed in a number of ways, the most important of which are socioeconomic, educational, and ethnic identity. Our focus here will be primarily on ethnic diversity in the church. While the early church initially consisted mainly of Jewish-background believers, they came from a wide variety of cultural and linguistic contexts. When tensions arose between them, the apostles did not attempt to resolve the conflict by separating them into homogeneous units, but instead appointed leaders from a variety of ethnic groups (Acts 6.1–6). Social and class distinctions were abolished by exhorting masters to fellowship together with slaves as brothers in Christ (1 Cor 7:17–24; Phlm 1:8–16).

Aubrey Sequeira argues that "while homogeneity in churches simply *reinforces the status quo of society, the biblical evidence shows us that the gospel broke down and cut down across ethnic, social, economic, and cultural barriers in ways never before seen in history*" (Sequeira 2015, 31–32; italics in original). Jesus and the apostles never encouraged ethnocentrism, but rather called Christians to embrace one another in spite of their differences.

Sequeira takes a stand against the church growth theory of Donald McGavran, and its "homogeneous unit principle" according to which the church grows most rapidly and easily along the lines of homogeneous units. Sequeira contends that "while the 'homogeneous unit principle' emphasizes seeking to win people by not offending their ethnocentric sensibilities, Jesus's approach is radically different—Christ lays the axe to the root of ethnic pride" (Sequeira 2015, 33).

While McGavran insists that the Jew-Gentile separation was not an ethnic issue, Sequeira asserts that though there are some points of discontinuity between the Jew-Gentile divide and modern ethno-cultural divides, there are enough points of continuity to warrant the parallel. Furthermore, the New Testament does extend the call to unity beyond "Jew" and "Gentile" to include categories like "Barbarian" and "Scythian," which are ethnolinguistic categories (Col 3:11).

In the New Testament, unity in Christ trumps all other issues of identity, and the call to embrace the "other" encompasses all categories of "otherness," and takes shape in the form of life together in the local church" (Sequeira 2015, 35). The book of Acts demonstrates clearly that churches were not established or separated along ethnic, socio-cultural, or class lines. While people may prefer not to cross racial, linguistic, or class barriers when becoming Christians, failing to do so does not conform to any normative biblical pattern. The reality is that reconciliation to God also brings a person into a community "where people find their identity in Jesus Christ rather than in their race, culture, social class, or sex, and are consequently reconciled to one another" (Sequeira 2015, 34).

It should be acknowledged that diversity is not the same as reconciliation and the goal of reconciliation goes beyond diversity. As Jarvis Williams helpfully points out, "an assembly of the United Nations is multiethnic and diverse, as is the army, or the local public high school, or so many other groups. Yet such settings hardly enjoy the racial reconciliation of the gospel" (Williams 2015, 9). Patrick Cho, writing about the challenge for Asian churches in North America to become more multiethnic, comments that "most cultures do not want a melting pot as much as an acknowledgment of cultural identity. To use a culinary analogy, perhaps *a truly multiethnic church would look less like a monochrome chowder and more like a varicolored minestrone*" (Cho 2015, 67; italics added).

This observation is particularly helpful, as it emphasizes that unity in diversity does not necessarily lead to or require uniformity. The image of a colorful cauldron of minestrone soup conveys a helpful message. Other helpful metaphors might include a multicolored tapestry or a colorful mosaic. Both of these pictures evokes the image of diversity in harmonious unity. The overall unity does not subsume the identity of its individual components, but rather its composite nature enhances the overall beauty and contributes to its harmony.

Working toward Reconciliation and Diversity

What is needed for the church to fulfill its calling to be a light to the nations, a royal priesthood representing Christ, and demonstrating the transforming power of reconciliation? In 2 Corinthians 5 Paul argues that our reconciliation with God transforms believers into agents of reconciliation, as he "reconciled us to himself through Christ and gave us the ministry of reconciliation" (2 Cor 5:18). Miroslav Volf writes, "Though reconciliation of human beings to God has priority, reconciliation between human beings is intrinsic to their reconciliation to God" (Volf 1998, 7). Obviously, such a ministry cannot be fulfilled unless this reconciliation extends to one another.

Reconciliation with God and with One Another

Reconciliation has only recently been recognized as a significant missiological theme. However, starting with Miroslav Volf in 1997, and continuing during the last two decades, the topic has received significant attention at various gatherings (for a helpful overview, see Rowan 2010, 54). Volf argues that in order for Christian communities to become peacemakers and reconcilers in situations of ethnic conflict, they need to not only understand the biblical message of reconciliation, but more importantly to comprehend "the inherent social meaning of reconciliation" (Volf 1998, 12).

Too often, according to Volf, reconciliation has either been reduced to restoring one's individual relationship with God or replaced by the pursuit of social justice and liberation. He argues for an understanding of reconciliation with both vertical and horizontal dimensions, and says, "though grace is unthinkable without justice, justice is subordinate to grace" and "though reconciliation of human beings to God has priority, reconciliation between human beings is intrinsic to their reconciliation to God" (Volf 1998, 7).

Forgiveness and reconciliation on the individual level are often difficult enough, but these issues become even more challenging on a group level. Myanmar society, with its deep-rooted and entrenched divisions, presents a daunting task for the church to be a reconciled and reconciling community. A major contributor to this problem is the fact that identity (both individual and communal) is usually bound up with ethnicity (Volf 2010, 37). Quoting Jacob Neusner, Volf challenges Christians to consider that "the ultimate allegiance of those whose father is Abraham can be only to the God of 'all families of the earth,' not to any particular country, culture, or family with their local deities" (Volf 2010, 39). Elaborating on how God's election of one man, Abraham, can serve as an instrument of blessing for all nations, Volf explains the connection between universality and particularity as follows:

> The oneness of God requires God's universality; God's universality entails human equality; human equality implies equal access by all to the blessings of the one God; equal access is incompatible with ascription of religious significance to genealogy; Christ, the seed of Abraham, is both the fulfillment of the genealogical promise to Abraham and the end of genealogy as a

> privileged locus of access to God; faith in Christ replaces birth into a people. As a consequence, all people can have access to the one God of Abraham and Sarah on equal terms, none by right and all by grace. (Volf 2010, 45)

Thus, through faith in Christ all of humanity is welcomed into God's family. Christians need to avoid creating a new, separate culture, by which they would isolate themselves from their own community. While stepping with one foot outside their culture, they should remain with the other foot within it. Although separate and different, they still belong. These are the paradoxes of the Christian church: united yet diverse, separate though still belonging, fostering community without exclusion.

However, inclusion is not the end point. In order to move from inclusion to embrace another step is needed: forgiveness. In a fractured and divided society like Myanmar, this is a sensitive topic. The reality is that almost all people consider themselves victims in one way or another. Minorities have experienced violence and harassment perpetrated by the majority Bamar, while many Bamar themselves would argue that they, too, have been victims of army and police brutality. Even the military will contend that they have been obliged to use force because of provocations by the armed ethnic groups (Walton 2012, 16).

Few people are prepared to acknowledge responsibility for their role in the continuing conflicts in the country (Walton 2012, 20). Consequently, the vicious cycle of violence, suffering and hatred continues, making a resolution to the conflict more difficult. Volf's portrayal of the situation is as poignant as it is tragic: "If perpetrators were repentant, forgiveness would come more easily. But too often they are not. And so, both victim and perpetrator are imprisoned in the automatism of mutual exclusion, unable to forgive or repent and united in a perverse communion of hate" (Volf 2010, 210).

Even if there was a recognition of responsibility and culpability, the harm and suffering can never be undone. The only way out is through forgiveness, because "unless people manage to forsake their determination to 'get even,' there can be no new beginning, no transformation of relationships. Everyone will remain imprisoned in a particular history or mythology, recycling old crimes and hatreds" (Van Essen 2014, 18, quoting Hannah Arendt, 1959, *The Human Condition*, 213). Volf's argument is not that forgiveness will necessarily bring suffering to an end—in fact forgiveness may be considered in itself a form of suffering—but that it allows the one who forgives to move beyond the wrongdoing and to focus on the future, rather than continuing to dwell on the past.

Robert Schreiter points out that reconciliation is first and foremost the work of God. However, when examining reconciliation between people, he stresses that God's reconciling work begins with the victim. God's healing work in the victim sometimes makes it possible for the victim to forgive the wrongdoer even before repentance takes place (Schreiter 2004, 6). This may result in a transformation of both the victim and the wrongdoer. Suffering, although not good in and of itself, can acquire meaning in the context of Christ's suffering. However, reconciliation will only be complete once God has eradicated all suffering. For Christians to extend to those from other ethnicities the grace they themselves have received, they need to embrace the reality of their own reconciliation with God and with one another. Reconciliation is inherently connected with diversity and inclusivity.

The Missional Impact of an Inclusive Community

Buddhism has traditionally absorbed a variety of local customs, rituals, and practices. Christianity, on the other hand, has tended to define clear boundaries between what is and what is not acceptable in terms of religious practice (Zam Khat Kham 2015, 125). While sensible, this has created the notion among Buddhists that Christians are rigid and intolerant. This impression of Christianity as exclusionist and restrictive is bolstered by the perception that church membership is predominantly based on ethnic identity and affiliation.

In order to overcome such perceptions, the church needs to consider its nature as the body of Christ, its calling as an inclusive community, and its composition as a multiethnic mosaic. Recognizing these aspects of the church will be a vital component in working toward a more missional model of the church in Myanmar. This chapter does not afford the space to discuss a contextualized gospel presentation for Myanmar. However, several recent publications have addressed this topic, highlighting the need for a more honor-shame based approach (e.g., Vaughn 2015; Mischke 2015).

Summary and Conclusion

It is hoped that this chapter will contribute in some way to a flourishing of the church in Myanmar, inspiring and enabling God's people to demonstrate the reconciling power of the gospel and the multicolored nature of the body of Christ. The church in Myanmar has a long and rich history going back more than two hundred years. It is well-established among the predominantly Christian minorities in the country. The next step would be for the church to become a community where people from all of Myanmar's ethnic groups will find a spiritual home.

Christians are in a unique position to build bridges to each of Myanmar's ethnic communities, reaching out in forgiveness and love. If they are able to overcome their hurts and wounds, Christians could bring genuine reconciliation and become true peacemakers in this country, which has for so long been ravaged by conflict and hostility. As Myanmar churches become more missional among their own people groups, may they also awaken to their missionary calling across borders to other Buddhist countries such as Thailand, Laos, and Cambodia. With that missionary calling comes the responsibility and privilege to proclaim God's reconciling love, just as they themselves have received and experienced reconciliation with God and with one another.

References Cited

Note: *Most Burmese author names are listed in the order given and referenced in full, since in Myanmar there is no distinction between first and family name.*

Cho Cho Myaing. 2013. "Forgiveness toward National Reconciliation in Myanmar from Christian Hji Perspective." MDiv thesis, Myanmar Institute of Theology.

Cho, Patrick. 2015. "Helping Asian Churches Become Multi-Ethnic." In *Multi-Ethnic Churches*, edited by Jonathan Leeman, 65–68. 9Marks Journal IX. Washington DC: 9Marks.

Cockett, Richard. 2015. *Blood, Dreams and Gold: The Changing Face of Burma.* New Haven and London: Yale University Press.

Duh Kam, C. 1997. "Christian Mission to Buddhists in Myanmar: A Study of Past, Present, and Future Approaches by Baptists." DMiss thesis, United Theological Seminary.

Fleming, Rachel. 2016. *Hidden Plight: Christian Minorities in Myanmar.* United States Commission on International Religious Freedom, 9–20, https://www.uscirf.gov/sites/default/files/Hidden%20Plight.%20Christian%20Minorities%20in%20Burma.pdf.

Foulkes, Francis. 2008. *Ephesians.* Olivetree Bible Study Digital Edition. Vol. 10. Tyndale New Testament Commentaries. Downers Grove, IL: InterVarsity Press.

Gravers, Mikael, ed. 2006. *Exploring Ethnic Diversity in Burma.* NIAS studies in Asian topics. Copenhagen: Nordic Institute of Asian Studies.

Hesselgrave, David J., ed. 2010. *Missionshift: Global Mission Issues in the Third Millennium.* Nashville, TN: Broadman and Holman Publishers.

Kawl Thang Vuta. 1983. "A Brief History of the Planting and Growth of the Church in Burma." DMiss thesis, Fuller Theological Seminary.

Keener, Craig S. 2009. *Romans.* New Covenant Commentary Series. Eugene, OR: Cascade Books.

Maung Shwe Wa. 1963. *Burma Baptist Chronicle*. Edited by Genevieve Sowards and Erville Sowards. Rangoon: Burma Baptist Convention.

Mischke, Werner. 2015. *The Global Gospel: Achieving Missional Impact in Our Multicultural World*. Scottsdale, AZ: Mission ONE.

Mitton, C. Leslie. 1989. *Ephesians*. New Century Bible Commentary. Grand Rapids, MI: Eerdmans.

Ngun Ling, Samuel. 2014. *Christianity through Our Neighbours' Eyes: Rethinking the 200 Years Old American Baptist Missions in Myanmar*. Yangon: Judson Research Center—MIT.

Osborne, Milton. 2004. *Southeast Asia: An Introductory History*. 9th ed. Crows Nest, Australia: Allen and Unwin.

Rowan, Peter A. 2010. "Proclaiming the Peacemaker: The Malaysian Church as an Agent of Reconciliation in a Multicultural Society." PhD diss., Open University, All Nations Christian College.

Schreiter, Robert J. 2004. "The Theology of Reconciliation and Peacemaking for Mission." In *Mission, Violence, and Reconciliation*, 11–28. Sheffield, UK: Cliff College Publishing. http://www.ehcounseling.com/materials/_applied_theology_of_reconciliation.pdf.

Sequeira, Aubrey. 2015. "Re-Thinking Homogeneity: The Biblical Case for Multi-Ethnic Churches." In *Multi-Ethnic Churches*, edited by Jonathan Leeman. 9Marks Journal IX. Washington DC: 9Marks.

Thant Myint-U. 2007. *The River of Lost Footsteps: A Personal History of Burma*. London: Faber and Faber.

Van Essen, Jelle P. 2014. "Recognizing Reconciliation: The Role of Culture on Post World War II and Post-Cold War Reconciliatory Processes and Acts of Apology." MA thesis, Erasmus University Rotterdam.

Van Gelder, Craig. 2000. *The Essence of the Church: A Community Created by the Spirit*. Grand Rapids, MI: Baker Books.

Vaughn, Brad. 2015. *One Gospel for All Nations*. Pasadena, CA: William Carey Library.

Volf, Miroslav. 1998. "The Social Meaning of Reconciliation." *Occasional Papers on Religion in Eastern Europe* 18, no. 3. http://digitalcommons.georgefox.edu/ree/vol18/iss3/3.

Volf, Miroslav. 2010. *Exclusion and Embrace: A Theological Exploration of Identity, Otherness, and Reconciliation*. Nashville, TN: Abingdon Press.

Walton, Matthew J. 2012. "The 'Wages of Burman-Ness:' Ethnicity and Burman Privilege in Contemporary Myanmar." *Journal of Contemporary Asia* 43, no. 1. https://www.tandfonline.com/doi/full/10.1080/00472336.2012.730892.

Williams, Jarvis J. 2015. "Racial Reconciliation, the Gospel, and the Church." In *Multi-Ethnic Churches*, edited by Jonathan Leeman, 8–12. 9Marks Journal IX. Washington DC: 9Marks.

Woodward, J. R. 2013. *Creating a Missional Culture: Equipping the Church for the Sake of the World*. Downers Grove, IL: IVP Books.

Zam Khat Kham. 2015. "Burmese Nationalism and Christianity in Myanmar: Christian Identity and Witness in Myanmar Today." PhD diss., Concordia Seminary. http://scholar.csl.edu/phd/22.

Chapter 11

Community-Based Reconciliation

A Case Study of the Sawi Peace Child Story

Yakubu Jakada

It is difficult to have meaningful progress in an atmosphere where peace is absent, and this includes areas of mission endeavors. In a generation where conflicts and violence are becoming normative, it is high time for mission agencies, churches, and missionaries to see the reconciliation of communities where they work as an important aspect of the missionary task. To underscore this importance, Robert J. Schreiter a leading Roman Catholic Missiologist, suggested that "reconciliation and healing provide a new paradigm for mission" (Bevans and Schroeder 2004, 390). Peace in communities can open doors for the gospel and or ensure the continuity of the gospel witness.

In the Peace Child story of Don Richardson, the peace that came to the Sawi people group from the concept of the "Peace Child" opened the door for them to receive God's "Peace Child" sent to the world. The writer argues that genuine reconciliation in a community that will produce lasting results is community-based; it emerges from the culture, initiated, implemented, and defended by the community. The communities referred to in this study are unreached communities who are still in need of the gospel. They may be non-Christian communities or communities of nominal Christians who are still considered unreached. Apart from being enemies of God (Rom 5:10), some of these communities are in conflict within themselves or with neighbors. Reconciliation is needed to be able to maintain an active gospel witness among them.

Karl Barth defined reconciliation as

> restitution, the resumption of a fellowship which once existed but was then threatened by dissolution. It is the maintaining, restoring, and upholding of that fellowship in face of an element which disturbs and disrupts and breaks it. It is the realization of the original purpose which underlay and controlled it in defiance and by the removal of this obstruction. (Barth 2004, 24)

In support of Barth's claim, Jim Van Yperen wrote, "Conflict is first and foremost a broken fellowship. Reconciliation is the process of restoring broken relationships" (Van Yperen 2002, 99).

Peace comes into the individual or community when fellowship is restored and meaningful progress results. This chapter argues that people groups and communities have in them the resources that can bring about peace referred to here as a *handle*. The Sawi had the "Peace Child," Rwandans "Gacaca" and South Africans had "Ubuntu" as handles that were key to the peace process (The handle here means the resources found within the community or people group that could be used to bring about peace and reconciliation).

The missionary's role is to encourage the community to seek peace and help them find the handle within the community that agrees with Scripture and can be used to bring about reconciliation. This chapter discusses conflicts, their sources, and how they affect mission work. We will also discuss the need for reconciliation and how to find and use the handle for reconciliation—especially in communities or people groups that are a target for mission engagement or already engaged communities. All Scripture references are from the New International Version of the Bible.

Case Study[1]

The Sawi people group of Irian Jaya in Indonesia is a distinct tribe with its own worldview, set of legends, and a sense of humor. At the time Don went as a missionary, this people group honored treachery as an ideal in their society. Their heroes were men who were able to form friendships with the purpose of betrayal (Richardson 1974, 8). The betrayed friend is often killed and eaten. The Sawi expression for this practice according to Richardson is "to fatten with friendship for slaughter" (Richardson 1974, 34). The Sawi communities were constantly at war with each other. Richardson, describing the frequency of violence in Sawi communities, said, "we lived among three villages of such men ... we counted fourteen battles fought within sight of our home during the first two months we lived among the Sawi. After that, we lost count" (Richardson 1974, 186).

Don and Carol Richardson worked tirelessly to see these communities embrace peace, but their efforts yielded very little fruit. Only when the Richardsons threatened to leave the community was the solution found within the culture of the people. Don was told, "Tuan, you've been urging us to make peace, don't you know it's impossible to have peace without a peace child?" (Richardson 1974, 201). The Sawi, because of the philosophy of treachery, suspected every demonstration of friendship except one, which is, "if a man would actually give his own son to his enemies, that man could be trusted! That, and that alone, was a proof of goodwill no shadow of cynicism could

---

1 This case study is from Don Richardson's book, *Peace Child*.

discredit" (Richardson 1974, 206). Peace and reconciliation require assurance of sincere goodwill from both parties in conflict.

Richardson's threat of leaving sparked a tumult of discussions in the three communities, which went on deep into the night. That night, the leading men from both warring factions—including Kani, Mahaem, Maum, Hato, Kaiyo, Kigo, and many others—came to plead with Don and his family not to leave the area with the promise, "tomorrow we are going to sprinkle cool water on each other." Cool water is Sawi idiom for making peace (Richardson 1974, 193).

The following day, there was a family in each warring community that was able to donate a male child as "Peace Child" that was given to an enemy community. When the child was presented in each community, those who accept the child as a basis for peace came out to lay hands on him. These included the young and old, male, and female who filed eagerly to lay hands, sealing their acceptance of peace with the enemy community. This ceremony took place in both communities. This was followed by the beating of drums and singing and dancing and exchange of gifts "such as axes, machetes, knives, shells, or necklaces of animal teeth" (Richardson 1974, 204). Those who exchanged gifts also exchanged names. The Sawi people group made peace and consequently embraced Christ the Prince of Peace. Fifty years after leaving the mission field, Don Richardson and his children visited the Sawi people group and still found vibrant and growing Christian communities.

A World Full of Conflict

Just like the Sawi people group, we live in a world full of conflict. On the global scene, it has been reported that in 2020, there were thirty-four armed conflicts. In Africa, there were fifteen conflicts, nine in Asia, six in the Middle East, three in Europe, and one in America (Alert 2021). The conflicts left seventy-nine million people forcibly displaced and two hundred and thirty-five million people in need of humanitarian assistance (Alert 2021). Countries affected by these conflicts include Cameroon, Ethiopia, Libya, Mali, Mozambique, Lake Chad region (Nigeria, Chad, and Niger), Western Sahel Region, Democratic Republic of Congo, Somalia, South Sudan, Afghanistan, Armenia, Azerbaijan, Iraq, Syria, Myanmar, Yemen, and many others. Currently, the international community is confronted with the invasion of Ukraine by Russia. There are also local conflicts involving ethnic and religious groups in communities that the international community may not be aware of.

For the sake of clarity, we need to discuss different types of conflicts including political conflicts involving nations and governments, and ethnic conflicts involving people of different ethnic nationalities, or within the ethnic group itself. There are also religious conflicts, both intra- and interreligious, economic conflicts having to do with resource control, geographic conflicts arising from disputes about boundaries, and cultural conflicts over what is considered offensive to the culture of a people. There are also family conflicts and personal or interpersonal conflicts which can impact communities. Conflicts in communities involve some or all of the above-mentioned variables.

To understand conflicts, we need to be informed about the causes of conflicts. These causes are diverse and, in some cases, very deep and not easily discernible. In our case study, the causes of the conflict among the Sawi communities included a combination of tribal, ethnic, and cultural factors. Ariaraja Wesley in his book *Not without My Neighbour* wrote, "Merely to state that, 'Muslims are killing Christians' in Nigeria or 'Christians are killing Muslims' in Bosnia involves over-simplification. Although religious affiliation or background provides a collective identity to the group, most conflicts are caused by a combination of historical, ethnic, tribal, racial, economic, and political factors that calls for closer analysis and considered response" (Wesley 1999, 16). To buttress this point, Peter Awoniyi in his article, "Inter-Religious Dialogue: Tool for Peaceful Co-existence in Nigeria a Religiously Pluralistic Nation" wrote:

> There are historical memories of wars, hatred, etc. among the world religions. Some of these memories are loaded with misunderstandings, exaggerations, unclarified historical details, unhealed anger handed from generation to generation. There are at least records of crusades and jihads in the world, also there are such [conflicts] at National, State, and Local Government levels.[2] These memories may not be easily forgotten, but the adequate response is to face them honestly, directly, and with hearts ready for truth and reconciliation. (Awoniyi 2012, 509)

Awoniyi's assertion is not limited to religious conflicts only—these complexities can be found in ethnic and community violence as well. In most cases, causes of conflict are a complex mix that require a great deal of discernment and wisdom to get to the root of the matter. This complexity makes the study on community-based reconciliation relevant and important because insiders can discern complexities that it is difficult for outsiders to understand.

> Causes of conflict are a complex mix that require a great deal of discernment and wisdom.

---

[2] Local Governments are the lower level of administration in the Nigerian Government.

Community Conflicts and Mission

A community is a place where people live or a platform where people meet. These people(s) have something in common that makes them a community such as a geographical location, a government, a culture, a religion, and/or common interest. Conflicts in the community grossly affect people physically, psychologically, spiritually, economically, sociologically, etc. Conflicts have created hatred, bitterness, and suspicion. When there are incessant conflicts in a community, people tend to move to places where they will be safe. In some cities in northern Nigeria, for example, conflicts have created communities that are exclusively for Christians and communities exclusively for Muslims with mutual suspicion. In this kind of situation, it is difficult to cross over to the "enemy" community to reach them with the gospel (Jakada 2020, 146–47). Missionaries living in that kind of context are living in danger.

It is well known that conflicts have interfered with or even prevented the work of evangelism. In our case study, the conflict prevented Don Richardson from doing much evangelizing until there was reconciliation and peace among the Sawi people. In some cases, conflicts have closed or wiped out mission work—examples abound in northern Nigeria and other places in the world bedeviled by conflicts where communities have been displaced or wiped out. Examples of the negative impact of violence and conflicts on missions can be seen in what happened to *Ekklesiyar Yan'uwa a* Nigeria (EYN)[3] churches. As reported by its president, Boko Haram has:

> Inflicted permanent damage on EYN that has changed the history of the Church. 36 Districts out of the 50 EYN District Church Councils have been destroyed, 6 DCCs are partially closed and only 7 DCCs are unaffected directly. Out of 456 Local Church Councils, 278 have been destroyed and out of 2,280 Local Church Branches, 1,390 have been destroyed. In summary, a total of 1,674 churches or worshipping centers have been destroyed. (Godspecial 2018, 9)

This report provides an example of what violence can do to the work of missions. In some cases, even when the displaced communities are rebuilt, the opposing forces insist that churches are not replaced. In this case, the work is gone apart from some future divine intervention of God. Conflicts also weaken the work of missions—several vicious attacks have discouraged missionaries and their converts. In some cases, there is a decline in membership and workforce on the mission field. Members and supporters are sometimes discouraged when they will have to use their meager resources to rebuild

---

[3] *Eklesiyar Yan'uwa a* Nigeria EYN is an indigenous church with roots in the Church of the Brethren, headquartered in the Northeast of Nigeria.

what has been destroyed after each attack. Believers facing incessant attacks in northern Nigeria and other parts of the world need cooperative support and encouragement from the body of Christ.

However, despite the negatives of conflicts as they affect missions, there are some positive aspects to consider. Some believers become strong in the faith when they pass through difficulties. This truth is evidenced by the resilience of believers in areas of the world affected by persecution. Conflicts have brought about forced migration. When believers are thus forced to migrate, some end up becoming missionaries in their new locations—they plant new churches and reach out to their host communities. People from closed countries are sometimes forced by conflict to migrate to the West or other places where there is Christian influence. Non-Christian migrants provide new missions opportunities to host Christian communities. Even though conflicts present some benefit to missions, they are not the ideal context to do missions. The Scriptures enjoin believers to live in peace and reconcile to one another. Where there is peace, there is progress. Missions will thrive in the context of peace, hence the importance of reconciliation.

Reconciliation in Scripture

In Scripture, God himself is the first initiator of reconciliation. When man fell in the Garden of Eden, God came looking for him wanting to reconcile man back to himself. This reconciliation move continued with the call of Abraham and his descendants—the nation of Israel. The climax of this reconciliation move took place in the fullness of time when "God sent his Son, born of a woman, born under the law" (Gal 4:4) to mediate this reconciliation through his death on the cross. The goal of biblical reconciliation is peace which might eventually open doors for the gospel as it happened among the Sawi people group.

Reconciliation in Scripture is three-dimensional. Reconciliation with God our Creator, reconciliation with fellow human beings, and reconciliation with oneself. This reconciliation is expected to bring about three dimensions of peace. As Ken Sande puts it, peace with God, peace with others, and peace with yourself (Sande 1991, 30–31). The first dimension is peace with God. At the fall, man became an enemy of God because of sin: "for all have sinned and fall short of the glory of God" (Rom 3:23). But "while we were God's enemies we were reconciled to him through the death of his Son" (Rom 5:10). As such, every human being needs to be reconciled with his or her Creator. A believer in Christ has made peace with God when he places his faith in the Lord Jesus Christ and is justified.

The second dimension is peace with yourself. The result of the experience of peace with God is man's personal experience of peace within himself.

Ken Sande affirmed that "Through Christ, you can also experience genuine peace within yourself." He added that "Internal peace is a sense of wholeness, contentment, tranquility, order, rest, and security" (Sande 1991, 31).

The third dimension is peace with others. Genuine peace with God and ourselves results in peace with others. Romans 12:17–21 enjoin believers who are children of God to "live at peace with everyone" (v. 18), and goes on to show how to do so by loving our neighbors and also our enemies, "If your enemy is hungry, feed him; If he is thirsty, give him something to drink; In doing this, you will heap burning coals on his head" (v. 20). Jesus Christ said in the beatitudes, "Blessed are the peacemakers, for they will be called children of God" (Matt 5:9).

Reconciliation and Mission

Like Jesus Christ, the Apostle Paul in 2 Corinthians 5:18–20 emphasized peace and reconciliation but connected reconciliation to mission. He said that God has reconciled the world to himself through Christ. This reconciliation, as the writer of this chapter sees it, is completed yet ongoing. Completed in the death of Christ as a sacrifice for sin, yet ongoing because the reconciliation that was completed must be proclaimed to those who have not yet heard so that they too can embrace it and place their faith in Christ through whom the reconciliation was made possible.

This fact makes reconciliation the primary task of missions. We are made his ambassadors, representing God in the ongoing work of reconciliation among nations and people groups. To effectively represent him, God has given us "the ministry of reconciliation" and the "message of reconciliation" as well (2 Cor 18, 19). In this sense, as missionaries, we take the gospel, the message of reconciliation, to people who are yet to be reconciled to God. Missionaries here have a dual role to play especially in conflict-ridden communities: to lead them to be physically reconciled to each other and also to lead them to reconcile with God as Don Richardson did in our case study.

Building upon Paul's teaching on reconciliation, Ott, Strauss, and Tennent discussed the missiological perspective of reconciliation in terms of "vertical" and "horizontal" reconciliation (reconciliation with God and fellow humans). They commented that "vertical reconciliation is … foundational to horizontal reconciliation, to evangelism, to church planting, to philanthropy, and to justice." They added, "we maintain that reconciliation is more than just a task of mission; it is central to the overarching purpose and nature of mission" (Ott, Strauss, and Tennent 2010, 97). They insist that "the restored relationship with God, and its attendant restored human relations, is central to the message of the gospel" (Ott, Strauss, and Tennent 2010, 97).

Bevans and Schroeder in *Constant and Context*, take a more practical approach as they propose different levels of reconciliation that the church, as well as missionaries and mission agencies can pursue. One level is personal reconciliation. This has to do with "violence done to certain individuals that leaves terrible emotional scars on the victims, scars that may take a lifetime to heal" (Bevans and Schroeder 2004, 391). The missionary has a responsibility to be involved in the reconciliation of people who have been deeply and personally hurt.

Cultural reconciliation is another level "where cultural identity has been ignored, disparaged or stolen from them altogether" (Bevans and Schroeder 2004, 391). This type of violence is often done to minority people groups who, in some cases, are rated as second-class citizens. Their culture is often despised, and their rights denied. For them to ascend the social ladder, they must deny their cultural identity and identify with the dominant culture.

Another level is political reconciliation. In some countries, certain segments of the nation are deeply hurt through the denial of their fundamental rights as citizens. To achieve reconciliation at this level, there must be national commitment such as happened with the Truth and Reconciliation that took place in South Africa. The presence of Desmond Tutu shows that the church was deeply involved in the reconciliation process (Tutu 2019).

There is also reconciliation within the church itself. This reconciliation could involve conflicts within the local church, within the denomination, or even inter-denominational conflicts. I would also add community reconciliation which may involve ethnic and or religious conflicts because missionaries go to communities or ethnic groups to do ministry. This element reinforces the importance of this chapter to practitioners of missions.

Community-Based Reconciliation

Community-based reconciliation is a theoretical assumption that true and genuine reconciliation in a community or ethnic group that will last is community-based. By *community based* I mean that the handle used to bring about or negotiate reconciliation should emerge from the community just as the handle that brought peace to the Sawi people group originated from the myths and legends of the community itself. As noted above, community conflicts are often multilayered and complex. The chapter raises a concern that most reconciliation initiatives come from outside the communities and from people who hardly understand the multilayered complexities of such conflicts. Some of the initiatives are government initiated, which is intended to accomplish political goals. Some initiatives come from foreign funded organizations or companies as partners. These reconciliation initiatives from partners outside the community must carry out the process that aims to accomplish the desires and aspirations of the sponsors.

The missionary, church, or agency coming from outside into the community to help mediate reconciliation should come in first as learners who will learn about the people and the source(s) of the conflict and respect the desire, intelligence, and judgment of the people. They should accept the fact that the people of the community are the ones that have been going through the ordeal of the conflict and can suggest the best solutions to their problems. The missionary should pray and trust the Lord to help him lead the community to find the handle that will bring reconciliation and peace.

The "Peace Child" became the handle for the Sawi people group and the "Ubuntu" philosophy served as the handle for the Zulu people in South Africa. *Ubuntu* means "I am because we are" which was essential to the success of the Truth and Reconciliation held in South Africa after the apartheid regime (Radzik 2019). In Rwanda, the *Gacaca*[4] courts, the *Ingando* (civic re/education camps), "*Itorero* (civic re/education academy) and *Ndi Umunyarwanda* (Rwandaness)" and *Umuganda* (community work) (Sentama 2022, 15–16) are examples of community-based resources used to bring about reconciliation. The case of Ubuntu and Gacaca concepts reinforces the argument that the handle for peace must be found within the community or people group.

It is important to note that the handle for reconciliation can be found in but not limited to the following: (1) the culture of the people (their myths, legends, stories, proverbs, symbols, rituals, etc.); (2) the history of the people or community (some have written history and oral history should not be neglected. Some conflicts are historical and there is the possibility of finding the handle in the history); (3) the religion of the people, whether past or present religion (beliefs, practices, teachings, symbols, rituals, and liturgy of their religion(s) could suggest a handle for peace and reconciliation); (4) the economic system of the people group or community (so many conflicts have economic undertones); and (5) the local administration and government (political or traditional).

In trying to find the handle, it should be noted that not all communities are mono cultural or mono religious. Urban, suburban, and semi-urban communities are often diverse, especially because of globalization resulting in

---

[4] The Gacaca traditional system of justice in Rwanda consisted of an informal, local system of participatory and restorative justice in which people, especially community elders, used to sit together in Gacaca (the "grass" or "lawn") and settle their disputes with the aim of reconciling conflicting parties (Sentama 2022). The Gacaca is said to be one of the most powerful tools used in the Rwandan peace and reconciliation.

increased global migration (Whiteman 2006, 66–67). Engaging the religious, ethnic, and cultural diversities existing in the community is a major way of finding the handle for peace in the context of diversity.

The Role of the Missionary, Church, or Mission Agency

The first thing you should do as a missionary or mission agency is to seek to study to be able to understand the people group or the community. Understanding their culture and the way they live and run the community is very important. Understanding them will better enable you to guide and work with them. This will enable you to best respect their opinion and sense of judgment. The missionary has the role of helping the community navigate the handle within the context of the people group or community. You should not influence them with any external agenda but allow them to pursue an agenda that is natural to them. The Sawi people were already aware of the handle, but some people groups or communities may not be—that is why they need the missionary as a guide.

> The missionary has the role of helping the community navigate.

The handle should be studied in the light of Scripture to be sure it does not contradict the Bible. When Biakadon[5] was taken as a peace child to the enemy community, Don followed to be sure that the ritual did not include some kind of Canaanite human sacrifice (Richardson 1974, 198–99). If that were the case, he was prepared to do all he could to rescue the child and return him to his mother. If the handle contradicts Scripture, it can block the Christian witness and close future doors.

With the handle found, the community should be allowed to confront themselves with the truth of what is going on. They should be trusted with the ability to negotiate reconciliation. This negotiation may take time because they may need to build trust among themselves for the reconciliation to be effective. It is also possible that the handle may fail to yield positive results. A new handle should be looked for and if found, the process should be repeated. There should be no end to the search for peace.

In the case where the community is diverse such as in cities, suburbs, or semi-urban communities, the missionary, agency, or church should engage the diversity(s) found in the community. The most effective way to engage the diversity is through dialogue. About dialogue, Ariarajah wrote, "Dialogue is not so much about attempting to resolve immediate conflicts, but about building a 'community of conversation,' a 'community of heart and mind' across racial,

---

5 The child donated as Peace Child from one of the communities.

ethnic, and religious barriers whose people learn to see differences among them not as threatening but as 'natural' and 'normal'" (Ariarajah 1999, 13–14).

In communities, it is possible for the dominant culture to be rated higher and minority culture looked down upon as noted above. In reconciliation negotiation, all ethnic groups, all religious groups, and all cultural groups should be treated as equal partners at the negotiation table.

The church, mission agency, and the missionary should see prayer as their primary responsibility. We rely on God to uncover the right handle that will bring peace, and on the Holy Spirit to convict people of truth and accept it. The community as a mission field may not be able to pray for themselves, they will need to have intercessors in the missionary, mission agency, and mission church. It is possible to have a few disciples at the time of the conflict, enlist them in prayer and teach them the need for peace from Scripture, so they can be the leading agents of peace in those communities.

Conclusion

This chapter on "community-based reconciliation" using the Sawi "Peace Child" story as case study argues that *true and genuine reconciliation in a community that will produce lasting result is community-based*. The need for peace and reconciliation in a world full of conflict underscores the importance of this chapter. We have reflected on conflicts around the world and discussed how conflicts relates to and affect mission. We also discussed biblical perspectives of reconciliation, and reconciliation as a missionary mandate. Further, we discussed community-based reconciliation which is the heart of the chapter.

God in his provision has blessed each community and people group with resources in their culture, traditions, history, religion, government, and way of life that can be useful in overcoming their problems. These resources are referred to here as the *handle*. The Sawi "Peace Child," the Rwandan Gacaca, and the Ubuntu of South Africa are examples of handles that reinforce the concept of community-based reconciliation. This chapter conclusively affirms that the most effective and long-lasting reconciliation that can bring about lasting peace is community based and should be pursued by missionaries and agencies who seek to bring about peace in communities for the prospect and or progress of missions.

References Cited

"Alert 2020! Report on Conflicts, Human Rights and Peacebuilding." Escola de Cultura de Pau, July 8, 2021. https://reliefweb.int/report/world/alert-2021-report-conflicts-human-rights-and-peacebuilding.

Ariarajah, S. Wesley. 1999. *Not Without My Neighbor: Issues in Interfaith Relations*. Geneva: WCC Publications.

Awoniyi, Peter Ropo. 2012. "Inter-Religious Dialogue: Tool for Peaceful Co-existence in Nigeria a Religious Pluralistic Nation." In *Indigenization of the Church in Africa: The Nigerian Situation in Honor of Dr. Ezekiel Bamigboye*, edited by A. A. Akande, M. Audi, and O. B. Oladejo, 495–510. Ibadan, Nigeria: Baptist Press (Nig.) Ltd.

Barth, Karl. 2004. *The Doctrine of Reconciliation*. Translated by G. W. Bromiley. New York: Continuum.

Bevans, Stephen B., and Roger P. Schroeder. 2004. *Constants in Context: A Theology of Mission for Today*. Maryknoll, NY: Orbis Books.

Godspecial, Moses O. 2018. *Understanding the Ongoing Bloodshed in Nigeria*. Lagos, Nigeria: Global Christian Communications.

Jakada, Yakubu. 2020. "Early Christian Responses to Persecution and Their Implications for Christians in Northern Nigeria." A dissertation submitted to the Faculty of Asbury Theological Seminary, Wilmore, Kentucky.

Ott, Craig, Stephen J. Strauss, and Timothy C. Tennent. 2010. *Encountering Theology of Mission: Biblical Foundations, Historical Developments, and Contemporary Issues*. Grand Rapids, MI: Baker Academic.

Radzik, Linda. 2019. "Reconciliation" *Stanford Encyclopedia of Philosophy*, revised August 2, 2019. https://plato.stanford.edu/entries/reconciliation/.

Richardson, Don. 1974. *Peace Child: An Unforgettable Story of Primitive Jungle Treachery in the 20th Century*. Ventura, CA: GL Publications.

Sande, Ken. 1991. *The Peacemaker: A Biblical Guide to Resolving Personal Conflict*. Grand Rapids, MI: Baker Book House.

Sentama, Ezechiel. 2022. "National Reconciliation in Rwanda: Experiences and Lessons Learnt." *European University Institute*, February 28, 2022. https://cadmus.eui.eu/bitstream/handle/1814/74338/QM-09-22-105-EN-N%5B54%5D.pdf?sequence=1&isAllowed=y.

Tutu, Desmond. 2019. "Truth and Reconciliation Commission, South Africa." *Encyclopedia Britannica*, updated March 20, 2023. https://www.britannica.com/topic/Truth-and-Reconciliation-Commission-South-Africa.

Van Yperen, Jim. 2002. *Making Peace: A Guide to Overcoming Church Conflict*. Chicago: Moody Press.

Whiteman, Darrell L. 2006. "Anthropological Reflections on Contextualizing Theology in a Globalizing World." In *Globalizing Theology: Belief and Practice in an Era of World Christianity*, 52–69, edited by Craig Ott and Harold A. Netland. Grand Rapids, MI: Baker Academic.

Chapter 12

Effective Discipleship for Reconciliation

Case of Genocide against the Tutsi in Rwanda

Kwizera Emmanuel

Reconciliation as the Mission of God (*missio Dei*) to the Broken World

Reconciliation is the message of the church. It is not a topic for countries that have gone through war, genocide, and other kinds of trouble that we see around the world. It is a biblical concept taught by Jesus Christ, and later upheld by the life and ministry of the first disciples. In Matthew 18:15,[1] Jesus said; "If your brother or sister sins, go and point out their fault, just between the two of you. If they listen to you, you have won them over." And in Matthew 5:23, 24 Jesus says "Therefore, if you are offering your gift at the altar and there remember that your brother or sister has something against you, leave your gift there in front of the altar. First go and be reconciled to them; then come and offer your gift."

Pauline teachings emphasize the Christian theology of peace and reconciliation. 2 Corinthians 5:19–20 say, "God was reconciling the world to himself in Christ, not counting people's sins against them. And he has committed to us the message of reconciliation. We are therefore Christ's ambassadors, as though God were making his appeal through us. We implore you on Christ's behalf: Be reconciled to God." And in Romans 12:18–19, Paul commands the church in Rome to live at peace with everyone: "If it is possible, as far as it depends on you, live at peace with everyone. Do not take revenge, my dear friends, but leave room for God's wrath, for it is written: 'It is mine to avenge; I will repay,' says the Lord."

Reconciliation should be part of the discipleship offered anywhere and at any time. As we will discuss in this paper, reconciliation and discipleship should not only be regarded as church programs, materials, projects, academic

---

[1] Unless otherwise noted, all Scripture quotations are from the NIV.

knowledge, or only a theological argument; they should be a lifestyle of every believer of Jesus Christ as the mission of God to his people.

The central meaning of reconciliation is the restoration of a right relationship. Reconciliation includes a concept of justice, which restores. We, as God's missionary people, need to restore reconciliation as God's mission (Gallagher and Hertig, 2017). I would say that the ministry of reconciliation between God and men and between people has been entrusted to the church, and this is God's mission to the world. "Mission was not made for the church; the church was made for mission—God's mission" (Wright 2006, 62).

> Reconciliation and discipleship ... should be a lifestyle of every believer of Jesus Christ.

Our mission is wholly derived from God's mission. It addresses the whole of God's creation, and is grounded at its center in the redeeming victory of the cross (The Lausanne Movement 2006). The apostolic church in the book of Acts describes God's intention to unfold his reconciling mission in his kingdom as it points to the person of Jesus Christ and works toward God's vision of a united and just society. "The biblical conviction that God is active in the world, active in human history through people he calls and sends, is at the heart of mission" (Escobar 2003, 86).

The concept of *togetherness* was at the center of the life of disciples. In Acts 2:44–47 it says:

> All the believers were *together* and had everything in common. They sold property and possessions to give to anyone who had need. Every day, they continued to meet *together* in the temple courts. They broke bread in their homes and ate *together* with glad and sincere hearts, praising God and enjoying the favor of all people and the Lord added to their number daily those who were being saved. (Emphasis mine.)

I would argue that the proclamation of the gospel through evangelism, growing new converts into disciples, and pursuing the holistic spiritual transformation of communities, are inseparable from God's mission of reconciliation. The center of reconciliation is our Savior Jesus Christ in whom God was reconciling the world to himself.

However, some of the pragmatic atheists built a case to reject Christian faith based on the hatred, division, and broken community that is present in the countries where Christianity is the majority. They argue that if Christianity is a true religion, we shouldn't hear of conflicts in churches, genocides, and civil wars in those countries. Religion has been an enormous multiplier of tribal suspicion and hatred (Hitchens 2009, 61). Many people who take an intellectual stand against Christianity do so against a background of personal disappointment by fellow Christians and churches (Keller 2009, 51). How can we be Christians and still live with hatred and anger? How can we live with slavery, apartheid, ethnic and racial hatred, family dislocation, and divorce? What has gone wrong with our evangelization and Christian discipleship? What can we do to become "ambassadors of reconciliation"? (The Lausanne Movement 2011).

As I will discuss in the next section of this chapter, the case of genocide against the Tutsis in Rwanda, left many questions related to Christian faith and its perspective of humanity and the creation. I would say that people are the focus of God's love and God is on mission to redeem creation. "Our mission means our committed participation as God's people, at God's invitation and command, in God's own mission within the history of God's world, for the redemption of God's creation" (Wright 2006, 23).

Any injustice or disrespect for human life—whether in the form of racism, tribalism, colonialism, hate speech, or economic exploitation, is an affront to the Creator who made every one of us in his own image (*imago Dei*). God longs for each one of us to live whole, complete, and fulfilled lives, rejoicing in God's love for all humanity in Christ Jesus. The narrative of the salvation in Christ Jesus reflects God's plan to reconcile to himself all things, through Christ Jesus. This reality should be the content of an effective discipleship model in our churches.

Part I: The Case of God's Mission in Rwanda

Introduction

Before the 1994 genocide against the Tutsi, the country of Rwanda was described as the most Christian country in Africa. The general population census of 1991 showed that Rwanda was 89 percent Christian, with a large proportion of Roman Catholics (62 percent), followed by Protestant denominations (27 percent), then traditionalists (8 percent), a few Muslims (1.5 percent) and other religions (0.5 percent). The genocide against the Tutsi people in Rwanda started on the night of April 6, 1994 and ended after one hundred days.

Although the exact number of people killed in the genocide is unknown, official Rwandan government documents estimate that the number is 1,074,017. As I mentioned above, many families record painful stories of the way their loved ones were killed. This includes the story of my grandfather, Oscar Rwasibo, a Presbyterian pastor, and my grandmother, who were killed by some of the elders of his church in Karongi district in Rwanda. According to the testimonies given by his neighbors, my grandfather decided to go into their church after many nights trying to hide in bushes. Both of them were killed there.

The hardest questions after the genocide against the Tutsi were "how do you rebuild a new community of offenders and offended, who will continue to worship in the same church, share the same market, farm the same land, and send their children to the same schools?" I would say that describing the case of reconciliation in Rwanda requires an understanding of its spiritual and socio-political history. The next part of this chapter looks at the two major missiological events of Christianity in Rwanda: (1) introduction of Christianity in Rwanda, and (2) the East African Revival.

Christianity in Rwanda

In the late nineteenth century, Roman Catholicism was the first Christian mission to arrive in Rwanda, when the country was part of German East Africa (1891–1919). In 1900, white fathers established their first mission station. In 1946, Catholic missionaries successfully made Christianity a state religion after the conversion of the King of Rwanda, Mutara III Rudahigwa (March 1911–July 25, 1959). He was the first Rwandan king to convert to Catholicism and take a Christian name: Charles Léon Pierre. Historians argue that his father had refused to convert to Christianity, and the Rwandan Catholic Church eventually considered him as anti-Christian and as an impediment to their civilizing mission. Rudahigwa had been secretly introduced to Christianity by Leon Class who was the head of the Rwandan Catholic Church since 1929, and was groomed by the Belgians to replace his father.

In 1946, King Mutara III Rudahigwa dedicated the country to Christ, effectively making Christianity a state religion. In Rwandan culture, a king was a symbol of God, he was God's representative on earth. This conviction spearheaded a wave of baptisms in the protectorate. This was described by theologians as a "Constantinian wave of conversion," which saw 95 percent of Rwandans baptized as Catholics. Rwanda was declared the most Christian country in Africa.

East African Revival

In the 1930s, East African countries experienced a great revival movement known as the "East African Revival." Its effects have been more lasting than almost any other revival in the church history of Africa. The East African Revival, which is also known in Uganda and Rwanda as the *Balokole*, translated in English as "saved ones," started at the hill of Gahini in the Anglican Church of Rwanda (Church 1981, 32). This spread to the whole region, as well as other countries, even beyond Africa.

It is very hard to know how this movement started. "This question did not interest many men and women who met the Lord through the East African Revival (MacMaster and Jacobs 2006, 25). Revival does not depend on people; it is evident that God always works through his people to accomplish his mission. For this movement, two names did recur as being the founders and key influencers of the revival: Joe Church from England, who was a medical missionary in Rwanda and Simeon Nsibambi from Uganda. They both had concerns about their church and had been praying for God to renew his church, his people. The appeal of the Keswick message in East Africa was evidenced in the rapid spreading of the revival, juxtaposed against the dead "formalism" and "modernism" of the Church of Uganda (Church 1981, 182–86).

While Joe Church was still a student, he became actively involved in the Cambridge Inter-Collegiate Christian Union (CICCU). This group was considerably influential among Christian students interested in foreign missions. From the late 1880s onward, Cambridge was a significant hotbed for a number of promising young foreign missionaries. Church's years at the CICCU were crucial to his spiritual and theological formation. A book popular in the CICCU at that time, *How to Live the Victorious Life*, had a profound influence on his religious conviction. The book represented the Keswick theology flourishing in the CICCU that emphasized the post-conversion experience of a second blessing, or "spirit-filling," and a strong desire for the higher Christian life.

The revival started in a small Bible study group, telling people about the joy of the filling of the Holy Spirit and the victorious life. These groups grew into a team, and they would go preaching on weekends, especially in the markets or other places where people were willing to listen. People began joining those small groups, to ask for advice and to pray with them. Revival came to East Africa in various ways, like hidden sins confessed, restitution for thefts or injuries, or the coming together of two or three or four seeking to know and do God's will.

Scholars of the East African Revival movement argue that the church in Rwanda, mainly those who have experienced revival like the Anglican Church of Rwanda, recall the memory of the revival, and this has been a theological and historical framework to explain both what happened in Rwanda in the years leading up to the genocide and to encourage reconciliation and healing in the post-genocide state, through reviving the traditions of movement such as: public confession of sins, love of your neighbors, hospitality, avoiding involvement in any political matters, etc.

I would say that these historical events, missionary work, revival, and later a genocide, should bring a theological debate on God's mission and the Great Commission. I do not agree with Richard K. MacMaster and Donald R. Jacobs who asserted that "Rwanda's Tutsi and Hutu people could have been spared decades of bloodshed if they had embraced the reconciliation power of Christ. That was the tragedy of Rwanda. God gave them the answer on their woes, but they repeatedly rejected the Prince of Peace. Some people ask why the revival failed in Rwanda. It did not fail, it was rejected" (MacMaster and Jacobs 2006, 259).

As I will discuss in the next part of this chapter, my argument is that the East African Revival inspired repentance of the hatred and divisions. However, the 1959 revolution and the weakness of the church as an institution in the face of social crises and its accompanying massacres quenched the fire of the revival before it had produced lasting results (Rutayisire 1995, 114).

Revival in the Process of Reconciliation

Scholars of the East African Revival agree that this revival brought people together and its character as a holiness movement created harmony and oneness among the people who were part of this movement. This reconciliation and repentance of hatred and division were even impactful to the life of missionaries in East Africa, as there were missionaries who remarkably confessed their own sins of feeling racially superior. Thus, the scholars of the East African Revival argue that the attitude of some missionaries toward the political organization of the country and their unwillingness to allow the revival message to penetrate deep social and ethnic issues within colonial Rwandan society, became the barrier to the revival creating an inter-ethnic Christian fellowship in Rwanda. The movement touched mainly people at the grassroots level, but some nobles and even high-ranking chiefs like Ruhorahoza of Bugesera and Mbaraga of Kanage were among the new committed Christians in Rwanda.

Part II: Post-Genocide Rwanda: Journey of Reconciliation

Introduction

As I mentioned in the first part of this chapter, the 1994 genocide against the Tutsi in Rwanda, left the country devastated in all aspects and had a significant effect on the life and the mission of the church. The genocide sparked a critical attack on the church in Rwanda, which was blamed for failing to stop the massacres. The question is, "should we analyze the testimony of the church based on individuals who refused to kill their neighbors because of their faith in Christ Jesus, or should we consider the church as an institution?" Some theologians proposed that for the analysis of this issue, the church should be considered as an institution, while others suggested that the church should be looked at as individuals in a church community.

However, in the aftermath of genocide, the country of Rwanda started the journey of healing, restoration, and reconciliation in Rwanda. This has been a difficult journey, especially with the background of the church as an institution, which not only did not teach about reconciliation enough before the genocide, but also was involved in the genocide. The other complication has been the fact that the church leaders themselves were hurting as they are part of the community. So, it took time for some to heal and reconcile themselves before they could even consider including reconciliation in their programs.

Other challenges include the high cost of reconciliation such as repentance, forgiveness, healing, and accepting the shame, guilt, and stigma, associated with the process of reconciliation in the hurting community. To some, the cost has been so high that they have abandoned it all together. But for those who accepted the cost and allowed the cross of Jesus Christ to be a place of reconciliation, they have witnessed a real and deep transformation in their lives, their communities, and the nation in general.

This is the case for young people who have been willing to come together under the cross of Jesus, repent of their own sins and stand in the gap for the sins of their families and forefathers. They bring their pain to the cross of Christ and have found their brothers and sisters who brought their own pain and forgiveness to the cross. Right there, Jesus has been uniting people, communities, and the nation as well. After the genocide of 1994, the church was covered with shame and accusations of her role in the genocide. The amazing thing is that despite the questions, the Protestant church, which includes mainline and evangelical branches, continues to grow.

Church Growth Post-Genocide

Genocide analysts and many writers thought that genocide put an end to Christianity in Rwanda, mostly due to its involvement. But to our surprise, the national census shows that the Protestant church has experienced a significant growth since the genocide. The national statistics on religion in Rwanda showed that in 1991, Romans Catholic were 62 percent, Protestant denominations were 27 percent, Traditionalists were 8 percent, Muslims were 1.5 percent, and other religions 0.5 percent. According to the national census in 2012, Roman Catholic were 43.7 percent, Protestants 37.7 percent, Seventh Day Adventists 11.8 percent, Muslims 4.5 percent, those who did not state any religion 1.3

percent, Jehovah's Witness 0.7 percent, non-religious beliefs 0.2 percent, and traditional religion 0.1 percent.

To my knowledge, there is no scientific research done to explain the dynamics of church growth, but according to Antoine Rutayisire responding to the question if anything changed after genocide answered, "Yes and no!" He argues, "Yes, because we now know the message, we should preach to heal the wounds of our nation. And no, because not many people are preaching it and those who preach it are not doing it with intentionality—that is, preaching until we see change!" He claims that the church in Rwanda had re-introduced the new perspectives on: (1) sin and alienation; (2) preaching the crucified Christ; (3) the identity; (4) the mission of the church; (5) social relationships; and (6) the power of our unity: mission and reconciliation (Cameron 2012, 67).

Part III: Rediscovering the Theology of Reconciliation for Discipling the Post-Genocide Generation

Introduction

A reflection on the post-genocide generation is very vital, mostly to prevent the cycle of violence and to build a future hope in the process of reconciliation. African theologians, researchers, and psychologists have noted two major challenges of the post-genocide generation: (1) passing on the trauma/transgenerational trauma; and (2) looking for political and theological answers. Professors of psychology and psychopathology at the University of Rwanda argue that it is mostly the 15- to 25-year-olds who experience traumatic attacks during the commemorative events. We asked ourselves, "Why does this group experience trauma, even though they were not yet born during the genocide?" I would say that the church is called to proclaim stories of hope to inspire reconciliation for the post-genocide generation. As we discuss in this paper, the post-genocide generation is looking for theological answers. These answers can be found through the story of hope and inviting them to believe in that story.

Finding True Identity in the Image of God

The question of identity, who we are, the identification to our ethnic or racial groups, has been the key factor to political and socioeconomic division. This division has led many countries to internal conflicts such as the case of genocide against the Tutsi in Rwanda or the apartheid in South Africa as well as the segregation and racism in the United States. The order in the process of how God created human beings, in his own image (*imago Dei*) is very vital for us to be God's earthly representatives. According to Genesis 1:26, God's image and God's likeness come before the full authority to have dominion over other creatures, and not the other way around. God says, "let us make mankind [human beings] in our image, in our likeness so that they may rule."

The *imago Dei* makes human beings different from other creatures like animals and makes them able to bear spiritual gifts. Functioning like God, reason, think, make choices, have relationships, communicate with the Creator and know his will. The message of the cross has brought a repentance of ethnic divisions and the restoration of the *imago Dei*. As the ethnic identity has been used as a dividing factor, the biblical narrative of *imago Dei* has been used as a theological reflection to study and assess root causes of conflict and the mission of God to redeem and restore the broken community for his glory.

The narrative of the mission of God in creation was that God created human beings in his own image, male and female, he created them. We should not have all these sorts of divisions, if we see each other in God's image. The only physical image with which God is represented is the human being—the one who can hear, understand, speak, and embody the divine Word, but the true representation of God has been lost (Treier 2019, 150). However, Paul wrote in Romans 3:23, "for all have sinned and fall short of the glory of God," and this justifies the human crises in its different forms. Human beings have failed to exercise their dominion over the earth and worship God without the image of God.

The good news of salvation we have in Christ Jesus is a story of creation, redemption, restoration, and justification of human beings. Ephesians 4:24 says, "To put on the new self, created to be like God in true righteousness and holiness." And Colossians 3:10 says, "Being renewed in knowledge in the image of its Creator." The church is called to redeem us in all aspects of our life and bring back God's righteousness at the center of our culture. Any sort of dehumanization, racism, genocide, and many more, are actions of destroying God's image.

> Any sort of dehumanization, racism, genocide, and many more, are actions of destroying God's image.

Reflecting on the 1994 genocide against the Tutsi in Rwanda, I would agree in saying that racism, slavery, genocide, and other forms of dehumanization, are acts of denying God. Theologically, racialization violates the equal dignity of all humans as bearers of the divine image (Treier 2019, 160). In fact, 1 John 4:20 says; "Whoever claims to love God, yet hates a brother or sister is a liar. For whoever does not love their brother and sister, whom they have seen, cannot love God, whom they have not seen."

Plurality and unity, which is also present in the triune nature of God, is a characteristic of God's created order. Racism is a moral problem, and the church exists to promote and preserve morality (Prior and Chatraw 2019). In Colossians 1:13, Paul writes, "For He has rescued us from the dominion of darkness and brought us into the kingdom of the Son he loves." We need the cross of Jesus Christ at the center of reconciliation.

Integrating the Cross of Jesus Christ at the Center of the Theology of Healing

The theological concept of the need of a wounded healer to heal the wounded soul has been used for the spiritual healing of wounds and trauma after the genocide against the Tutsi in Rwanda. These represent Jesus Christ as the person who understands wounded people because he was also wounded. In the case of Rwanda, survivors of the genocide needed someone that they could trust and who can feel and heal their wounds. The self-identification to the suffering of Jesus Christ brought healing and forgiveness.

On the other side, how do we present the cross of Jesus as a cause of repentance to the oppressors and the cause of forgiveness to the oppressed? In Psalm 103:2, 3, the psalmist mentions two benefits we get from God: "Praise the LORD, my soul, and forget not all his benefits, who forgives all your sins and heals all your diseases." We often preach about Christ our sin bearer to call people to repentance but rarely call people to offload their pain, frustrations, anger, hatred, and bitterness on the cross. This is the message the offended must hear in order to heal. It is only when people have been healed that they can forgive. And many times, we preach the cross without touching on those issues of perpetrators and offenders. When preached pertinently, this message leads the offender to confessing and repenting, facilitating the coming together. Only when the offender confesses and asks for forgiveness, and the offended has healed and is ready to forgive, can real reconciliation happen. And the cross of Jesus Christ is the ideal place for such a happening.

The message of the cross of Jesus Christ should bring inner healing and hope through repentance, forgiveness, and lament. I would agree with other scholars of reconciliation, that the practice of lament grounds the journey of reconciliation. Lament is not despair. It is not whining. It is not a cry into a void. Lament is a cry directed to God. It is the cry of those who see the truth of the world's deep wounds and the cost of seeking peace. It is the prayer of those who are deeply disturbed by the way things are.

My argument is that physical suffering often affects our relationship with God and with others, and has an impact on all the aspects of our life. The Scriptures say in Proverbs 17:22 "A joyful heart is good medicine, but a crushed spirit dries up the bones." This experience is a reality for every human being, to ask themselves questions in the midst of painful experience such as genocide: Why suffering? Why me? Where is God? Does he care? Does he know everything? If God knows everything, does it mean that he knew that genocide would happen? If he is almighty, why does he not stop evil doers?

In Psalm 42:3, the psalmist says in his lament to God, "My tears have been my food day and night, while people say to me all day long, 'where is your God?'" Heartfelt cries and existential questions operate at the core of healthy theology, and suppressing them is more hurtful than a confession of ignorance (Kapic 2017). Suffering keeps us isolated from God, throughout the journey of pain; instead of understanding YHWH as God of love, mercy, and compassion, sufferers see him in a false image. One of the survivors told me that he thinks that God was dead during the genocide, another one thinks that God is powerless in times of pain and suffering.

Throughout the Bible, we see lament as a spiritual discipline of God's people. In Psalm 56:8, David writes "Record my misery; list my tears on your scroll— are they not in your record?" The theological argument is that lament will not solve all of the genocide survivors' questions on the theology of suffering, but it provides a genuine space to bring their suffering to God's attention and allow God to help them cope with it. To lament is to respond to God's plan in the story of creation, salvation, and redemption.

Part IV: Implication for the Global Church

The story of Rwanda is a story of the mission of God to redeem and restore a broken community, and what happened in Rwanda can happen anywhere. This section will cover some of the lessons that the global church can learn from Rwanda.

Our Responsibility in the Mission of God of Reconciliation

In the history of the church, many times, Christians have failed to defend people who are oppressed or protect those who are in danger. The biblical narrative of Cain and Abel in the Genesis 4:4–10, portrays the sinful nature of jealousy and irresponsibility. When Cain killed his brother Abel, God asked "where is your brother Abel?" Cain replied, "Am I my brother's keeper?" Then, the Lord said, "What have you done? Listen! Your brother's blood cries out from the ground" (Gen 4:10). Christians are called to be the light and the salt of the world. Matthew 5:14–16 says:

> You are the light of the world. A town built on a hill cannot be hidden. Neither do people light a lamp and put it under a bowl. Instead, they put it on its stand, and it gives light to everyone in the house. In the same way, let your light shine before others, that they may see your good deeds and glorify your Father in heaven.

The church should be the hope of the hopeless by living out reconciliation with one another and being committed to peacemaking. Reconciliation to God is inseparable from reconciliation to one another. God's plan for the integration of the whole creation in Christ is modeled in the ethnic reconciliation of God's new humanity (The Lausanne Movement 2006). Isaiah 53:5 says, "But he was pierced for our transgressions, he was crushed for our iniquities; the punishment that brought us peace was on him, and by his wounds we are healed." Psalm 103:2–3 portrays the message of reconciliation: "Praise the LORD, my soul, and forget not all his benefits—who forgives all your sins and heals all your diseases."

Discipleship Framework

The framework for effective discipleship for reconciliation in Rwanda is the stories of people of hope reflected in four aspects. First, the theological aspect is the cross of Jesus brings reconciliation between God and his people and between people themselves. Christians have been called to preach and live God's message of repentance, forgiveness and healing. The radical love that recognizes God's image in everyone is an integral part of God's demand for justice. As human beings, they were all created by God and entitled to the protection of the church (the holy places and those who accepted a life of discipleship expressed through love and justice). Those who did not accept those demands failed to accept God's presence and the kingdom of peace and justice in Rwanda (Aguilar 1998, 67).

Second is the sociological aspect where offended and offenders (survivors and perpetrators) live together. In Rwanda, people have made a choice to stay together. Genocide survivors and perpetrators live in the same neighborhood and their descendants go to the same school. The biblical response to a divided community is to facilitate unity. Third is the ecclesiological aspect. God's mission to the church is to be a multi-ethnic church and worship YHWH. He rejoices in diversity. Revelation 7:9 says "After this, I looked, and there before me was a great multitude that no one could count, from every nation, tribe, people and language, standing before the throne and before the Lamb. They were wearing white robes and were holding palm branches in their hands."

The fourth aspect is anthropological. Interethnic marriages between Hutu and Tutsi have been a beautiful story of reconciliation. This has restored friendship between families and removed hostility for future generations. The process of reconciliation is helping Rwandan people to restore their cultural values such as promoting the national identity *Ndi Umunyarwanda*, literally translated as "I am Rwandese." The model of discipleship in Rwanda, is not only the curriculum but the kind of life people live. However, reconciliation is a journey that requires commitment from the country and its people.

Jesus's Model of Discipleship

In many countries, Christian leaders have lost their moral authority by not living what they preach. Communities are transformed by the kind of lives we live, rather than the position we have or what we tell them; this is the biblical discipleship model. We need to restore the Jesus model of discipleship—an invitation to become like him, our Rabbi. Jesus, our Savior-King was born into a rabbi-disciple culture. In this culture, a rabbi would invite disciples to follow and learn from him. The church was born in a discipleship paradigm, a culture where a rabbi invested in their disciples. When the center of the church moved from Jerusalem to Rome, the culture of discipleship was replaced by a culture of consumption (Geiger and Peck 2016, 56).

The ministries of the church, including reconciliation, have become only programs and materials rather than a lifestyle of discipleship. Our communities long to see and experience the reality of reconciliation, and the world should learn from the journey of reconciliation in Rwanda. The church in Africa and Africans in diaspora need to collaborate and engage with the global mission of reconciliation. We need Christian leaders with a "kingdom paradigm" for holistic community transformation wherever the gospel is being preached.

As I conclude, reflecting on the last twenty-eight years after the genocide against the Tutsi in Rwanda, I want to stress that living together is possible. We are the product of our past but not the prisoners of it. We cannot change the past, but the church should respond to God's mission of reconciliation. Effective discipleship for reconciliation is possible and should engage all the aspects of our life—our thinking and our living. It requires intentionality and should be part of discipleship anywhere and at any time. There is a cost to working for reconciliation, especially when the society is already divided. However, if we pursue reconciliation before division occurs, it can even serve as a preventive measure. The message of reconciliation in our churches goes beyond theory and materials. It is a lifestyle for every disciple of Jesus Christ as a way to respond to God's message of reconciliation.

References Cited

Aguilar, Mario I. 1998. *The Rwanda Genocide and the Call to Deepen Christianity in Africa*. Eldoret, Kenya: AMECEA Gaba Publications.

Cameron, Julia E. M. 2012. *Christ Our Reconciler: Gospel, Church, World*. Downers Grove, IL: IVP Books.

Chatraw, Josh, and Karen Swallow Prior. 2019. *Cultural Engagement: A Crash Course in Contemporary Issues*. Grand Rapids, MI: Zondervan.

Church, J. E. 1981. *Quest for the Highest*. Australia: Bookhouse Richmond Road.

Escobar, Samuel. 2003. *The New Global Mission*. Downers Grove, IL: IVP Academic.

Gallagher, Robert L., and Paul Hertig. 2017. *Contemporary Mission Theology: Engaging the Nations*. New York: Orbis Books.

Geiger, Eric, and Kevin Peck. 2016. *Designed to Lead*. Nashville: B&H Publishing House.

Hitchens, Christopher. 2009. *God Is Not Great: How Religion Poisons Everything*. New York: Hachette Book Group.

Kapic, Kelly M. 2017. *Embodied Hope: A Theological Meditation on Pain and Suffering*. Downers Grove, IL: IVP Academic.

Keller, Timothy. 2009. *The Reason for God: Belief in an Age of Skepticism*. New York: Penguin Books.

Lausanne Movement. 2006. "Rediscovering the Gospel of Reconciliation." *Lausanne Movement*. https://lausanne.org/content/rediscovering-the-gospel-of-reconciliation.

Lausanne Movement. 2011. "The Cape Town Commitment." *Lausanne Movement*. January 25, 2011. https://www.lausanne.org/content/ctcommitment#capetown.

MacMaster, Richard K., and Donald R. Jacobs. 2006. *Gentle Wind of God: The Influence of the East Africa Revival*. Scottdale, PA: Herald Press.

Rutayisire, Antoine. 1995. *Faith under Fire. Testimonies of Christian Bravery*. London: African Enterprise.

Treier, Daniel J. 2019. *Introducing Evangelical Theology*. Grand Rapids, MI: Baker Publishing Group.

Wright, Christopher J. H. 2006. *The Mission of God: Unlocking the Bible's Grand Narrative*. Downers Grove, IL: IVP Academic.

Chapter 13

An Invitation to the Table

Stories of Mission, Reconciliation, and Food

Andrea Chang and Nelson Chang

Reconciliation is at the center of God's missional purpose in the biblical narrative. From the creation story in Genesis, to Israel's narrative, Jesus's life and ministry, as well as the life of the church, God weaves reconciliation into the fabric of the entire biblical narrative. Interestingly, a focused view on this biblical narrative not only shows the importance of reconciliation but also that food is often present in this reconciliation.

Throughout the Old Testament, food is found in the reconciliatory narrative of the Bible. In the creation story, God creates food for the nourishment and sustenance of life (Gen 1:29). Adam and Eve partake in this nourishment, but their disobedience in eating of the fruit from the tree of the knowledge of good and evil results in consequences for them. Food is still needed for their sustenance, but they now suffer the pain of toiling for that food (Gen 3:4–19).

Food is also used for reconciliation in the Joseph narrative (Gen 37–50). This story tracks the Israelite people migrating from their homeland to Egypt because of the lack of food due to famine. This migration leads to reconciliation between Joseph and his family. Another example of food in the Old Testament is Moses in Exodus 16, where God sustains Israel with supernatural manna in the wilderness, leading to a deeper trust in him. Also, in Leviticus 23, the people of Israel find restoration with God through the establishment of feasts and festivals. Throughout the Old Testament, food is present in the reconciliatory narrative of God and his people.

The importance of food and reconciliation continues in the New Testament in the life and ministry of Jesus. Through the culmination of his life, death, and resurrection, followers of Jesus are reconciled with God (Rom 5:10). This reconciliation is the foundational truth of the good news of Jesus for humanity. Jesus speaks of this good news when he declares himself as the bread of life, alluding to the spiritual renewal found in him through his salvific death and resurrection (John 6:35). In the parable of the sower, Jesus uses the analogy of sowing seeds to produce food as an explanation of the different responses toward his reconciliatory good news (Matt 13:1–23; Mark 4:1–20; Luke 8:4–15).

After his resurrection, Jesus appears to his disciples in John 21 following a long night of unsuccessful fishing and helps them miraculously catch fish. He then invites them to bring some of the catch to eat breakfast with him. During this meal together, Jesus restores Simon Peter to the ministry calling on his life. Many other examples of Jesus's life showcase the importance of food and reconciliation. Whether it is the parable of the great banquet (Luke 14:15–24), the miraculous feeding of the crowds (Matt 14:13–21; 15:32–39), or the parable of the mustard seed (Mark 4:30–32), these glimpses of Jesus's life and ministry connect food with the reconciliatory purpose of his life.

The church continues this theme of food and reconciliation in the New Testament. In accordance with Jesus's example and teachings, his followers devoted themselves to the fellowship and breaking of bread together (Acts 2:42–47). A significant moment for the church is found in Acts 10:1–11:18, where food plays an essential role in breaking barriers between Jews and Gentiles with the interaction between Peter and Cornelius, the Roman centurion. This is a pivotal moment for reconciliation of God's people because here they begin to fully apply the life and teachings of Jesus to transform and become a new *ecclesia* that is diverse and inclusive, with food being a common medium and vehicle for this reconciliation.

The biblical pattern continues today with the church fulfilling God's missional mandate to be participants in his reconciliation. 2 Corinthians 5:19 says, "God was reconciling the world to himself in Christ, not counting people's sins against them. And he has committed to us the message of reconciliation." Throughout the generations, the church has been sent on mission and tasked with the message and action of reconciliation, involving both spiritual renewal through Christ and practical life-giving restoration in the lives of all people. Throughout these transformative and compassionate interactions, food is often present.

> Throughout the generations, the church has been sent on mission and tasked with the message and action of reconciliation.

Case Study: An Invitation to the Table

This chapter is a case study called "An Invitation to the Table," an initiative that weaves reconciliation, mission, and food together through the powerful medium of narrative. This case study details stories told or birthed over Sunday afternoon meals through the Newcomers Fellowship at The Peoples Church, where congregation members extend hospitality to newcomers and share a meal together. It will highlight five important elements that surfaced from these meals that contribute to reconciliation through food while walking alongside diverse people from around the world as they make their journey of life and faith in a new country. These five elements are *commonality, conversation, culture, community,* and *communion.*

Humans have lots in *common*, such as basic needs, a desire to be loved, to feel safe, to belong, and to have purpose. In recognizing and highlighting these commonalities, people can begin building bridges with one another through open and honest *conversation*. These bridges unlock the door to celebrating differences of identity and *culture* through the act of sharing. Through these intentional actions, a new *community* is formed, and people move from being welcomed toward the sense of belonging. Finally, mission and reconciliation around shared meals center people in Christ so they can experience the restorative *shalom* of *communion* with God and with each other.

This case study will highlight these five elements of reconciliation in "An Invitation to the Table" using the medium of narratives and stories of participants encountered at these meals. These narratives give a glimpse of the heart of Jesus found in his parable of the great banquet: a redemptive story of an intentional invitation to eat food as a medium and vehicle of restoration and reconciliation (Luke 14:15–24).

Commonality

A light gust of air blew from the kitchen across the dimly lit room carrying a warm aroma of sweet and spicy herbs as Jung and Olabiyi prepared the dining tables for lunch. As the scent reached them they glanced at each other, wondering what today's lunch would be. Last week several Korean guests treated the group to Bibimbap, a flavorful smorgasbord of mixed rice with bar-b-que Korean beef, assorted vegetables, and a golden sunny-side up egg on top. They served kimchi on the side, which was a bit spicy for most people that day, causing the water pitchers to be emptied and filled more than usual. The week before was a delicious Eggplant Parmesan. It had the taste of Italian authenticity because the chef was an Italian-trained African cook, who sought refuge in Italy when conflict arose in her home country, but later made Canada her home. Jung and Olabiyi grinned with anticipation because lunch was always special at Newcomers Fellowship.

Toronto is one of the most multicultural cities in the world with more than 430,000 immigrants arriving every year (Singer 2021). By being in this city, The Peoples Church has the privilege of serving hot meals for these newcomers to Canada every Sunday at their Newcomers Fellowship lunch. Jesus's example of radical hospitality models the loving posture of welcoming the strangers in our midst, and the Newcomers Fellowship strives for this convivial experience every week. Elegant black tablecloths drape the tables, along with a centerpiece for the season, and upbeat international music playing faintly in the background—there is a place setting for anyone who wants to join. Care and consideration are put into each preparatory detail at this lunch because that is how members of the church would treat any guests who entered their own home.

This radical hospitality showcases the first commonality with the guests: the desire to be safe, welcomed, and feel a sense of belonging. Reconciliation often starts with the acknowledgment of these basic human needs. As strangers in a new country, many newcomers do not have connections, friends, or family. Therefore, offering a safe space for them to find support and companionship is immensely important for their health and wellbeing. Instilling a sense of safety is the first step to building trust for a healthy relationship, and eventually leads to restoration and reconciliation.

This meal highlights another commonality: the human need for food which is necessary for life, sustenance, and nourishment. This common need for food brings people to the table and opens many opportunities for support and companionship, while also pointing directly to the need for God. According to Wirzba, eating "establishes a membership that confirms all creatures as profoundly in need of each other and upon God to provide life's nutrition and vitality" (Wirzba 2011, 2). This common need for food is a unique design of God, but food need not only be a necessary part of humanity's common physiological design, it can also be enjoyable. With the many different ethnic diaspora groups in Toronto, it is easy to find different recipes to satisfy diverse palettes and explore new, adventurous flavors. Therefore, people are grateful for both the nourishment and the diversity of food. "To say grace or offer a benediction of thanksgiving over a meal is among the highest and most honest expressions of our humanity" (Wirzba 2011, 179).

As the preparations for lunch finish, the guests begin to arrive. They trickle in slowly and form a beautifully diverse mosaic of individuals from different parts of the world all gathered in one place. Despite their differences—whether the color of their skin, their various unique physical features, the ethnicity they belong to, or the nationality they claim—they are all created by God and share a common humanity with one another. This diverse setting might be a small glimpse of how God's reconciled church is described in Revelation 7:9 ESV as "a great multitude that no one could number, from every nation, from all tribes and peoples and languages, standing before the throne and before the Lamb."

As the Newcomers Fellowship lunch commences and people start to eat together, a low hum of voices begin to get louder as conversations turn to the sharing of stories. Here another commonality arises: shared migration stories. During the lunch, the migratory nature of humanity is intentionally acknowledged. Referencing current scientific theories of historical human migration (Ness 2014, 70), as well as the biblical migration narratives including Abraham (Gen 12-20), the people of Israel (Gen 32, 35, 46; Exod 12-19; 2 Kgs 25:11-26), and the scattering of the early church (Acts 8:1) lead to the conclusion that all humans have a migration story. This recognition helps build an inclusive and welcoming environment for all newcomers to Canada. Whether a person is a Canadian citizen, immigrant, asylum seeker, refugee, international student, or temporary worker, they all have a "how did you get here?" story and are welcome at the Newcomers Fellowship lunch. Sharing these common migration stories help to reconcile newcomers' current migration challenges by showing that they are not alone in their migration and that migration is as old as the first biblical stories of Adam and Eve. These shared commonalities surface from meals together, and the birth of reconciliation begins to appear.

Conversation

The midday sun threw an elongated shadow across the multicolored flag-lined wall as the young woman sneaked in earlier than normal one Sunday afternoon. Ava strolled in slowly, sitting at a freshly decorated table in the far end of the room. Mai would have missed her if not for the faint blurred movement she saw out of the corner of her eye. With a startled jump, Mai turned her head to find Ava quietly fiddling with her smartphone. Mai smiled at her and waved. Unlike her normal demeanor, Ava returned Mai's gesture with a half-grin out of one side of her mouth and a slight nod of her head acknowledging to Mai that she had been seen. Without saying one word to each other, Mai could sense there was something upsetting Ava.

After fleeing as a refugee from a Middle Eastern country, Ava had arrived in Canada only a few months before. She heard about the Newcomers Fellowship while living at a refugee transition house in Toronto and had been attending the Newcomers Fellowship lunch for several weeks. Even with only a basic understanding of English, Ava was often smiling, pert, and happy to attend.

Mai contacted a volunteer leader who spoke Ava's native language. They slowly approached her. Before any words could be said, Ava must have read the non-verbal cues on the leader's face because without warning the sun's bright rays exposed the tears glinting in her eyes that welled up as she began to sob uncontrollably. Mai and the other leader sat with Ava for the next few minutes, supporting her through her grief and saying silent prayers for God's comfort to sooth her pain.

Ava eventually composed herself. Through tears, she informed the volunteer that she was grieving for her home country. Although she was grateful to be living in Canada, she missed her country and her family. She longed for her people to be as free as she was. She longed to be back home but knew that it was too dangerous for her to go back now. The volunteer listened, nodded, gestured, acknowledged her pain, and prayed with her.

Communication can be challenging for people like Ava. It is often like participating in a slow waltz without any instruction in the art or practice—a forced, ungraceful effort with more questions afterward than when you started. Many newcomers typically try to communicate through broken English or go back-and-forth between translation applications on their smartphones. Learning to communicate through non-verbal cues and gestures becomes immensely important. In moments like this incident with Ava, followers of Jesus must be led by the Holy Spirit while also increasing their competency in intercultural communication skills, awareness, and sensitivity to make conversations easier and to avoid misunderstandings.

Different cultures often feature differences in communication styles. Understanding these differences can increase a person's effectiveness in communication. Learning about communication dynamics such as high and low context communication, as well as direct and indirect communication are critical to effective conversations between different cultures (Meyer 2014, 39). Along with these communication skills, intercultural intelligence can help a person understand, communicate with, and effectively interact with people across cultures. Learning more about someone's unique culture can enable you to compare different cultures with minimal bias and to better understand differences between different cultures.

Unconsciously, all people bring their own cultural frame of interpretation to any situation and therefore reliance on the Holy Spirit for guidance is important for discernment. Through the leading and reliance of the Holy Spirit, communication focuses less on talking and more on listening to understand. This leads to a communicative posture that is patient with a willingness to listen more intently and be less judgmental. Through the help of the Holy Spirit along with better intercultural communication skills, reconciliation can begin to happen effectively between different cultures.

In the intentional moments of conversation and communication together over a meal at the Newcomers Fellowship, reconciliation begins to happen through deepening personal understanding, compassion, and the sharing of life with one another. Eating a meal together not only nourishes people's physical bodies but also leads people to more awareness of the world they find themselves in, and inspires them to be more present in the lives of the people in that world. As Wirzba says, "Because eating is something we regularly do, it can be the training ground where people learn to articulate their fears and worries, but also name the many sources of nurture and help that are evident at the table" (Wirzba 2011, 28).

Leaders at the Newcomers Fellowship have learned to not only empathize by saying "I understand," but also to show love through action, welcoming the stranger and acknowledging their hurt through compassion. They may use non-verbal communication like holding hands (when appropriate) and compassionate smiles to communicate gestures of welcome. They offer tissues for tears, hugs for sobs, and ask permission to pray. "Hospitality fosters empathy, for it brings people together, face to face, in a time of intentional listening" (Arrington 2017, 30).

Ministry leaders will often stay with a person in pain throughout the day. They will walk to the food line together for comfort just to return to the table to sit down to eat and talk more. They ask intentional questions and sensitively inquire about topics such as their families back home, what they miss about home, their favorite places to go, or activities they miss doing. Throughout it all, they actively listen, often leaning into the conversation to show interest.

Gathering together at the table for food opens opportunities for restoration and reconciliation through conversation. Good communication skills applied with grace, compassion, and love is effective in engaging others toward reconciliation. Christ first engaged humanity for reconciliation, and only through his compassionate love can people fully engage with others from different cultures on a deeper level. This level of engagement often does not happen quickly because building trust among one another takes time and intentionality. Eating at the table together slows people down to truly be present with others, redeeming the fast-paced, busy culture humanity has created for itself and reconciling it with God's ever-present kingdom culture.

Culture

George savored his slices of homemade pizza one Sunday afternoon. He enjoyed it so much that he quickly scarfed down a second helping before others at his table were finished with their first slice. As George politely waited for them to finish their first serving before going for a third helping himself, Jenni, the group leader, noticed his head tilted slightly upward gazing thoughtfully at a blank wall. Jenni watched him for several minutes deep in thought before his concentration finally broke when others at the table got up for more pizza. George quickly jumped out of his seat and immediately joined the crowd for more pizza. George was grinning ear to ear as he sat back down at his table and Jenni asked him, "George, you seemed like you were in deep thought earlier. Is there something on your mind?"

George replied, "Yes. I have a few questions and maybe you can help answer them. Is pizza considered Canadian food? Is pizza not Italian food? If pizza is considered Canadian food, when and how did this distinction happen? And if pizza is Canadian, are Italians upset over this?"

Jenni grabbed her plate and looked at George with a grin then sarcastically said, "I think it is time for me to get more pizza."

Navigating culture can be a complex endeavor. George's questions speak to this reality by highlighting the connection of food, ethnicities, culture, and reconciliation. "Cooking and eating practices are often not only symbolic but also tangible and concrete ways that ethnic identities are preserved by migrants in multicultural societies" (Reddy and Van Dam 2020, 1). George's comments illustrate that food is a distinctly important part of a person's culture and that reconciliation through food is complicated. George and Jenni eventually had a long conversation about group social and cultural identities. Their conversation identified three ways that these identities impact culture: (1) the impact of these identities within the construct of immigration and settlement over a long period of time; (2) the impact of these identities within the emergence of multicultural cities; and (3) the impact of these identities with the increase of global migration of people across the world.

The insights they shared with each other were complex and deserving of focused attention. The importance for this case study is the certainty that maintenance of food types and eating practices are an inherent part of a group's cultural and ethnic identity. But the challenge for reconciliation of group cultural dynamics is paradoxical. A group trying to keep their identity intact while generously sharing it with others, does not result in the maintenance of their culture. When they share their culture and practice reciprocity by having others share their culture with them, both cultures begin to transform. The result is the fusion of that mix and the formation of a new group culture. Thus, food such as pizza can be both Italian and Canadian.

This case study found that the activity of true reciprocal sharing is a vital way to engage other cultures in reconciliation. Along with sharing different types of food with one another, many Newcomers Fellowship activities centered on sharing Canadian cultural experiences with newcomers, as well as celebrating the various cultures in the group. Some Canadian activities include helping newcomers to experience and understand nuances of Canadian culture, food, celebrations, practices, and norms. Newcomers were invited to experience activities such as ice skating in the winter, apple picking in the fall, hiking nature trails in the spring, and visiting cottages in the summer. These experiences also come with the unique food offerings available during those seasons. Canadian food is tied closely to the culture, as well as with the season in a particular Canadian region.

The sharing of Canadian food and culture is also an exercise in reciprocity. The Canadian team members at the Newcomers Fellowship ask the newcomers questions about their own cultures so they can learn more about them. By intentionally asking questions and making sincere efforts to get to know others around the table, the Canadian team members not only learn about a newcomer's culture but also about their needs. This reciprocity brings mutual joy and encouragement, but for newcomers especially it is an invitation toward belonging and reconciliation.

Another way cultures are shared is by intentionally celebrating cultural holidays. It is regular practice at the Newcomers Fellowship to celebrate Canadian holidays like Canada Day, Thanksgiving, and Remembrance Day along with the important holidays of newcomers and their cultures as well. The Canadian Thanksgiving holiday is a great example of using food to share the Canadian culture with newcomers. During this celebration a big meal with traditional Canadian dishes is served. Volunteers provide an explanation of each dish and its significance to the celebration. This celebration also includes the story of indigenous peoples and their different views toward Canadian Thanksgiving, as this is an important part of the past, present, and future of Canadian culture.

Many diverse Canadians are also able to share how their individual families celebrate Canadian Thanksgiving and the many different foods in their traditions. In reciprocal manner, groups such as Brazilians and Koreans shared how they celebrate a Thanksgiving holiday in their home countries with food, activities, and dress. Other cultural holidays that have been celebrated include Lunar New Year and Nowruz. Newcomers gravitate toward this reciprocal sharing. They bring different food to share and explain with joy the significance of each dish within the holiday. This type of sharing goes beyond simply sharing food, but the sharing of culture, which is deeply personal and heartfelt, resulting in a reconciliatory understanding of each person to the other. Much of the sharing is bittersweet because many newcomers miss celebrating these holidays with their families and their home communities, but despite this fact, they are grateful for the opportunity to share their culture in their new home country along with their new community.

Community

Jane gently placed the kettle on the stove. Opening the cupboard, she reached for a tin box with colorful artwork depicting a canary and a cup. It reminded her of a similar box her mother kept personal items in when she was a child back in her home country. As she opened the box, she did not find personal items but was welcomed by an aromatic treasure trove of dried tea leaves in pouches. They were blended with various herbs and spices such as bergamot, lavender, cardamom, rose pedals, and so much more. She thought of her mother again and then of her father. She remembered the many times she made tea for them, as well as the many guests they would regularly host in their home. Many of these guests were extended family who lived in the same building. She smiled, remembering the joy and safety she had with this community.

She removed several pouches from the box and began ripping them open to expose the tea leaves neatly packed in semitransparent nylon bags. As she continued ripping the pouches open, a cold chill shot through her body that tensed her neck and shoulders. She thought about how her previous life and community tore apart because of conflict within her country, resulting in her fleeing her home and seeking refuge in Canada. She would never make tea for that community again. She would never be welcomed back home again.

The kettle sang with a high-pitched wheeze and sent up swirls of transparent steam into the air that signaled the water was boiling. Jane walked over to the kettle and gently moved it off the stove. She delicately poured the steaming water into a teapot with the tea bags. She smiled again. The simple act of brewing tea was something she always enjoyed doing. But today, it brought more than pleasure because it was purposeful and redemptive. Today she was brewing tea for the new community she belonged to, and it brought hope for her future.

It is hard for anyone to leave their family, their community, and their way of life to start something unfamiliar and new somewhere else. For newcomers to Canada, regardless of the reason they come to Canada, it is a difficult journey. There are so many barriers to becoming established in a new community, such as the struggle to find employment and adequate housing, English language comprehension, establishing relationships, and belonging to a community.

Surfacing from this case study is the fact that every newcomer to Canada not only wants to belong to a community but desires to be an integral part of their new community. They do not want to only receive support from the community but to give back to the community. As human beings, they want to feel like their skills are needed, wanted, and appreciated. Oden points out that it is "seductive, even dangerous, for the host to view herself as the helper. The would-be act of hospitality becomes an act of condescension and failure to see, either one's own need or the true identity of the stranger as Christ" (Oden 2001, 109).

So how can a host use their privilege to restore dignity and purpose to the lives of others? At the Newcomers Fellowship, this is accomplished by becoming aware of each newcomer's abilities and desires. Volunteers ask questions like, "What are you passionate about?" or "What are some of your skills and talents?" They intentionally provide opportunities for newcomers to help restore their dignity and purpose within the Newcomers Fellowship and their new community.

One of the most heartbreaking findings from this case study are the stories of many newcomers unable to find jobs in their profession or field of educational training because their credentials are not equivalent to Canadian standards. There are newcomer surgeons, therapists, and dentists whose education meets the requirements to get into the country but is not good enough to practice their profession. Unfortunately, many of these newcomers find themselves working in jobs that are well beneath their educational training and expertise. The opportunity to become re-trained, re-educated or certified by Canadian standards are limited because of the steep financial burden of the education system. Jane is one of these examples.

Jane came to Canada as a refugee. In her home country, she was an accountant. It has been difficult for her to settle in Canada because she is unable to work as an accountant. With her educational training unrecognized, lack of Canadian work experience, and limited connections in Canada, she turned to her cooking skills for an entry-level job at a restaurant. The Newcomers Fellowship helped her complete the Food Handlers certificate and journeyed with her until she got settled.

In time, she started her own business as a caterer and the Newcomers Fellowship became one of her first clients. Jane continues to serve with the Newcomers Fellowship to support others just as she was supported. They have given her leadership responsibilities by having her plan the Newcomer Fellowship meals, manage a team of volunteers, and oversee a food budget. Jane is now in a position to teach others about hospitality. As DeBorst says, "Hospitality is not merely an expression of compassion toward the other; when the host is humble enough to be hosted, it opens a two-way street in mission" (DeBorst 2015, 198).

Jane has progressed from being a participant and recipient of the community to using her gifts and talents to give back to the community as a leader. The mission of reconciliation through a new community includes investing in people to assist with restoration of their purpose, dignity, and hope in the future. "The promise borne by the reciprocal dialectic of host and stranger is the emergence of a new world of shared meanings" (Ogletree 2003, 4).

Communion

Beatrice loves bread, especially when it is freshly baked from the oven with its warm, delicate, and milky soft texture wafting an inviting earthy, sweet smell that so easily permeates a home. People who are only aware of the stereotypes of her East-Asian heritage would not imagine that she prefers bread over other Asian food staples such as rice or noodles. But Beatrice grew up baking and eating bread. From a young age, she found baking to be such a magical and mysterious process. Who knew that taking a dry powdery substance and mixing it with ingredients such as milk, water, sugar, eggs, and yeast, can be baked in a hot oven to result in a fluffy loaf of edible goodness? As she got older she learned of the scientific transformation that takes place in the mixing of these ingredients to change flour into dough, as well as the chemical reactions of yeast working through that dough to rise and proof so the heat from the oven can truly bring the bread to life. Little did Beatrice know that a similar transformation would happen in her life as she began sharing her love of bread with others at the Newcomers Fellowship lunch.

Beatrice came to Canada as an immigrant who did not know much English. She was not a Christian but was invited by a friend to attend the ESL classes offered at a church. Through this same friend, she heard about the Newcomers Fellowship lunch and showed up one Sunday afternoon for the meal. "I was not a Christian but everyone was so nice and hospitable that I always felt welcomed here."

Beatrice started attending regularly and allowed herself to gradually learn more about the Bible, Jesus, and why Christians are so hospitable. After each meal she was invited to join the ESL Bible study class. "At first, I came for the meal, but I stayed because I was curious and I also wanted to build friendships and learn English." Beatrice continued attending for two years and like the proofing of dough, her heart was slowly transformed. "It took a long time, but I was not rushed. I come from an atheist background and I needed to be sure that God was changing my heart." Beatrice has professed Christ as her personal Lord and Savior and recognizes that he is the true bread of life.

An Invitation to the Table

Inviting people who are vulnerable and at the margins of society into something new with Christ is what happens around the table at the Newcomers Fellowship. It may not start with a sermon or a gospel presentation, but rather an intentional invitation for a hot meal to experience what it is like to be in communion with Jesus Christ. Just as the grace of Jesus is extended to all humans through his death and resurrection on the cross, it must also be received by humans through faith in him according to Ephesians 2:8. Not everyone accepts the grace of Jesus Christ, and not everyone accepts the invitation to relationship, reconciliation, and communion. "When this healing takes place, a healing that is glimpsed at the Eucharistic table in the eating that people do, relationships are transformed so that they witness to true life" (Wirba 2011, 147). The community of the Newcomers Fellowship is humbly grateful to witness people like Beatrice who find restoration and reconciliation in communion with God and with others.

Jesus inaugurated communion during the Last Supper where he enjoyed a meal with his closest friends and disciples (Matt 26:17–29; Mark 14:12–25; Luke 22:7–38). For the disciples, this was a special, annual Passover meal, but for Jesus this was something more. Along with celebrating the Festival of Unleavened Bread, Jesus knew this was his last meal with his disciples, but the beginning of a new celebration. When Jesus invited his disciples to this table, he had a plan and a purpose that would forever impact their lives. From the shared meal together, to the washing of their feet, to the breaking of bread, and the drinking of the cup, the disciples witnessed Jesus's humble, cleansing, and restorative example which demonstrated to them a new way of life. The disciples would understand later that this Last Supper was an invitation to exercise their faith in Christ by spiritually feeding on him through the bread and cup as a symbolic way to be in communion with God.

Just like Jesus, the Newcomers Fellowship welcomes and invites newcomers to the table to share food and to share an experience with Christ in very practical and restorative ways. "Food is about the relationships that join us to the earth, fellow creatures, loved ones and guests, and ultimately God" (Wirzba 2011, 4). Although spiritual renewal is a major focus for the Newcomers Fellowship, their method for this happens through hospitality and welcoming. Many guests who join the Newcomers Fellowship are not Christians nor will they become Christians during their time with the Newcomers Fellowship. Despite this reality, the unwavering response toward newcomers is to serve and shower them with the love of Christ. Welcoming with radical hospitality introduces them to a different way of experiencing Jesus and an experiential communion that happens through his multifaceted reconciliation.

Conclusion

Food is an immensely important yet often overlooked vehicle for mission and reconciliation. The findings from this case study point to the fact that eating together is vital for a community of people to experience restoration and *shalom* of communion. But too often, God's people have taken for granted the power of hospitality and the generosity of sharing food. At the table commonalities are discovered, conversations go deeper, cultures are explored, community is formed, and communion is experienced. Therefore, an invitation to the table is an invitation to mutual relationship and sharing oneself with others.

> God's people have taken for granted the power of hospitality.

The potential outcome of this hospitality is beautiful communion with God and with others, but it is not without challenges. An invitation to the table also introduces possible conflict with others. God's people will risk being hurt by making themselves vulnerable to strangers, along with the potential that their hospitable commitment may never be fruitful. Despite these challenges and risks, an invitation to the table is more than worth the venture because it is an invitation for both the guest and host to draw nearer to God's kingdom.

As servants of God, inviting people to the table is an essential tool for reconciliation because it models the heart of God throughout the Bible and the example set by Jesus Christ. This is God's invitation to take part in his redemptive story of intentional welcome and celebratory feasting as a way toward restoration and reconciliation with him.

References Cited

Arrington, Aminta. 2017. "Becoming a World Christian: Hospitality As a Framework for Engaging Otherness." *International Journal of Christianity and Education* 21, no. 1: 26–38.

DeBorst, Ruth Padilla. 2015. "At the Table Their Eyes Were Opened: Mission As Renouncing Power and Being Hosted by the Stranger." *International Bulletin of Mission Research* 39, no. 4: 198–202.

Meyer, Erin. 2014. *The Culture Map: Breaking through the Invisible Boundaries of Global Business*. New York: PublicAffairs.

Ness, Immanuel. 2014. "Part 1: The Peopling of the World during the Pleistocene." In *The Global Prehistory of Human Migration*, edited by Peter Bellwood, 69–228. West Sussex, UK: John Wiley and Sons.

Oden, Amy. 2001. *And You Welcomed Me: A Sourcebook on Hospitality in Early Christianity*. Nashville: Abingdon Press.

Ogletree, Thomas W. 2003. *Hospitality to the Stranger: Dimensions of Moral Understanding*. Louisville, KY: Westminster John Knox Press.

Reddy, Geetha, and Rob M. van Dam. 2020. "Food, Culture, and Identity in Multicultural Societies: Insights from Singapore." *Appetite* 149.

Singer, Colin R. 2021. "Canada to Dramatically Increase Immigration to More than 400,000 per Year." *Immigration.ca*, May 11, 2021. https://www.immigration.ca/canada-to-dramatically-increase-immigration-to-more-than-400000-per-year.

Wirzba, Norman. 2011. *Food and Faith: A Theology of Eating*. New York: Cambridge University Press.

Chapter 14

The Missional Fruit of Reconciliation
The Impact of Armenian and Turkish Reconciliation over the Armenian Genocide

James Jacob Pursley

To date, the Armenian-Turkish Peace Initiative (henceforth, ATPI) reconciliation meetings are undoubtedly the most historic reconciliation meetings ever to take place in the twenty-first century. Though the first official ATPI meeting took place from August 28–30, 2014, and others have followed in recent years, similar meetings were held as early as 2007.[1] The covenant commitments, such as *The Pasadena Covenant*, that came out of ATPI are unprecedented. They are between the descendants of the victims and perpetrators of the Armenian genocide.

The purpose of these meetings is biblical reconciliation for the advancement of the kingdom of God. The two parties in need of reconciliation were the descendants of the victims of the Armenian genocide—Armenians, Greeks, and Syriacs, and the descendants of the perpetrators of the genocide—the Turks and Kurds. The fruit of these meetings has led to a prayer and missions movement among Armenian Christians for the Turkish world.

This Armenian prayer and missions movement is truly extraordinary considering the legal restrictions of ethnic Christian communities living under *dhimmitude* during the Ottoman Empire, and the attempted eradication of the Christian communities in Turkey that began in 1915.[2]

---

1 The first ATPI meeting was documented in the short film, *The Journey to Reconciliation*, Vimeo, 2015. This film is password protected as names and faces are shown and could be a security risk.

2 In Ye'or's book, "Dhimmitude represents a domain which embraces the social, political, and religious relations of different human groups" (Ye'or 2003, 21). "An Armenian *dhimmi* belongs to the civilization of dhimmitude" (Ye'or 2003, 22). Mark Durie, in his work, *The Third Choice*, explains that a *dhimmi* person is to be belittled, and disgraced by their Muslim captors. Therefore, *dhimmitude* are the conditions that perpetuate the *dhimmis*' humiliation. Examples of this are: (1) paying *jizye* tax—a tax to be paid to Muslim captors because of the dhimmis' unbelief, (2) propagation of the *dhimmi*'s faith among Muslims is forbidden, (3) *dhimmi*s are restricted from public display of their religion (no crosses, bells, loud singing etc…), (4) *dhimmi* testimonies in court are not valid against a Muslim, (5) *dhimmi*s are forbidden to teach or critique Islam, (6) *dhimmi*s are not allowed to hold public offices or exercise authority over Muslims, and (7) *dhimmi* house structures had to be smaller and lower than Muslim houses (Durie 2010, 141–45).

The Missional Fruit of Reconciliation

The first section of this chapter attempts to summarize the historical facts of the Armenian genocide. It is quite lengthy for the following two reasons: (1) most people are not aware of the Armenian genocide, and the impact it has had on Christian communities; and (2) the brutal and gruesome history may help the reader understand the significance of reconciliation.

The second section will provide a short description of the spiritual darkness and turmoil resulting from the genocide. The third section will highlight the researcher's ethnographic observations. As a participant observer, translator, and organizer of reconciliation meetings between Armenians and Turks over the genocide, the researcher has taken detailed notes. These observations will include quotes from the participants translated into English from Turkish and Armenian. The fourth section will describe the missional fruit which has resulted from these reconciliation meetings.

The Pasadena Covenant

The Pasadena Covenant is an unpublished document drafted by Turk, Kurd, and Armenian Christian leaders at the first Armenian Turkish Peace Initiative (ATPI) reconciliation meeting, located in Pasadena, California on August 30, 2014.

> As recipients of God's grace and redemption called to be truth-tellers and peacemakers in our broken world, we acknowledge the reality of evil and seek God's blessing on the nations.
>
> We, the participants of the first Armenian-Turkish Pastors Initiative (ATPI), affirm that together in Jesus Christ we are a chosen race, a royal priesthood, a holy nation, God's special possession, that we may declare together the praises of him who called us out of darkness into his wonderful light. Once we were not a people, but now we are the people of God; once we had not received mercy, but now we have received mercy.
>
> We Turkish pastors, with humble and contrite hearts have come at the invitation of our Armenian brothers in Christ to apologize and seek their blessing and forgiveness. We have no words that can undo what our ancestors have done; yet in Christ we receive their love, hospitality, forgiveness and fellowship. We joyfully receive their partnership in the gospel to reach the people of our nation for Christ.
>
> As recipients of God's grace and forgiveness, we Armenian pastors accept the repeated apologies of our Turkish brothers for the horrors inflicted on the Christian peoples of the Ottoman Empire in 1915 and forgive them without condition or demand. We release them and the Turkish church of any generational culpability. Furthermore, we ask forgiveness from our Turkish brothers in Christ for our people's failure

and unwillingness throughout the centuries to share the love and mercy of Jesus Christ with their neighbors.

Together, as God's chosen people, holy and dearly loved, we clothe ourselves with compassion, kindness, humility, gentleness and patience, committing ourselves to bear with each other and forgive one another any grievances from the past, in the present or in the future; to forgive as the Lord forgave us. We will love one another and bind ourselves to each other for the sake of the gospel in the unity Christ gives.

As people redeemed by the blood of Jesus Christ, Turkish and Armenian Christians, we stand together for the truth, identifying and denouncing evil and the works of the evil one, whether acts of violence or attitudes of vengeance or condemnation. We covenant together both in prayer and action to seek the unity of the Spirit in the bond of peace for our peoples in Christ.

We covenant together both in prayer and action to build genuine relationships between our churches and ourselves to see the land of our peoples reached with the gospel of grace and peace.

This is a new beginning.

—The Pasadena Covenant

A Brief History of the Armenian Genocide from 1894–1923

Before 1894, a third of Turkey's population was Christian. According to Ottoman records, in the late nineteenth century, out of eleven million people, there were around 3–4 million Christians living in Turkey, 2.6 million of them Armenian (Balakian 2003, 51; Shaw 1977, 241; The History Place 2000).[3] In what are today considered Turkey's spiritually darkest provinces, Muş, Bitlis, Ağrı, Tunceli, Malatya, Van, and Batman, half of the population living were Christians. Pre-genocide, there were thousands of missionaries in Turkey. There were several Christian universities such as: Euphrates College at Harput, Elazığ, the Central Turkey College in Antep, Girl's College of Theology Seminary in Maraş, Anatolian College of Marsovan, International College of Smyrna, and the Robert's College in Istanbul (Balakian 2003, 25–26).

In the province of Sivas alone there were twenty-five Christian schools, with one school educating over fifteen hundred students (Severance and Severance

---

3 The number of eleven million accounts for the entire population of the area of modern-day Turkey during the Ottoman Empire, and not the entire Ottoman Empire's population of the late nineteenth century. Aaron O'Neill, a statistician for Statista, has calculated that in the 1860s Turkey's approximate population was eleven million (O'Neill 2022).

2012, 118, 273). There were thousands of churches all over the country in every province. Sivas had a population of three hundred thousand Christians, and Anatolian College located in the town of Merzifon, from 1886 until the genocide, had graduated 2,425 students (Severance and Severance 2022, 253; History of Anatolia College 2022). In the center of the city of Kahramanmarash during the late 1800s there was one church that held two worship services every Sunday. The first service had one thousand in attendance; the second service had fifteen hundred attendees. During that time one-third of Kahramanmarash's residents were Christian, a total of thirty thousand believers (Blincoe 1998, 63).

Some of the ethnic Christians had their own Christian villages, some of them lived in minority quarters in larger cities, separated from the Muslims. The minorities were forced to pay *Dhimmi* taxes to the Ottoman government—*jizye*. They also had to pay extortion—*haraç* to Kurdish *Axas* (chiefs) for protection and host Kurds in their homes, feeding them and taking care of them during the winters (Balakian 2003, 42).

Christians had no equal rights, and in some regions had to wear clothing that distinguished them from Muslims. The Muslims would steal their young sons and conscript them for military service—*devşirme*, and for all intents and purposes these men were the work-slaves for the Muslims, and these women were sex-slaves for the Muslims—*jariye* (Balakian 2003, 41).

Türkiye Türklerindir is a popular phrase in Turkey which means "Turkey belongs to the Turks."[4] This was first said in July of 1921, and by that time this was true. Turkey had gotten rid of the Christian problem and their schools. Turkish Muslims thought of the Christians as dogs or pigs and called them *gavur* (infidel). Even today, the word *Ermeni* (Armenian) is used in the Turkish language to degrade someone.

> Turkish Muslims thought of the Christians as dogs or pigs.

In 1890, Abdul Hamid II, from his palace at *Yıldız* Park, said that he would take care of the "Armenian problem" (Balakian 2003, 35–36). He made good on his word, and from September of 1894 until 1896 Hamid released his forces, the *Hamidiye*, which were made up of Kurdish soldiers. During those two years Christians throughout the country were massacred, up to two hundred thousand Christians (Balakian 2003, 110, 123).

All over the country the Muslims burned the churches down where the Christians were hiding and taunted the Christians before killing them saying, "Where is your Christ now? Where is your Jesus? Why does he not save you?" (Balakian 2003, 82). They killed the men, raped the women, stole their property

---

4 In this context the word Turks is equivalent to the word Muslims. This phrase is purposely used to exclude religious minorities and demean other ethnicities.

and valuables, razed churches and villages, and turned hundreds of churches into mosques. In every province there were massacres (Balakian 2003, 59–60). As they would set fire to the churches full of Christians and before they would slaughter or rape, they would shout the *tekbir*, that is, *Allahu akbar*, meaning "Allah is greater" (Balakian 2003, 112).

Accounts of what happened in Gaziantep during this time are chilling: screams of women and children, the shouts of men among gun shots, and the Muslim women and men both cheering about what was happening as they massacred and plundered Christian homes (Blincoe 1998, 98). Blincoe, commenting on the events from Gaziantep writes: "There is blood on the hands of the Kurds. They tore open the homes of peaceful Christians. Having no light of their own, they extinguished the light in those around them. When Kurds turn from the devil to follow Christ, they will cry for shame over the sins of their fathers" (Blincoe 1998, 99).

These massacres were and are known all over the world, but they were systematically denied by the Ottomans, and they shifted the blame saying, "they attacked us too" or "they were rebellious" (Balakian 2003, 115).

During the year 1915 the *Tehcir* law passed; this law was a forced displacement and exile of the Christians. It was during this time that Turkey completely erased any memory of Christianity by sending them out of the country, killing them on the way, and leaving them without food or medical care. Many Christians were forced to leave in the winter and could not take their small children with them. Many naively thought that they would return to their homes and villages.

Before 1915, however, there was another massacre that took place on April 13, 1909, in the province of Adana, and modern-day Osmaniye. Here, upward of twenty-five thousand Christians were massacred by Muslims, and their homes pillaged and destroyed (Balakian 2003, 154).

April 24, 1915, is the official Armenian Genocide Day of Remembrance. Beginning this day, Armenian intellectuals were rounded up in Istanbul (Balakian 2003, 179). They were imprisoned and killed (similar to the *Ergenekon* camps in Turkey of 2008). There were mass burnings of Armenians and Assyrians all over the country (Blincoe 1998, 126). In the Trabzon region, Muslims took women and children out in boats and systematically drowned them in the Black Sea (Balakian 2003, 267). Scholars have estimated that in the year 1915 alone, between eight hundred thousand and one million Christians were killed (Balakian 2003, 179).

Peter Balakian refers to the research of the largest body of genocide scholars in the world to establish the number of genocide victims: "The Association of Genocide Scholars of North America conservatively assess that more than a million Armenians were killed, and probably somewhere between 1.2 and 1.3 million. Some historians put the figure at about 1.5 million, which spans the period from 1915 to 1922, when the last waves of killing took place" (Balakian 2003, 196).

According to the *Tehcir kanunu* (deportation law), and the *Sevk ve İskân Kanunu*, all property, including land, livestock, and homes belonging to the Christians was to be confiscated by the authorities (Kévorkian 2011, 176). The Christians were sent to deportation control centers and stations located in Sivas, Muş, Erzurum, Diyarbakır, Bitlis, Elazığ, Adana, Yozgat, Amasya, Çankırı, Maraş, Antep along with Izmir and various smaller areas (Balakian 2003, 176).

Christians were forced into cattle cars and were also marched to the deserts of Syria. Many of them died of disease and starvation, or they were killed along the way. They were robbed of their possessions and when those who were left alive arrived in Syria they were systematically massacred. The most well-known area for the massacre against the Christians is called Deir ez-Zor in Syria. Here Armenians were crowded into caves and a primitive form of a gas chamber was used for mass extermination (Balakian 2003, 176).

Exposure, starvation, clubbing, drowning, immolation, poison gas used at internment camps, and many other means were used to murder the Christian population, resulting in the Armenian genocide. As we will see in the next section, the extermination of the Christians, and expulsion of the missionaries was spiritually devastating for the country of Turkey.

The Resulting Spiritual Darkness

After the Armenian genocide, and specifically after the founding of the Turkish Republic in 1923, missionary work in Turkey came to a halt. Ethnic Greek, Syriac, and Armenian Christians had been systematically massacred or had fled to other lands. Aside from the Armenian genocide, the Christian ethnic populations continued to decline after 1923 due to ongoing pogroms and the forced migration of the Greek population in Turkey.[5] The Assyrian Christian population also suffered during this time with an estimated 250,000 killed (Blincoe 1998, 126).

Christian property was confiscated, and any light of the church and gospel was snuffed out. Aside from the loss of personnel due to the genocide, new Turkish regulations forced missionary societies to close their schools and missions (İdris 2012, 63–65). Turkey was plunged into spiritual darkness from

---

5 The Greek population in Turkey before 1923 of approximately 250,000, was reduced to 110,000 after 1923. Today the estimated Greek population is around 2,500 (Canefe 2008, 26).

1923 until the first missionaries returned to Turkey in the 1960s. It has been estimated that there were only ten Turkish Christians in all of Turkey in the 1950s (Pikkert 2006, 234). The first missionaries arrived in 1961 for an initial survey trip. Not until 1966 did the first missionary teams finally return to Turkey after the genocide (Pikkert 2006, 235).

Later in the 1970s, more missionary organizations began to establish their works.[6] By 1978 it is estimated that there were only fifty converts to Christianity (Pikkert 2006, 235). Patrick Johnstone's book, *Operation World* has designated Turkey as the least reached country in the world, and this designation has been agreed on by missiologists since 1978 (Pikkert 2006, 235).

Turmoil and Division

The Kurds and Turks have been in conflict since the founding of the Turkish republic.[7] One example out of dozens of massacres committed against the Kurds was the Zilan massacre. The Zilan massacre of Kurdish Muslims took place in the Ararat region by the Turkish forces in 1930, and over fifteen thousand were killed (Batman 2021; Cumhuriyet 1930). Over 220 villages were destroyed, and five thousand women, children, and elderly were massacred during this time. According to the front page of the *Cumhüriyet* newspaper July 13, 1930, "*Temizlik başladı: Zeylân deresindekiler tamamen imha edildi. Bunlardan tek bir kişi kurtulmamıştı.*" Translated as: "The Cleansing started: In the area of Zilan, all were annihilated, not even one person was left alive" (ANF News 2019). These Kurdish massacres are reminiscent of the fulfillment of the curse of Jotham among the leaders of Shechem and Abimelech.[8]

The two parties, the Kurds and the Turks, have been divided and killing each other since the Armenian genocide. According to records since 1979, total casualties on each side is estimated between 40,000–250,000, with 17,000 missing, and over three million people displaced. Additionally, some three thousand Kurdish villages have been razed (Yeni Şafak 2015; Koivunen 2002, 104; Gunter 1998). The Turkish government also has been torturing and killing its own people over politics in one coup after another (Göç 2016).

Despite the spiritual darkness and turmoil, the missionary movement toward Turkey has grown since 1978. The number of Muslim background believers

---

6 An example is the United Church of Christ, which did not start their work in Turkey until the 1980s (Global Ministries 2014).

7 In this article, Hürriyet Gazetesi lists every Kurdish rebellion and faction since the founding of the republic until 2008 (Birand 2008).

8 Jotham cursed Abimelech for the massacre of his seventy brothers. The curse was fulfilled three years later with rebellion and infighting of Abimelech's supporters. See Judg 9 and Prov 26:2.

has also grown to an estimated seven thousand. There are approximately 175 national fellowships. These new believers, together with Armenian background Christians, began the reconciliation over the genocide in 2007.

The next section consists of Turkish and Armenian Christians' own responses to the reconciliation meetings. These responses were recorded in detail, and a few selections were translated by the researcher. The researcher was a participant observer and translator, therefore this section also contains the researcher's ethnographic observations.

A Turkish Pastor's Journey to Reconciliation[9]

To be clear, the idea to, "go ahead and ask the Armenians for forgiveness," did not just come from nowhere. In fact, it began with my editing a book in the Turkish language called *Beklenen Uyanış*, in English *The Expected Awakening*, which was written by a beautiful person, a close friend, and a colleague of mine in the ministry in Turkey, Sebastian James.[10] Before reading this book, I had never given this topic much thought. My ideas were not much different from those of the people you would meet on the streets in Turkey. Without a doubt, I was greatly influenced by the nationalism of where I was born and raised. My family and social group also affected my thinking. I am from Osmaniye, Turkey.

After reading this book, I began to question the historical "facts" that had been taught to us as Turks. I learned a foundational truth that prepared me to journey to Pasadena: God wanted us to repent for the sins that were committed by our forefathers, so that the people of this country, which we serve, can be delivered from the curse of this sin, and for a spiritual awakening to come. Repentance, confession, and asking for forgiveness was necessary.

On my journey to Pasadena, I had many thoughts running through my head. Is it really necessary that I apologize to my Armenian brothers and sisters? Because I did not do anything! Would my apology mean anything to them? Will they accept my apology? Oh, but what if they reject us! What if they are angry! Will they really forgive us? Should I hug them? Maybe just extending my hand to them would be better.

I cannot remember a time in my life that asking for forgiveness and apologizing was this difficult. Think how shameful and frightening it is to look into the eyes of hundreds of Armenians and say, "Please forgive us for the sins,

---

9   The following section is a Turkish pastor's thoughts on participating in the ATPI and subsequent reconciliation meetings. The text was translated from Turkish into English by the researcher. The pastor's name has been omitted for security reasons.

10 Sebastian James was used by the researcher as a pseudonym for this book's author.

savagery, and genocide that my fathers committed against your fathers." For a moment I tried to put myself in their place and thought, "If I was an Armenian what would I do? Would I forgive?" This was very difficult for me, yet I had great inner peace.

God gave me peace because we were going to a church. The Armenians were our brothers and sisters. Just as we Turks, they were also children of God who had been forgiven of their sins. They knew what it meant to forgive and to be forgiven. The same Spirit which was in us, was also in them. It was not necessary for me to be reluctant. As I thought about this truth, a peace fell over me. Furthermore, God wanted us to do this. So, I had to be obedient as well.

I arrived in Pasadena with these emotions. We first met with the Armenian brothers who were leading the meeting. We spoke about subjects like, "What steps will we take? After this, what was the next step in the process which would have to be done? How will it continue?"

During a break in one of the meetings, one of my Armenian brothers there caught my eye, and I thought, "I need to ask forgiveness from this Armenian named Shishmanian. It will be good practice for me. At the same time, he looked very proud."

Before going over to him, though my mind was plagued with the same worries I faced on my journey to Pasadena, I memorized what I was going to say. At the same time, I was trying to think of more flowery wording. I went straight up to him and began to say what I had planned. I had just started speaking, when Shishmanian put his arms around my neck and hugged me. At that moment I felt overwhelmed and as if I owned the world. I wanted to continue to speak, but it was like my tongue was tied and my throat was in a knot. I was only able to embrace him and cry. It was an unbelievable feeling, and all my worries went away.

The thing that really moved me during this first encounter, was to see that my Armenian brother was already prepared to forgive. He was only waiting for me to take the first small step.

After we finished our meetings among the leaders, we arranged a large meeting of Armenian brothers and sisters at a nearby church. Prior to the meeting, our Armenian mothers and sisters had prepared Armenian food for us. The food was very familiar to us, as it was much like our Turkish food. It looked just like our food, and even the names were the same—*sarma* and *dolma*. This experience in Pasadena with Armenians made us feel like we were at home. It was like the food was speaking to us. During these meetings we realized that we were alike in many ways—our land, our food, and my face even looks Armenian, and Armenians look like me.

Hundreds of Armenians, young and old, came to the meeting and listened to us. Each one of the Christian Turkish leaders spoke, asked for forgiveness and apologized. While we were speaking, they were crying, and we were crying. Our tears intermingled and words were unnecessary. That picture explained everything. I can still see it so clearly.

That day, in the most vivid way I had ever seen, I became a witness to God's grace, which flows among people—the grace which is shared. That day I experienced again to the very marrow of my bones, the joy of forgiveness, asking for forgiveness, and of grace.

Since the meeting I have felt that this should have been displayed for the whole world to see. Through formal media channels we should have shown Turkey, Armenia, and the entire world how Turks were going to the Armenians, apologizing, asking forgiveness, and the Armenians were embracing the Turks, both drowned with tears. What we should have done a hundred years ago, and what politics or politicians could never achieve, we could have shown the world that God's children and the church are able to accomplish, to the glory of God.

Throughout the days in Pasadena this was the beautiful picture God showed me, and this was the message. From what I observed at this time, the main message that God put in my heart was the picture of the Armenian and the Turk embracing each other.

This was a godly picture that will make an unbelievable contribution to changing hearts, and will break racism, fear, prejudice, and the denial of the genocide by the Turks who live in Turkey, and still have fear in their hearts and are reluctant to make amends for the genocide.

Ethnographical Observation[11]

Can enemies reconcile? The answer is a resounding yes. Christians have been reconciled to God through Jesus Christ alone, and through Christ alone they can reconcile with each other:

> All this is from God, who through Christ reconciled us to himself and gave us the ministry of reconciliation; that is, in Christ God was reconciling the world to himself, not counting their trespasses against them, and entrusting to us the message of reconciliation. Therefore, we are ambassadors for Christ, God making his appeal through us. We implore you on behalf of Christ, be reconciled to God. (2 Cor 5:18–20)

This past week I witnessed the grandchildren of the offenders come together with the grandchildren of their victims. The Turks and Armenians

---

11 These are the researcher's thoughts and observations from the ATPI meetings, August 28–30 of 2014.

came together because Jesus Christ had reconciled them to God through the cross. They came together because Jesus Christ is at the center of their hearts and lives. They came together because their King is the Prince of Peace and the author of reconciliation. They came together because they heard the voice of their Shepherd and followed him.

Both parties had been at enmity with God, both had sinned against God, both had received God's salvation, forgiveness, and reconciliation. Both parties had received without condition. Both groups offered apologies with many tears, embraced each other, forgave each other, and forged friendships that will last for eternity.

The Turkish pastors at first felt apprehensive: Would the Armenian leaders accept them and their apology? The Armenian pastors did not know what to think, many of them were not even aware of God's work among Turkish and Kurdish people or the existence of the Turkish church.

Throughout the meetings there were many remarkable statements that impacted me greatly. Below are the Armenian pastors' responses to the Turkish Christians when they apologized for the genocide:

- "I would have never believed that I would have witnessed something like this in my lifetime."
- "I hated you and your people, my grandfathers even killed some of you."
- "We forgive you, without condition, without demand. We forgive you."
- "We were forgiven so much, we forgive you."
- "Please forgive us for not taking the gospel to your people when we had the chance."
- "I am in total shock."
- "I now want to take my congregants to the country of Turkey, to their historical villages to meet with the villagers there."
- "We bless Turkey, we stretch out our hands and take away the curse from Turkey, and we ask for God's mercy for Turkey."
- "We love you, accept you as our brothers, and embrace you."
- "How can we partner with you and work together in Turkey?"
- "It is only Jesus Christ that could do something like this."

The Missional Fruit of Reconciliation

Stories of the atrocities were passed down to these Armenian pastors from their forefathers. All was still fresh in their minds and was revived with the presence of Turks. When the Turkish pastors asked for forgiveness and confessed generational sins, Turks and Armenians, old and young alike began to weep uncontrollably; they embraced each other and offered forgiveness and acceptance. This was a major breakthrough for many of the Armenian Christians as well, as they have held grudges for so long, and had never released the object of their pain and anger to Christ until now.

> Turks and Armenians, old and young alike began to weep.

The Turkish Christians confessed the sins of their fathers and below are some of their memorable quotes:

- "What kind of people were we and what would cause us to do such horror?"
- "My grandfather explained that we would put our rifles on the ground, bayonets fixed toward the sky, and run the babies through in their bassinets until the river was flowing with their blood. In Sivas we committed genocide. Please forgive us."
- "As Turkish Christians we have faced some persecution, but nothing in comparison to what you as a people went through."
- "Because of what our forefathers did there is a curse upon our nation, our people, and our churches."
- "We believe that we as the church must lead in acknowledging our people's sins. If the church cannot do this, how do we expect the government to do this?"
- "Thank you for accepting us, thank you for inviting us, thank you for forgiving us."

Friday evening of August 29th, we had an open reconciliation event for the Armenian community. Among the Armenian Christians that were present, there were over one hundred Turkish-speaking Armenians. These Armenians had learned Turkish from their grandparents who had escaped the genocide. Our Turkish brothers were surprised when they were greeted and spoken to in their own language. The Armenians shared their stories and offered forgiveness to them in their own tongue. Both sides believed that they were building a bridge between their two communities. Both groups believed that they had foundations to build on their side of the bridge, and that this meeting was the beginning.

The ATPI meetings culminated with the drafting of *The Pasadena Covenant*, (a joint document written by both Armenian and Turkish pastors). Aside, from a drafted document, Armenian churches in diaspora and in Armenia committed to pray for Turkey and to send missionaries to Turkey. The next section summarizes the missional fruit in Turkey from 2014 to the present.

Fruit of Reconciliation: Prayer and Sending of Missionaries[12]

Prayer and missions are inseparable. In 2014, a movement began among the churches in Armenia that had participated in the reconciliation meetings. Monday through Friday, every morning at 8:00 a.m., church members gather to pray for Turkey. This movement began to grow as more reconciliation meetings took place, and more and more Armenian church leaders and members participated. Since 2016 other diaspora Armenians repatriated to Armenia to help fuel the prayer and missionary movement for Turkey.

I have estimated that since 2014 at least three hundred short-term Armenian missionaries have ministered in Turkey.[13] Their ministries have been varied. Some Armenians have gone directly to Turkish Protestant churches via invitation and served alongside existing local fellowships. Other Armenian missionaries have targeted the unreached and unchurched areas of Turkey. They have established friendships, and their focus has been evangelism. Many of these short-term missionaries visit for a month at a time and continue itinerant missionary work on a regular basis.

Aside from the short-term movement, approximately eighteen long-term Armenian missionaries and church planters are currently working among Turks and Kurds.[14] The majority of these missionaries have moved to and started new churches in unreached, unengaged areas of Turkey. These missionaries have joint partnerships with Protestant Turkish churches in their endeavors to advance the kingdom of God. At the time of this writing there are at least thirty more Armenians preparing for the mission field in Turkey.

These selected testimonies of Armenian missionaries are evidence of the missional fruit of reconciliation:[15]

---

12 For security reasons the names, organizations, and places have been omitted. This section is short and vague to protect the security of the Armenians serving in Turkey.

13 This number is calculated according to the ministries based out of Armenia that mobilize, equip, and send to Turkey. It is the researcher's opinion that this number is much higher, as there are diaspora Armenians and other ministries that the researcher is unaware of that have been focusing their mission work to Turkey. *Christianity Today* covered a story on the Armenian and Turkish Reconciliation movement and the resulting missional fruit (Casper 2020).

14 This number is based on the researcher's knowledge of the existing Armenian missionaries. This number is probably higher based upon a number of Armenian denominations that may have sent their own missionaries.

15 These testimonies were translated by the researcher from Armenian into English.

The Missional Fruit of Reconciliation

- "God promised the Turks to me, and God wants their heart, and we need to help them give their hearts to God. God has kept this promise by allowing me to go to Turkey and be equipped to serve. I love them. And I have a heart for them."
- "I want to concentrate on Turkey for missions. It is God's command. I was not prepared to go before, but now my God is preparing me for great things."
- "I love Turkey. This is from God. And God is preparing us because there are prophecies that our church will do much in Turkey. We are in God's work here, and we are praying for Turkey. God will work there."
- "I am ready to be a missionary to Turkey. It was difficult for me to forgive, but while I was there, and in prayer, God changed my heart."
- "I was scared and angry. God changed my heart while I was there, and now I can stay and serve. I can go."
- "While I was looking at our forefathers' lands, I was angry, and did not want to forgive the Turks. I was uncomfortable while I was there, then the Holy Spirit spoke to my heart, and told me I must change my heart. He then said, 'Do you want these lands back so bad that you wish there would be another genocide, and all of the Kurds die?' God changed my heart while I was there."
- "I feel I must now learn Turkish and prepare to go long-term."
- "We here have so much Bible knowledge and we are prepared. It is easy for us to share the gospel in Armenia. Since we are so blessed, the Turks, through us must also be blessed. We need to have fire and passion for our neighbors."

One observer of these short-term Armenian missionary teams to Turkey stated: "It seems impossible to forgive, especially for Armenians to forgive the Kurds (over the genocide). And the Armenians have now forgiven the Kurdish peoples. When the Armenians forgive the Kurds, the Kurds then will learn to forgive the Turks for what has happened to them. This begins with the Armenians—going and forgiving and will be an example for the Kurds to follow with the Turks."

Timeline of Turkish and Armenian Reconciliation[16]

- 2007: A Turkish pastor travels to Yerevan, Armenia in October of 2007, and offers his apologies to Armenian Christians (Shahverdyan 2018, 1).[17]
- Fall of 2008: James Jacob Pursley travels from Turkey and begins to speak at churches in Armenia. He acts as an ambassador for some Turkish churches and offers apologies on their behalf concerning the genocide.
- 2009: Rafi Shahverdyan and a team leave Armenia and arrive in Turkey to connect with James Jacob Pursley, along with Armenian and Turkish churches to seek reconciliation (Shahverdyan 2018, 13).[18]
- 2009–2014: James Jacob Pursley begins networking with Armenian and Turkish Christians to facilitate reconciliation meetings both in Turkey and Armenia (Shahverdyan 2018, 50–51).[19]
- 2013–2014: The book, *The Expected Awakening in Turkey, Confession to Revival: Written to the churches in Turkey* is written and published. James Jacob Pursley writes this book to challenge Turkish Christians to confess and reconcile with Armenians, Syriacs, and Greeks (James 2014; Balancar 2014).[20]
- Spring of 2014: Around thirty Kurdish Christian leaders come together in Istanbul, Turkey. They bow themselves in prayer before the Lord and weep over what their ancestors did.
- Summer of 2014: First ATPI meeting occurs. Turkish and Kurdish pastors meet with Armenian leaders in Pasadena, CA for a reconciliation meeting. It is at this meeting that *The Pasadena Covenant* is drafted.
- Fall of 2014: Turkish pastors visit Armenian pastors in Yerevan for reconciliation.
- March 2015: Over one hundred Turkish and Kurdish and Armenian pastors come together in Istanbul for a reconciliation meeting.
- April 2015: Turkish/Kurdish pastors meet with church leaders in Yerevan, Armenia for reconciliation on the one-hundredth Commemoration of the Genocide (Baker 2015; Panorama 2015).

---

16 This list is undoubtedly incomplete and represents only what the researcher is aware of.
17 The researcher was not a part of these meetings to observe. I have since met with this pastor, and he has joined many of the subsequent reconciliation meetings.
18 Rafi recounts one of these meetings where the researcher served as a translator and connector for the Turks and Armenians.
19 Rafi records one of our visits to Armenia during the fall of 2009.
20 Casper in *Christianity Today*, Casper recounts the impact of the book *The Expected Awakening in Turkey*, and the reconciliation movement among Armenians and Turks (Casper 2020).

- April 24, 2015: The one-hundredth year remembrance of the Armenian genocide is commemorated.
- Winter of 2015: Turkish and Kurdish pastors meet in New Jersey with diaspora Armenians from the East Coast of the USA.
- April 2016: Turkish, Kurdish, and Armenian leaders conduct reconciliation meetings in Adana and Istanbul (Daeryeong Kim TV 2016, 0:00–0:34; Silk Wave Mission 2017).[21]
- 2017–2019: Reconciliation meetings continue to occur in the United States, Yerevan, and in cities and villages all over Armenia until the implementation of COVID-19 pandemic restrictions (Goddard 2017).[22]

Conclusion

These reconciliation meetings are no mere academic exercise. The Turkish and Kurdish Christians humbled themselves before God and man, confessed and repented. The Armenian Christians did what Jesus Christ commanded, "For if you forgive others their trespasses, your heavenly Father will also forgive you, but if you do not forgive others their trespasses, neither will your Father forgive your trespasses" (Matt 6:14–15).

The Armenians have committed to return to their ancestral villages in Turkey, meet with the villagers, pray, bless, and share the gospel with them. They have asked the Turkish churches to partner with them to help in their endeavor to re-evangelize their historical homelands. The bonds of friendship and missional fruit that have resulted from these meetings was only made possible by the God who reconciled them to himself.

References Cited

Anatolia College. 2022. "History of Anatolia College." https://anatolia.edu.gr/en/about/history.

ANF News. 2019. "Dewlet Şopên Komkujiya Zîlanê Ji Holê Radike!" [The state is erasing the traces of the massacre of Zilan!] *ANF News*, July 22, 2019. https://anfkurdi.com/rojava-sUriye/dewlet-sopen-komkujiya-zilane-ji-hole-radike-116107.

Baker, Barbara G. 2015. "Turkish and Armenian Christians Reconcile on Genocide Anniversary." *Christianity Today*, April 24, 2015. https://www.christianitytoday.com/news/2015/april/turkish-christians-reconcile-armenian-genocide-anniversary.html.

---

21 Our reconciliation meeting in Istanbul, Turkey, was televised live at Azusa Now, April 9, 2016. Rev. Joe Matossian led in a prayer.
22 Biola University covered one of these testimonies in their publication.

Balakian, Peter. 2003. *The Burning Tigris: The Armenian Genocide and America's Response*. New York: HarperCollins.

Balancar, Ferda. 2014. "Turkey Will Have No Peace until They Confront the Armenian Genocide." *Agos Gazetesi*, May 8, 2014. http://www.agos.com.tr/tr/yazi/7734/turkey-will-have-no-peace-until-they-confront-the-armenian-genocide.

Batman Gündem. 2021. "Cumhuriyet Dönemi Barbarlığından Bir Kesit—Zilan Katliamı." *Batman Gündem*, July 15, 2021. https://www.batmangundem.com/cumhuriyet-donemi-barbarligindan-bir-kesit-zilan-katliami/11246/.

Birand, Mehmet Ali. 2008. "Bugüne Kadar Kaç Kürt Isyanı Oldu?" *Hürriyet Gazetesi*, January 3, 2008. https://www.hurriyet.com.tr/bugune-kadar-kac-kurt-isyani-oldu-7957402.

Blincoe, Robert. 1998. *Ethnic Realities and the Church: Lessons from Kurdistan, A History of Missions Work, 1668–1990*. Pasadena, CA: Presbyterian Frontier Fellowship.

Canefe, Nergis. 2001. "The Legacy of Forced Migrations in Modern Turkish Society: Remembrance of the Things Past?" *Balkanologie Revue d'études pluridisciplinaires* 5, no. 1–2. https://journals.openedition.org/balkanologie/709.

Casper, Jayson. 2020. "Turks and Armenians Reconcile in Christ. Can Azeris Join Them?" *Christianity Today*, October 21, 2020. https://www.christianitytoday.com/news/2020/october/armenia-turkey-christian-reconcile-genocide-nagorno-karabak.html.

Cumhuriyet Gazetesi, 16 July 1930. https://www.gastearsivi.com/gazete/cumhuriyet/1930-07-16/1.

Daeryeong Kim TV. 2016. "Rev. Joe Matossian, an Armenian Pastor, Leads Prayer along with Ararat Awakening @ Azusa Now." July 8, 2016. YouTube Video, 2:54. https://youtu.be/3g0wV75dudM.

Durie, Mark. 2010. *The Third Choice: Islam, Dhimmitude and Freedom*. Australia: Deror Books.

Global Ministries. 2014. "The Past 50 Years of Mission in Turkey." *Global Ministries*, October 10, 2014. https://www.globalministries.org/the_past_50_years_of_mission_in_10_10_2014_1112/.

Göç, Anıl. 2016. "Ülke Tarihinin Utanç Tablosu: Türkiye'de Şimdiye Kadar Yaşanmış Darbe Ve Darbe Girişimleri." *Onedio*, July 16, 2016. https://onedio.com/haber/ulke-tarihinin-utanc-tablosu-turkiye-de-simdiye-kadar-yasanmis-darbe-ve-darbe-girisimleri-721503.

Goddard, Jessica. 2017. "Faith Fosters Forgiveness: Turkish and Armenian Christians Seek Reconciliation after Deep Held Hatred." *The Biola University Chimes*, October 10, 2017. https://chimesnewspaper.com/25963/archives/features/faith-fosters-forgiveness/.

Gunter, Michael M. 1998. "An Interview with the PKK's Ocalan." *Journal of Conflict Studies* 18, no. 2 (Fall). https://journals.lib.unb.ca/index.php/JCS/article/view/11697/12451.

İdris, Yücel. 2012. "A Missionary Society at the Crossroads: American Missionaries on the Eve of the Turkish Republic." Hacettepe University. *Cumhuriyet Tarihi Araştırmaları Dergisi Yıl* 8 Sayı 15. http://www.ctad.hacettepe.edu.tr/8_15/4.pdf.

James, Sebastian. 2014. *Beklenen Uyanış: Uyanış için Türkiye'deki Kiliselere İtiraf Çağrısı*. [The Expected Awakening: Confession to Revival: Written to the Churches in Turkey] Topkapı, İstanbul: Gerçeğe Doğru Kitapları.

Kévorkian, Raymond. 2011. *The Armenian Genocide: A Complete History*. London: I. B. Tauris.

Koivunen, Kristiina. 2002. "The Invisible War in North Kurdistan." PhD diss., University of Helsinki. https://helda.helsinki.fi/handle/10138/23401.

O'Neill, Aaron. 2022. "Population of Turkey 1800–2020." *Statista*, June 21, 2022. https://www.statista.com/statistics/1067119/population-turkey-historical/.

Panorama. 2015. "Turkish Christians Ask for Forgiveness." https://www.panorama.am/am/news/2015/03/17/hraparak/92210.

Pikkert, Peter. 2006. "Protestant Missionaries to the Middle East: Ambassadors of Christ or Culture?" PhD diss., University of South Africa. https://uir.unisa.ac.za/bitstream/handle/10500/722/thesis.pdf?sequence=1.

Severance, Gordon, and Diana Severance. 2012. *Against the Gates of Hell: The Life and Times of Henry Perry, a Christian Missionary in a Moslem World*. Eugene, OR: Wipf and Stock.

Shahverdyan, Rafi. 2018. *Armenian Bread Turkish Wine: A Real-Life Journey of Reconciliation*. Translated by Noah Watson. Yerevan, Armenia: Seko Print.

Shaw, Stanford J., and Ezel Kural Shaw. 1977. *History of the Ottoman Empire and Modern Turkey: Reform, Revolution, and Republic*. Vol. 2. *The Rise of Modern Turkey, 1808–1975*. Cambridge: Cambridge University Press.

Silk Wave Mission. 2017. "Armenia Turkey Peace Initiative Istanbul 2016: Is It Possible for Armenians to Forgive the Genocide of Killing 2 Million?" *Silk Wave Mission*, December 22, 2017. http://silkwavemission.com/board.php?board=english&page=17&command=body&no=925.

The History Place. 2000. "Genocide in the 20th Century: Armenians in Turkey, 1915–18." http://www.historyplace.com/worldhistory/genocide/armenians.htm.

"The Journey to Reconciliation." Vimeo, 2015. https://vimeo.com/114642734.

Yeni Şafak. 2015. "Nearly 7,000 Civilians Killed by PKK in 31 Years." *Yeni Şafak*, August 28, 2015. https://web.archive.org/web/20161011091853/http://www.yenisafak.com/en/news/nearly-7000-civilians-killed-by-pkk-in-31-years-2237092.

Ye'or, Bat. 2003. *Islam and Dhimmitude: Where Civilizations Collide*. Lancaster, UK: Fairleigh Dickinson University Press.

Appendix

Resources for Next Steps

As partners in EMS 2022, the World Evangelical Alliance's Peace and Reconciliation Network—commissioned to inspire and equip the global evangelical community to enable communities to live life in all its fullness—celebrates the insights of this compendium. At the same time, as was noted from the beginning of this anthology, one collective effort cannot address all areas of reconciliation. We agree with those crying out for more contributions in reconciliation missions theology and practice in areas such as Indigenous relationships, creation care, trauma-healing, gun-violence, and people migrations, to name a few. Perhaps what you have read in these pages will inspire you to add your own study, voice, and practice to equip the body of Christ for the transformative task in front of all of us.

At the same time, we recognize that reconciliation can be costly. Working in the often muddy terrain where reconciliation with God, ourselves, others (including enemies) and creation is required can be an overwhelming and lonesome task. In the words of Karl Barth, "How lonely are those who dare to speak about God" (Barth 1990, 49).[1] We might add: how lonely are those who work for the reconciliation God has spoken. If you have made it this far in reading this book you are likely one of these ministers of reconciliation, or eager to be equipped as one. As a way to encourage you, and to provide resources and ways to collaborate in reconciliation, God's mission through missions for all, we point you to the following:

Organizations and Networks

NAIITS An Indigenous Learning Community: https://naiits.com

Peace Catalyst International: https://www.peacecatalyst.org

Peacemakers Confessing Christ International: https://www.pcci.team

Global Immersion: https://globalimmerse.org

The Peacemakers Collective: https://www.thepeacemakerscollective.com

Healing Hearts Transforming Nations: https://hhtnglobal.org

Global Anabaptist Peace Network: https://mwc-cmm.org/en/global-anabaptist-peace-network

---

[1] Karl Barth, *The Gottingen Dogmatics: Instruction in the Christian Religion*, Vol. 1 (Grand Rapids, MI: Eerdmans).

Resources for Next Steps

Musalaha: https://musalaha.org

Civil Righteousness: https://civilrighteousness.org

Global Ethnodoxology Network (arts and trauma healing): https://www.worldofworship.org/home-announcement/arts-and-trauma-healing-course

American Bible Society Trauma Healing: https://ministry.americanbible.org/trauma-healing

Canadian Bible Society: Caring for the Wounded Heart, Trauma Healing Program: https://biblesociety.ca/caring-for-the-wounded-heart

A Rocha: https://arocha.org/en

World Freedom Network: https://wfn.worldea.org

Books

David Bosch, *A Spirituality of the Road*

John W. de Gruchy, *Reconciliation: Restoring Justice*

Grace Ji-Sun Kim and Graham Hill, *Healing Our Broken Humanity: Practices for Revitalizing the Church and Renewing the World*

David W. Shenk and Ahmed Ali Haile, *Teatime in Mogadishu: My Journey as a Peace Ambassador in the World of Islam*

Intotemak, *Wrongs to Rights: How Churches Can Engage the United Nations Declaration on the Rights of Indigenous Peoples*

John Paul Lederach, *The Little Book of Conflict Transformation*

John Paul Lederach, *Reconcile: Conflict Transformation for Ordinary Christians*

Ken Sande and Kevin Johnson, *Resolving Everyday Conflict*

Ken Sande, *The Peacemaker*

Brenda Salter McNeil, *Roadmap to Reconciliation*

David W. Shenk and Badru R. Kateregga, *A Muslim and a Christian in Dialogue*

Jim Van Yperen, *Making Peace: A Guide to Overcoming Church Conflict*

Miroslav Volf, *Exclusion and Embrace: A Theological Exploration of Identity, Otherness, and Reconciliation*

To network with other agents of reconciliation, peace, and holistic transformation, please feel free to reach out to Peace and Reconciliation Network: https://www.reconciledworld.net.

Manuel Böhm, PRN Director of Network Development
Phil Wagler, PRN Global Director

About the Editors and Contributors

Ken Baker spent twenty-four years church planting with SIM International in three West African countries, with five of those years spent in primarily Muslim contexts. Afterward he was US director of Culture ConneXions, a ministry which coaches churches in intercultural life and ministry. Currently he is the global team training lead for SIM International.

Jeanette Böhm worked in the financial sector and in Canadian mission contexts under The Alliance (CMA). Starting with church planting and advocacy work for anti-human trafficking agencies, she journeyed to a more holistic local mission. She is passionate about telling stories of reconciliation and contributes to the work of the Peace and Reconciliation Network (PRN). Jeanette is leading "Love Drayton," a New Venture of the CMA together with her husband.

Manuel Böhm has been working for the Peace and Reconciliation Network since its beginning in 2016. He holds a Master in evangelical theology and started his journey of a PhD to research network leadership at the University of Pretoria, South Africa. In Canada, he is linked to The Evangelical Fellowship of Canada and seeks collaboration and networking for peace and reconciliation.

Andrea and **Nelson Chang** emigrated from the USA to Canada in 2013 as international students. After graduating with MTS degrees from Tyndale Seminary, they became ordained missionary pastors with the CBOQ. Currently, Nelson is the pastor of Newcomers Ministry at The Peoples Church and Andrea is an assistant leadership consultant and research assistant with the TIM Centre in Toronto, Ontario.

Arend Van Dorp has worked with OMF in Southeast Asia since 1987, serving for thirteen years in church-planting and pastoral leadership training in Thailand, and then supervising mission teams throughout Southeast Asia for another twenty years. Since 2021 he has been involved in training and mentoring Hispanic mission candidates for East Asia.

Annette R. Harrison earned a PhD in sociocultural linguistics at the University of California, Santa Barbara. She and her husband served in Francophone Africa with Wycliffe Bible Translators/SIL International for twenty-three years, primarily in Bible translation needs assessment and training. She is currently the associate professor of intercultural studies at Corban University in Salem, Oregon.

About the Editors and Contributors

Geoff Hartt received his DIS degree from Western Seminary. He is the Executive Director of Hispanics for Christ, resourcing Hispanic church planting and providing theological education to Hispanic leaders across the Americas. He has been a local pastor for over twenty-five years and serves as an adjunct professor at Kairos University. He is the regional VP for Evangelical Missiological Society in the Northwest.

Alan Howell, his wife Rachel, and their three daughters resided in Mozambique from 2003 to 2018 as part of a team working among the Makua-Metto people. That work included discipleship, leadership training, sustainable development projects, and hosting Harding University students as interns each summer. Alan has an MDiv and is currently serving as the visiting professor of missions at Harding University.

Yakubu Jakada has served as an evangelist and church planter in Muslim northern Nigeria. He was also the pastor of Glory Land Baptist Church, Kano, and has taught missions and evangelism at The Baptist Theological Seminary Kaduna. He has a graduate certificate in Christian-Muslim relationships from Hartford International University of Religion and Peace, and a PhD in intercultural studies from Asbury Theological Seminary. He is currently teaching missions at Tri-State Bible College.

Emmanuel Kwizera was born and raised in Rwanda. He is currently pursuing his Masters in evangelism and leadership at Wheaton College. He serves as the international missions director with African Enterprise and is a proclamation evangelism catalyst of the Lausanne Movement.

Michael Hakmin Lee is associate professor of ministry and leadership within the Litfin School of Mission, Ministry, and Leadership at Wheaton College. He has written on the theology and philosophy of religions, race and ethnicity, theology of technology, religious mobility, and evangelical deconversions. Michael also serves as an elder in a local church and is an ordained minister.

Kazusa Okaya is a PhD candidate at Durham University. He has served as a campus minister for IFES Japan. He recently published "Tsumi no Yurushi (forgiveness of sins)" in *The Guide to the Apostle's Creed* (UCCJ press, 2022). He has translated numerous books into Japanese, including *Forgiving as We've Been Forgiven: Community Practices for Making Peace* (Jones and Musekura, 2010).

MICHAEL A. ORTIZ received his PhD from Seminario Teológico Centroamericano (SETECA) in Latin America and currently serves as vice president for global ministries at Dallas Theological Seminary and an associate professor in their missiology and intercultural ministries department. His primary academic interests relate to global theological education and contextualization. He also serves as the executive director of the International Council for Evangelical Theological Education.

JAMES JACOB PURSLEY has been a missionary in the Muslim world since 2002. He currently resides in Yerevan, Armenia, and is the dean of a missions school. Dr. Pursley's academic pursuits have been focused on the application of reformed presuppositional apologetics to Muslim apologetics, and discipleship of believers from a Muslim background.

JOHANNES REIMER (PhD) has recently retired as Professor of Missions Studies and Intercultural Theology at the Ewersbach University of Applied Arts in Germany and continues to serve as extraordinary professor of the University of South Africa. Born in a village for displaced Germans in Siberia, he grew up in the former Soviet Union becoming an aggressive Youth Communist Party Leader. Reimer studied theology in Germany, Belgium, the USA, and South Africa. He founded and co-founded numerous churches and agencies, including Logos International, St. Petersburg Christian University, Lithuanian Christian University, and the Peace and Reconciliation Network of the World Evangelical Alliance. He is the Director of the Public Engagement Department of the WEA.

AUBRY G. SMITH is a PhD candidate in intercultural studies at Columbia International University. After serving on the Arabian Peninsula, she and her husband Brady now work in Belfast ministering to asylum seekers. Aubry, a mother of three, is also a childbirth educator and has published two books on spiritual formation in childbearing.

AL TIZON earned his PhD at Graduate Theological Union and is affiliate professor of missional and global leadership at North Park Theological Seminary in Chicago, IL and lead pastor of Grace Fellowship Community Church in San Francisco, CA. Al has been engaged in ministry both in the Philippines and the United States and has authored or edited six books.

Visit us at missionbooks.org

Unity through Repentance:
The Journey to Wittenberg 2017

Thomas Cogdell | Paperback & ePub

Unity through Repentance is the story of God interrupting the lives and plans of an ordinary couple to invite them into the adventure of a lifetime, gathering all the major streams of Jesus-followers in Wittenberg on the 500th anniversary of the Reformation. God gave the vision; tested and confirmed the calling; formed an international leadership team; and inspired a series of gatherings dedicated to joining with Jesus through repentance, forgiveness, and praying John 17.

As he tells his story, Cogdell emphasizes spiritual formation and conflict resolution underscoring the importance of unity in the body of Christ for world evangelism. *Unity through Repentance* provides fresh inspiration for the global Church to fulfill Jesus' prayer for missions: Make them one ... so that the world will believe.

Teaching English for Reconciliation:
Pursuing Peace through Transformed Relationships in Language Learning and Teaching

Jan Edwards Dormer and Cheryl Woelk
Paperback & ePub

How can an English class become a transformative space for both teachers and learners? When the teacher intentionally uses strategies and builds skills for peacebuilding and reconciliation, the classroom can be a place where relationships and communication transform people. This text encourages those engaged in the teaching of English as a second or foreign language to first consider why we might strive to teach English for reconciliation, and then addresses the contexts, individuals, and resources which are involved.

www.ingramcontent.com/pod-product-compliance
Lightning Source LLC
Chambersburg PA
CBHW071235070526
44583CB00017B/2187